The Unfulfilled
Prime Minister

The Unfulfilled Prime Minister

Tony Blair's quest for a legacy

Peter Riddell

POLITICO'S

First published in Great Britain 2005
by Politico's Publishing, an imprint of
Methuen Publishing Limited
11–12 Buckingham Gate
London SW1E 6LB

A catalogue record for this book is available from the British Library.

ISBN 1 84275 113 1
Printed and bound in Great Britain by St Edmudsbury Press

Contents

To Avril and Emily, for all their love, inspiration and support.

Preface

This book aims to answer a simple question. After all the great hopes of May 1997 – the 'things can only get better' theme of the campaign – why didn't Tony Blair do better? I do not believe that his premiership has been a failure. Some things have got better. But the Blair record is mixed at best, especially by the standards he set himself before he became prime minister in 1997. Despite the friendly urgings of one of Blair's former advisers to put a question mark at the end of the title, I believe his premiership is unfulfilled, and is likely to remain so. There is a widespread sense of disappointment, of achievement not matching rhetoric – in part, of a wasted opportunity. Of course, the Iraq war was the dominant event of Blair's second term. But it is not just Iraq. The disillusionment is much deeper, and began much earlier. Opinion polls have shown that the hopes of voters in May 1997 have not been fulfilled. These hopes were exaggerated, though Labour played its part in fuelling them during the campaign. Yet it is not a one-sided story. The economy has grown steadily and inflation and unemployment have been low, while improvements have occurred in some public services. But the whole is unsatisfactory, rather bitty. Tony Blair's legacy is in doubt.

So many books have been written about Tony Blair and his government, including a couple by myself, that any author has to make a good case to add another to the full and sagging bookshelves. This book is intended to offer a

different approach and perspective. It is not another biography of Tony Blair
– of which there are already several good ones. Nor is it another 'kiss and tell',
'stab and spin', account of events since 1997, like the many already written by
departed insiders or journalists. These are often diverting and entertaining,
but only provide a very partial, indeed partisan, view. My focus is primarily
on performance, not on personalities or presentation, on the use of power
rather than its pursuit: what Blair and his government have achieved since
1997. How far has the Blair team lived up to the earlier promises? And, if not,
why not? And could his government have done better?

However, to explain what the Blair government has done inevitably
involves looking at the politics of New Labour, its origins and development,
the people and personal rivalries – particularly the complicated relationship between Tony Blair and Gordon Brown – as well as the policies.
But while most of the 'personality' books tend to ignore, or oversimplify,
what the government has done, so most of the 'policy' books by academics
have had little feel for the personalities. I hope to offer a bridge between the
'personality' and 'policy' books, while avoiding the fate of Blair's transatlantic bridge. I look at the broader questions of how far the Blair
government has changed Britain. This obviously involves foreign policy,
and particularly Europe, but I will not repeat the much fuller account of
the events of 2002–03 in my post-Iraq war book, *Hug Them Close: Blair,
Clinton, Bush and the 'Special Relationship'*. The focus there was primarily
on transatlantic relations. That only forms a small part of this book. I do
not go in detail over the by now familiar story of the run-up to the Iraq war,
the arguments over weapons of mass destruction and the Hutton and
Butler reports, except where they affect the overall assessment of Blair's
premiership.

My other main reason for writing this book now is because I believe that
much of the discussion about Tony Blair and New Labour has been wrong
headed, biased and grossly oversimplified. This misunderstanding and
distortion has not just, or even primarily, been from the right, where some
writers have admired Blair's stand on Iraq, if little else he has done. Much of
the criticism from the left has been even more unbalanced, not just from the
hard left, who have always disliked him, but also from previous allies like
Frank Dobson or Helena Kennedy. The decade and a half of failure and
division in the Labour Party before Blair's election as Labour leader has

tended to be forgotten. Moreover, the controversies over Iraq have distorted the broader assessment of his premiership. The criticisms of much of the establishment, notably the 'old and the bold' who have retired, have also often been based on a misreading of Blair. They have exaggerated the supposed virtues of earlier times, in fact, largely marked by economic decline and political failure. They have ignored how Blair's behaviour and conduct have changed during his eight years in power. Blair is often portrayed as phoney, a superficial media figure solely concerned with appearance, with little grasp of policy, or alternatively – and sometimes by the same people – as a traitor, a liar, who has betrayed both his party and the high hopes when he became prime minister. Blair is seen as having no coherent view, while anything the government has achieved is because of Brown, not him. For many on the right, and their media allies, the extra spending on public services has largely been wasted and nothing has really improved.

The truth is more complicated. I regard Tony Blair as a more substantial, though often ambiguous and elusive, figure than many of his critics who now spit out his name with venom. He has been Labour's most successful prime minister ever in electoral terms. He has led his party to three sizeable Commons majorities in a row (including two landslides), as opposed to the wafer-thin margins which Harold Wilson won in three of his four victories. Moreover, his government has many solid achievements to its credit, thanks to both Blair and Brown, which previous Labour administrations would have envied. While critical of Blair's record, I believe his analysis of what Labour needed to do in the mid-1990s was broadly correct. New Labour was probably the only viable path for a centre-left party in the mid-1990s. The alternatives had failed, and John Smith had not done enough to change Labour. However, while I am sympathetic with many of Blair's aims, particularly in the reform of public services, he has been both muddled in implementation and often cavalier in the exercise of power. In the process, he has deluded himself and created disillusionment amongst others.

One of the central paradoxes is the conflict between spin and substance, between promise and performance, between perception and reality. In its first term, the Blair government promised much more than it achieved, and left voters disappointed, as reflected in the fall in voter turnout in the 2001 general election, especially in strong Labour areas. In the second term, more was achieved, especially in the public services such as health and education, yet the government received at best just grudging credit. This was, in part, because of the ambiguities in Labour's ideological position which I explore over the following chapters. Labour won its third term in May 2005 not only with a much reduced Commons majority but also with a sharp fall in its share of the vote, to the lowest ever for a governing party. Several of what Blair regarded as his boldest policies, such as flexible tuition fees or the choice and diversity agenda for public services, have been opposed by many Labour MPs and supporters.

However, much of the explanation for both the mixed performance and the critical public view of this record can be traced to well before the 1997 election. Blair became Labour leader overwhelmingly because he seemed to offer his party the chance of a return to power after so many years in opposition. There were never that many committed Blairites: many more have been fairweather followers. Blair has always been more respected than liked. He has never been regarded as 'one of us' within the Labour Party. That is a big difference from Margaret Thatcher, who always spoke for her party's gut instincts, rather than just its electoral interests.

New Labour was created as an electoral rather than a governing strategy. Preparations for what to do in office were uneven, and limited by the overriding priority of not putting at risk electoral victory. The resulting language – the triangulation electoral tactics of distancing New Labour both from the Tories and from Old Labour, and the search for a 'third way' strategy – often confused people about what New Labour stood for, and deliberately masked the considerable continuities with the past. The priority was always winning, or rather, avoiding a repetition of past defeats. Minimising risks over tax and public spending meant that many of the initial policy commitments were muddled. Not enough thought went into what to do after being elected. Blair and his team had virtually no experience of government or of running any organisation. It took the new government a long time to come to terms both with Whitehall decision-making and, especially, with implementation of policy on the ground. These questions about the role of the state are fundamental to the unfulfilled nature of Blair's premiership. In its early days, New Labour raised expectations about what central government could do to improve public services and change people's behaviour without having a clear idea about how these goals could be achieved. That explains much of the later disappointment.

Moreover, when in office, Labour ministers found that their pre-election promises were often flawed and inadequate, and policies had to be substantially changed, in some cases reversed. There is nothing inherently wrong about modifying your policies when in power. Most governments – even self-consciously radical ones – find that policies devised in opposition have to be changed after they arrive in office. Such governments often have to reinvent themselves. The question is whether they then achieve a momentum and, above all, coherence. The first chapter tries to put Blair's aspirations and record in the context of previous radical administrations, both successful and unsuccessful.

The book then looks, successively, at the creation and shaping of New Labour and the adjustments and problems of handling government after 1997, before four substantial chapters examining the government's performance in four broad areas: the economy, public services, constitutional change and foreign policy. Inevitably, this means that several big subjects – such as the environment, Northern Ireland, the arts and the media – are neglected. Finally, I attempt to assess the Blair legacy and how it compares with the reforming administrations I discuss in the first chapter. One of the central themes is how Blair and his government changed course well before the Iraq war. Public doubts and disenchantment began during the first term, and if Iraq was the key event in his foreign policy, the key period in his domestic policy was the first half of 2000, when the government decided both on a substantial increase in public spending and on far-reaching reforms to public services. In retrospect, the flu epidemic and the shortage of hospital beds during the winter of 1999–2000 were crucial in changing the course of the Blair government.

Inevitably, this book is an interim judgement. Tony Blair is still in 10 Downing Street. But he is now obviously in the final phase of his premiership. At the time of writing, in mid-summer 2005, he has already been prime minister for longer than any of his predecessors over the past hundred years apart from Margaret Thatcher, with her eleven and a half years, and Asquith and Churchill, who both served a total of roughly eight years and eight months. If he remains in Downing Street, Blair will exceed the Churchill and Asquith tenures in late December 2005 and early January 2006 respectively. Blair has already served longer than such greats or near-greats as Lloyd George, Baldwin, Attlee, Macmillan and Wilson.

But few believe he has achieved as much as Attlee or Thatcher. If he had been an American president (as in so many ways he aspired to be), he would have left 10 Downing Street after two four-year terms at exactly the date when he celebrated his third election victory. As it is, he has become the first prime minister to set himself a time limit in office, albeit a lengthy one, after he sprung the surprise announcement in October 2004 that, while he would seek to serve a full third term, he would not seek a fourth term.

How long Tony Blair will serve is obviously highly uncertain, even more so after the sharp reduction in Labour's majority at the May 2005 general election. But, at the very most, he is now well into the last third of his period as prime minister and probably in the final quarter, maybe even much less. Much can still happen: just remember the impact of the 9/11 attacks or the Iraq war. But the main outlines of his premiership are clear, as are his successes and failures. There are limits to what he can achieve during his remaining time in office. Blair has already publicly acknowledged that his longstanding goal of entering the euro will not be achieved in this timescale. In many other areas too, his room for manoeuvre is more limited, both by time and by the reduction in his political authority, let alone Labour's Commons majority. His power is not as it was in his first term in office. What seemed possible in 1997 or 1998 now looks impossible, or, at least, very unlikely. So his record can now be assessed with greater confidence than even six months or a year ago.

However, the unexpected, and the tragic, can always happen to change the public's views of a prime minister. That was shown in the first week of July 2005, when Tony Blair went from the triumph of helping to secure the Olympics for London in 2012 – by when he will have long left 10 Downing Street – to the appalling tragedy of the terrorist attacks in London. At the same time, he was chairing the meeting of the G8, and other world leaders, in Gleneagles. The intelligence agencies had warned about the likelihood, even inevitability, of such attacks, which did not lessen the immediate shock and horror. These were reinforced a fortnight later when a further series of terrorist bombs in London failed to explode. Blair's sure handling of this extraordinary week – returning to London and going back to Scotland within a few hours – reminded everyone of his qualities as a leader.

In writing this book, I have drawn on my years of writing for *The Times* about Tony Blair and the rise and tribulations of New Labour, which has been the dominant political story for well over a decade. My sources are too many to list here, especially since many of the most valuable have been, or still are, senior advisers to Tony Blair and Gordon Brown, serving ministers and civil servants, who must necessarily remain anonymous. I would, however, mention Tony Blair himself, whom I have seen regularly for conversations in Downing Street over the years, as well as doing on-the-record interviews with him with Philip Webster and other colleagues at *The Times*. Tony Blair has always been courteous and good humoured, if, at times, elastic in reinterpreting events to try and make the best of the situation at the time. To him and my other contacts, my thanks for their insights over the years, as well as to all my colleagues on the political team of *The Times* for making daily journalism such fun. I would particularly like to mention Robin Cook who died suddenly in August 2005 as I was finalising the proofs. He was always open and stimulating. I have not changed any of my references to him, especially his large contribution on constitutional reform.

I would like to thank Sean Magee, with whom I have happily worked on several books over two decades and who was with Politico's, part of Methuen Publishing, until May 2005. He is the most encouraging and supportive of editors, even though he wondered at times whether, unless the book got finished quickly, the 'unfulfilled' in the title might apply to Gordon Brown rather than Tony Blair. He has continued to be involved in editing the book. I am also grateful to the team at Methuen Publishing, especially Emma Musgrave, for bringing out the book so promptly. A number of old friends have read parts of the book and have made several valuable suggestions. I would particularly like to thank Andrew Arends, Roger Liddle (chapter 6 on foreign policy) and Andrew Tyrie (chapter 4 on the economy). Naturally, they have no responsibility for what I have written.

My family – my wife Avril and nine-year-old daughter Emily – have, as always, been closely involved. They have tolerated my desire to write yet another book with patience and support, wondering when I would finish, as well as what I would say. My irreplaceable debt to them is recognised in the dedication.

Peter Riddell

August 2005

1

Making the Weather

'Survivor regimes do not usually arrive in office with any detailed set of plans stretching over the years, or, if they do, the plans have speedily to be rewritten under the pressure of events (Roosevelt came to power promising to balance the budget). Their first needs are to communicate a sense of confidence and to establish stability. Characteristically, they will then develop a "rolling agenda" which both expresses and renews a continuing sense of political purpose and builds on experience.'

Ferdinand Mount, article in *The National Interest*, 1988–89.

'You create a settlement that your political opponents have to come to an accommodation with, and at the moment the Conservative Party aren't in that position ... What we want to create is a situation where the great post-war settlement for welfare, for public services, for the type of country we are, is renewed and modernised thoroughly for today's world.'

Tony Blair, speaking at the launch of Labour's election manifesto, 13 April 2005.

Tony Blair had two aims in the years after he became Labour leader in July 1994. He wanted to be the first Labour prime minister to have two full terms in office, and he wanted to head a radical administration that would fundamentally change Britain. He has more than succeeded in the first goal, becoming the first Labour leader to win three full terms. But he has not achieved his second goal. His legacy and longer-term impact are in doubt. This book is about how Blair tried to achieve these two aims, and about how strategies for winning elections and for governing have often been in conflict.

Blair has seen himself as a transforming leader: one who, in Winston Churchill's famous phrase about Joseph Chamberlain, 'makes the weather'. He has never been satisfied with, or interested in, the political life as such. He is not a House of Commons man, even though he has been able to master the chamber at times. Perhaps reflecting his talents, and even instincts, as an actor, he has sought a more heroic role as leader. This has been reflected in the development of a deliberately 'presidential' image and style and in a conviction approach, particularly to foreign affairs. Yet, contrary to the criticisms on the right – say in the pages of the *Daily Mail* or *Spectator* – Blair has been much less concerned with the trappings of power than with its use. He has wanted to change Britain, even though his thinking and sense of direction have sometimes appeared muddled.

During his final election campaign in spring 2005, Blair talked, as in the quotation above, about trying to achieve a 'settlement' comparable with the post-1945 one. When pressed during an interview by *The Times* on 29 April, he said: 'I want to see public service and welfare reform pushed forward, further and faster, to the benefit of people. So, at the end of the third term, you have taken the historical settlement of the twentieth century on public services and the welfare state and refashioned it for today's world: more individualised, personalised services based on mutual responsibility, rather than a passive welfare state.' Earlier, at the launch of the Labour manifesto on 13 April in the Mermaid Theatre, Blair said his aim was to 'embed a progressive consensus that reflects the mission of our movement – combining economic prosperity and social justice, you create a fairer society but do so in a way that keeps your economy driving forwards, that equips your people for globalisation and the modern age, greater opportunity, and not just for a few.' This raised many questions of definition and implementation. But the ambition was clear, and, interestingly, shared by Gordon Brown, who at the same event said that he believed 'the 1997 settlement will in time be seen as important as the 1945 settlement.' The Chancellor of the Exchequer presented it slightly differently from Blair: as 'enabling not corporatist or controlling government, but enterprise, markets and labour flexibility its hallmark. An empowering, not a dependency-creating welfare state. Not monolithic, top down or impersonal but personal to all.'

So the two key figures of the government have seen themselves as historic reformers. However, their achievements, while more substantial than their critics allege, appear more elusive than those of earlier 'transforming' administrations. The very idea of a 'settlement' seems too ambitious to describe the record of the Blair government.

Blair has often compared his government with the two reforming centre-left administrations of the twentieth century – the Liberal government of 1905–15 and the Labour government of 1945–51 – and with the drive and impact of the Thatcher government of 1979–90. Other parallels, across the Atlantic, are with Franklin Roosevelt's peacetime administrations from 1933 until 1941 and, more ambiguously, with Bill Clinton's two terms in the White House from 1993 until 2001. All five were long-serving administrations in the sense defined in the quotation from Ferdinand Mount at the beginning of this chapter. The first four had considerable achievements to their credit: the last, the closest in time and sympathy to the Blair government, left a legacy of disappointment, and also a sense of promise unfulfilled.

All five earlier administrations provide revealing pointers by which to judge Blair's premiership. Indeed, not only has Blair frequently quoted the Asquith and Attlee governments as inspirations, he also sought to learn more about them. When he became Labour leader, he knew little about the party's history, as opposed to its current predicament. The late Roy Jenkins became a mentor to Blair during this period, encouraging his thinking about how to maximise the progressive forces of the centre-left. When he spoke in February 2000 at the centenary celebrations of the formation of the Labour Representation Committee, he seemed almost to regret that Labour had been formed as a separate party, as opposed to remaining with the Liberal Party. He often noted how the split between Labour and the Liberals in the first quarter of the twentieth century had permitted the dominance of the Conservatives for most of the following decades. The influences he cited were as much Liberals such as Beveridge and Keynes as democratic socialists like Tawney and Crosland. History became important to Blair, as a guide to the changes in the political landscape which he wanted to achieve. As leader of the opposition, he read a biography of Henry Campbell-Bannerman, in itself unusual since 'C-B' – Liberal prime minister from 1905 to 1908 – rivals Bonar Law's title as 'The Unknown Prime Minister'.

To take the five key administrations in turn:

• The Campbell-Bannerman and Asquith governments of 1905–15 helped change the view of what the state could do, away from the largely night-watchman role of the nineteenth century towards accepting responsibility for assisting the poorest through redistributive taxation. Most of the policies for which this government is best remembered were developed well after, rather than before, the Liberals won their landslide victory in the February 1906 election (having taken office the previous December). The election was largely fought on traditional radical and Liberal issues such as free trade versus protection, licensing reform, education and the use of Chinese labour in South Africa. G. R. Searle (2004, p. 361) notes in his history of the period how a study of Liberal manifestos in the 1906 election shows that while two-thirds mentioned 'Poor Law reform and pensions', social policy questions like these came seventh in frequency behind the more familiar issues. In the aftermath of the election there was no hint of what was in the offing. The policies that later emerged were devised by a combination of ministers such as David Lloyd George and Winston Churchill, civil servants and social reformers. The Liberal government was seen as faltering before Asquith took over from the dying Campbell-Bannerman in April 1908, and Lloyd George became Chancellor of the Exchequer and Churchill President of the Board of Trade. The administration then developed a second wind and a sharper cutting edge. The leading ministers proposed and enacted policies such as old age pensions, a limited national insurance scheme for the sick, disabled and unemployed, labour exchanges, a minimum wage in certain low paid industries, and an extended school meals service. This was financed by a combination of higher taxation, including a supertax on the wealthy, and direct contributions (for the insurance scheme).

The Lloyd George Budget of 1909 proved to be the most bitterly fought of the twentieth century, leading to the confrontation with the

House of Lords which the Asquith government eventually won after two general elections in 1910 and a lengthy constitutional battle. These successes both permanently curtailed the political power of the landed aristocracy in the Lords and laid the foundations for the development of a universal welfare state over the following half century. But they were only achieved thanks to a combination of strong leadership, risk-taking and political skill. The end of the constitutional crisis, nearly six years into the life of the government, proved the high point of its social and economic reforms. The Asquith government was increasingly preoccupied with Irish Home Rule before the outbreak of the First World War in 1914.

• The Attlee government of 1945–51 had as formidable a list of legislative achievements to its credit as its Liberal predecessor forty years earlier, but its political position was very different. All its key ministers, apart from Aneurin Bevan, had been senior members of the wartime coalition administration. Most had been involved in domestic policy and in thinking about postwar planning and reconstruction. They had been involved in a series of influential official inquiries, notably the Beveridge report in 1942, which was central to the development of policies to combat unemployment and to extend welfare protection. So, unusually, Labour's thinking about what to do was well developed when the Attlee government took office in July 1945. The party had specific plans for the nationalisation of the main public utilities, such as gas, electricity, coal and the railways, though its thinking was less coherent on health. But there was a reforming momentum from the start, and the legislative programme was ably directed by Herbert Morrison as Leader of the Commons. While many of these measures created considerable controversy, there was a widespread public acceptance of nationalisation of the main utilities, which had anyway come under considerable state control during the wartime years. The government not only fundamentally changed the boundaries between the public and private sectors, but also greatly expanded the universal welfare state. If the Attlee government is the prime example of a reforming team making a strong start, it began to run out of momentum and direction even before Labour's narrow re-election in February 1950. This was partly because of severe economic problems which led up to the 1949 devaluation of the pound and partly because many of the senior ministers were tired and/or ill. There was disagreement over Labour's future programme even before the outbreak of the Korean War in 1950 led to a big rise in defence spending, which created severe economic and political problems.

- The Thatcher government changed the terms of the political debate. Over a whole series of policy areas, what previously seemed impossible proved to be possible. The trade unions were tamed, while the nationalisations of the late 1940s were reversed: indeed, the boundaries between the public and private sectors were shifted back to include industries which had never previously been privately owned, like what became British Telecom. Yet, while many of the ideas about confronting union power and rolling back the state had been discussed privately before the election victory of May 1979, the Conservative manifesto had been cautious, concentrating mainly on the high inflation, strikes and other failures of the corporatism of the 1960s and 1970s.

  The evolution of what became known as Thatcherism was anything but smooth at the time, however coherent it has looked to some in retrospect. Legislation restricting the powers of the unions developed stage by stage. Similarly, the privatisation programme was only gradually extended to the monopoly utilities, such as gas, electricity and water, and the main legislation was only introduced in the second and third terms. Moreover, it was not until the Tories had been in power for seven years that attention really turned to reform of health and education.

  Much depended not only on the conviction style of Margaret Thatcher herself but also on the determination and clear-sightedness of ministers like Geoffrey Howe, Nigel Lawson and Norman Tebbit. The government showed courage in taking risky decisions, such as the tax-raising March 1981 Budget, over the Falklands in spring 1982, and during the long miners' strike of 1984–85. In each case, a different prime minister and a different government might have compromised. However, after faltering in the middle of the second term, the government developed fresh impetus, both to win a third term and to introduce a further tranche of privatisation. But the cohesion of the government was increasingly lost after the third victory in 1987 as disputes developed between Thatcher and other ministers over the poll tax, and then over European and exchange rate policies.

• The first two Roosevelt administrations from 1933 until 1941 have often been cited as the model for centre-left reforming administrations. (The New Deal was, for example, borrowed and adopted by Gordon Brown as the overall title for his welfare-to-work programme to reduce youth and long-term unemployment, announced in 1997.) The role of the federal government was greatly extended across the economy, especially during FDR's first term, as a result of a mass of legislation covering business behaviour, the unions and financial markets. Virtually none of this was promised during the 1932 election, when FDR fought a cautious campaign. As Patrick Maney, one of the best of his recent biographers, has written (1992, p. 43): 'With almost all political experts predicting victory for him, he clearly wanted to avoid saying or doing anything that would alienate any important bloc of voters ... Accordingly, Roosevelt spoke in code words and catchphrases, each intended to appeal to one group or another but each falling short of committing himself to a specific course of action.' The one exception, where he was unequivocal, was government spending. He promised to cut federal spending by 25 per cent. This reflected the conventional wisdom of the time that budgets should be balanced.

In office, FDR's policies were very different. As Maney notes (1992, p. 48), 'Roosevelt had only a vague idea of what he would do, but he nevertheless exuded the confidence of a man who believes that a solution to the depression could be found and that he was the one to find it.' His key role was as a communicator, an educator via his fireside chats on the radio, news conferences and speeches. Against the background of soaring unemployment and the closure of many banks, his main, initial achievement was to create a more positive mood, underpinned by fifteen major recovery and relief measures during the first 100 days alone. His administration did not produce full economic recovery, but it did show that democratic government could work. Implementation was not according to a clearcut plan. Nor was the president the only source of ideas. Congressional leaders also played a creative role. It was a matter of often brilliant, often confusing and often contradictory improvisation. New initiatives were tried, modified and replaced. FDR ran into serious political problems after his second landslide victory in 1936, particularly in his losing battle over the size and membership of the Supreme Court, reorganisation of the executive branch, and when a deep recession hit the American economy in 1937–38. Many of these difficulties were of the administration's own creation. As a result, the Republicans made sweeping gains in the mid-term elections of November 1938, and FDR's presidency looked headed for failure after two terms. FDR then showed characteristic resilience. But it was only the start of the European war in 1939, and of rearmament in the USA, that gave his presidency a fresh impetus.

• The Clinton presidency was a powerful influence on the Blair team's thinking. Many of New Labour's most characteristic features – particularly its campaigning techniques and slogans – were deliberately copied from what Bill Clinton and the New Democrats had done in the US (as is discussed in more detail in the following chapter). Clinton impressed New Labour by his ability to be seen as pro-business and economically competent. His main success, partly building on the elder Bush's vote-losing 1990 tax increases, was to take bold early action to reduce the federal budget deficit and to produce a sizeable surplus in his second term. Aided by Alan Greenspan of the Federal Reserve, the Clinton years were a period of sustained economic prosperity and low unemployment. That was Clinton's major achievement, along with a commitment to free trade. Otherwise his administration lacked focus and tripped itself up by a combination of being diverted into secondary issues (an early, unnecessary row over the policy towards gays in the military), failing to identify and pursue achievable objectives (notably by overreaching itself over health care reform in 1993–94) and by a series of scandals undermining its political authority (Whitewater, and then the Monica Lewinsky affair, which led to the impeachment proceedings in late 1998 and early 1999).

These five examples offer several lessons.

First, it does not matter very much what a party has promised before it takes office. What the Liberals said before the 1906 election and FDR during the 1932 campaign gave no guide to what they subsequently did. While Thatcher's instincts and prejudices were clear before May 1979, the full radicalism of her programme was not apparent. The conventional wisdom was that she would have to modify her policies in office, hence the famous 'The lady's not for turning' retort in her October 1980 party conference speech. Circumstances, such as the financial collapse of March 1933 at the start of FDR's first term, and the gradual evolution of policy when in office, usually matter far more in defining a government's subsequent programme. The Attlee government appears an exception but its ministers had developed new ideas in office as part of the wartime coalition, before the election of the Labour government in July 1945.

Second, flexibility and the ability to reinvent yourself are vital for both survival and success in office. That explains the achievements of the Asquith/Lloyd George team, of FDR and of the Thatcher administration. They learnt from their mistakes and from the difficulties of being in power. That made them bolder. This was linked to a sense of optimism and of direction. During their prime, these administrations conveyed an impression of confidence, of knowing where they were going. Only when that was absent did they lose their grip, sometimes temporarily – as the Thatcher administration did for the first half of 1986 after the Westland crisis; as FDR did in 1937 and 1938 after the Supreme Court debacle; and as Clinton did over the winter and spring of 1994–95 after the Democrats were routed in the mid-term elections. In each case, momentum was regained and a fresh impetus conveyed. The failure to find such a second, or perhaps third, wind after more than a decade in office, in both the wartime coalition and on their own after 1945, largely explains why Labour lost direction and fresh thinking in 1950–51.

Third, personal resilience is crucial, as shown by Asquith until 1914–15; by FDR throughout despite his polio; by Attlee and his senior ministers until 1950–51, when illness fatally undermined the government; by Thatcher until 1989–90, when she became isolated even from previously close allies like Lawson and Howe; and by Clinton, despite personal scandals and vilification by the Republicans and their media allies. Virtually all these leaders were hated by their opponents, and often subject to vicious personal attacks. Asquith was howled down in the House of Commons; FDR was widely seen as a class traitor by many Republicans, who called him 'that man'; Thatcher became a hate figure to many on the centre-left who have feared and disliked her; and Clinton was regarded as corrupt and unscrupulous by many American conservatives. Attlee tended to be patronised, but many other ministers, like Bevan and Morrison, were loathed by conservative England. Yet during their most successful periods in office these leaders brushed aside the personal criticisms, often turning them to advantage, as both FDR and Thatcher did.

Fourth, these leaders possessed, to varying degrees, what the late Richard Neustadt called the power to persuade. In his pathbreaking study of the American presidency (1990, p. 11 and pp. 30–32), he defined persuasion as the key power of the occupant of the White House. Neustadt quoted Harry Truman: 'I sit here all day trying to persuade people to do the things they ought to have the sense enough to do without my persuading them … That's all the powers of the president amount to.' This is allied to the 'bully pulpit' aspect of leadership, less to preach than to address a nation and to command and steer opinion. FDR had this ability above all others to mobilise public opinion, particularly outside his core supporters. Margaret Thatcher did the same, particularly among skilled workers, and what later came to be known as Essex Man and Woman. Clinton, though he was loathed by many Republicans, was a spellbinding speaker, especially to core Democratic audiences such as Afro-Americans. This ability was less true of the fastidious Asquith or the inarticulate Attlee, whose influence was more among their close colleagues at the centre.

Fifth, all these governments were prepared to take highly controversial and risky decisions. They did not opt for a quiet life. They believed political capital should be spent. Asquith staked all over the Lloyd George Budget of 1909; FDR did over the first 100 days programme and, less successfully and nearly fatally, over his 1937 proposals for Supreme Court and executive reorganisation; Attlee pressed on with Labour's ambitious nationalisation programme and extension of the welfare state despite adverse economic circumstances; and Thatcher did not flinch over sharply rising unemployment, the Falklands war and the miners' strike. All consequently defied earlier expectations and achieved more than had been forecast at the beginning of their times in office.

Sixth, and a related condition, successful administrations have a sense of priorities and proportion. They concentrate on the big issues and get them right. This does not mean that their plans have always been clear. Often they have not been. The early years of FDR's administration were a bureaucratic nightmare as competing schemes and initiatives were launched – all, however, with the common aim of reviving the US economy and reducing unemployment. Successful leaders are often flexible tactically, retreating when necessary in the face of political pressures, while keeping a clear eye on the strategic objectives. That was true of Margaret Thatcher in 1982 when she avoided a confrontation with the militant miners' union since she did not think the government was ready. There were insufficient stocks of coal at the power stations. She knew that a confrontation had only been postponed, not avoided, and was in a much stronger position when the battle came two years later. Similarly, successful leaders do not insist on the fine details of their plans, as long as the basic objective is secured. That was true of many of the Liberals' social reforms in 1909–11, as well as with the introduction of the NHS in the late 1940s. By contrast, Bill Clinton often appeared to get diverted into secondary matters, while the health proposals of 1993–94 foundered in a mass of detail because the administration, and particularly Hillary Clinton, were not prepared to be flexible. They would have done better to have followed the FDR example of having broad aims, in this case reducing the number without adequate health insurance, and then to allow Congress greater latitude in settling the details.

Seventh, all these leaders had secure political bases in their own parties during their periods of success. They have understood their parties and governed with, rather than against, their instincts. That was true of Asquith, Attlee, Thatcher, FDR and Clinton. All, at times, had problems with their parties: Attlee over foreign policy; Thatcher over the poll tax and, finally, Europe; FDR over his ill-judged 1937 legislative proposals. Most of the time these leaders had a fund of political capital and support in their parties which enabled them to overcome these problems. Such a fund stood Clinton in good stead during the Lewinsky impeachment saga when virtually all the Democrats stood behind him. Asquith lost office in December 1916 because of arguments with his coalition partners, the Unionists/Conservatives, and because of the ambitions of Lloyd George, not because of any upsurge of revolt from rank-and-file Liberals, most of whom remained loyal to him in the party split. Similarly, Margaret Thatcher was ousted because of a revolt by Conservative MPs and her Cabinet, not by party supporters, many of whom continued to revere her long after she had left Downing Street.

Eighth, all successful leaders have had allies and advisers upon whom they can rely, but no rivals at the top level. Asquith dominated his government until the First World War despite the critical, and growing, role of Lloyd George, though strains developed after the battles of 1909–11; Attlee survived because of the steadfast support of Ernest Bevin, despite recurrent plots to remove him involving Morrison and Cripps; Thatcher had a loyal band of allies and divided her critics, the Tory 'wets', until she fell out with her most effective lieutenants, first Nigel Lawson and then Geoffrey Howe, in the final eighteen months of her premiership; FDR worked through competing advisers and prevented any possible challenger becoming too powerful; while Clinton dominated his administration and outsmarted most of his political opponents, notably Newt Gingrich after the Republican takeover of Congress in November 1994.

Ninth, few leaders or administrations can retain the political initiative for any longer than seven or eight years at most. The pre-First World War Liberals ran out of steam after six years in office; the Attlee government was a spent force after five years; the Thatcher administration got a fresh burst of energy, and a third election victory, after losing its way in early 1986 but was increasingly divided and lacked coherence and direction in 1988–89; FDR had lost the political initiative on domestic policy after five years in 1937–38, and only regained it in 1940 because of the start of the European war; while Clinton stumbled and never really recovered after the Lewinsky revelations and his subsequent impeachment battles in 1998 and early 1999.

Tenth, the records of all these leaders show that political power is leasehold, not freehold. Few have recognised the signs of political mortality, that their authority and influence is waning. Asquith never appreciated the extent of his loss of power in 1915–16 before being ousted by Bonar Law and Lloyd George. In Attlee's case, the life of the administration was brought to a premature close by the death, illness, exhaustion and loss of a will to fight by its senior members. Thatcher never realised how she was becoming isolated and had increasingly lost the confidence of Tory MPs during 1989–90, that her time of glory and achievement had gone by then. She never recognised the warning signals of the always doomed leadership challenge from Sir Anthony Meyer in December 1989. Admittedly, she won 84 per cent of the votes cast, but that was a false reassurance. That is why she saw her departure a year later as a betrayal. FDR defied illness and declining physical powers to win a fourth term in November 1944, only to die less than three months after being sworn in again. Clinton was constrained by the post-FDR constitutional amendment restricting an American president to two terms, a maximum of eight years. But like many presidents operating under this limit, like Eisenhower and Reagan before him, Clinton achieved little in his final year or so in office when he was a lame duck. In Clinton's case, his authority had already been weakened by the impeachment battle.

There are several lessons here for Tony Blair. If you go through this checklist, he meets over half the tests for a successful political leader, but fails critical ones and is now directly confronting the two final measures of political mortality. Blair has shown himself not to be tied by the promises which Labour made in opposition. Much of his government's approach to public spending and taxes, and to the reform of health and education was, by the end of his second term, very different from the 1997 manifesto proposals and from the actions taken during the first two years in office. In that sense, Blair has shown the long-term survivor's classic flexibility and ability to reinvent both himself and his government. In later chapters, I show that the first six months of 2000 was the critical period for this readjustment.

Blair has also been personally resilient. While depressed and tired at times – notably in the spring of 2004, when he considered resignation – he has quickly bounced back, conveying an impression of energy and commitment. He has also generally been able to shrug off personal criticism, even when, cumulatively, the charges damaged his reputation for honesty and integrity. That may have been partly the actor's mantle, although he was sensitive to attacks on his wife Cherie. He has given the appearance of being much less worried about press assaults than, say, John Major or Harold Wilson, or for that matter Gordon Brown. The most that I have heard from him after a critical article or articles is: 'You have been a bit rough on me recently.'

He has also had the ability to persuade – again partly the skill of the actor. Even, or rather especially, at the most testing times, he has been a powerful persuader, willing to confront critics and criticism. What Alastair Campbell, his long-serving media adviser up to September 2003, described as the 'masochism strategy' involved Blair sitting in a studio facing hostile questioners. He did not always win them over. But his apparent candour generally won respect. Even when opinion polls showed a fall in his personal ratings, especially on measures such as trust and honesty, Blair still rated very highly on being a strong leader. He was always ahead of opposition leaders, not just a series of unpopular Conservative ones but also the popular Liberal Democrat leader Charles Kennedy.

However, Blair has fared less well on some other tests. He has been cautious on many domestic policies and reluctant to take controversial and risky decisions. He has appeared to be concerned, at times too concerned, about offending supporters. As discussed in later chapters, this is one of the paradoxes of his 'big tent' approach. He has deliberately occupied the centre ground in politics, thus squeezing his opponents out to the extremes. But his defence of the centre ground has also limited his options, and has involved ideological and policy contradictions. He and New Labour have been electorally successful by accepting many of the policies brought in by the Thatcher and Major governments, such as trade union laws, the privatisation of the main utilities and cuts in income tax rates. For all the talk of radicalism, they have worked within a broadly free-market framework in economic and industrial policy. By contrast, there were much clearer dividing lines during the Asquith, Attlee and Thatcher administrations.

Blair's reluctance to take risks was particularly true in the first term, when fears of the impact of a policy on Middle Britain (in practice, Middle England) or on business often led to Downing Street interventions to squash controversial initiatives by departments which might offend someone. This has been rightly contrasted with Blair's greater boldness in foreign affairs, or rather, the non-European parts of international policy. Blair has been cautious over specifically European issues such as the euro. His boldness has been more on security and military questions, where he has felt fewer domestic political constraints and his instinctive moralism has been given fuller play. That began with the Kosovo conflict in spring 1999 and developed after the 9/11 attacks, particularly, of course, over the

Iraq war in spring 2003. This led him to proclaim at the Labour conference that autumn that his government was 'best when boldest'. From the middle of his second term onwards, he did become bolder, notably over the introduction of semi-independent foundation hospitals in the National Health Service and over flexible tuition fees in higher education. But by then, largely because of the Iraq war, he was in a weaker political position.

However, the earlier caution and attempts at reassuring middle-class voters left people confused about what he stood for. What he believes in has been a frequent question. That would never have been asked of Margaret Thatcher or Attlee – though it could easily have been asked of Roosevelt or Clinton. In fact, Blair has had a clearcut set of ethical beliefs, though these have not translated into easy ideological categories.

He has had an instinctive feel for voters' aspirations. Wanting to widen educational opportunities, protect people against crime and anti-social behaviour, or ensuring that as many as possible benefit from globalisation have been admirable goals, but hardly distinctive. His flexibility about specific policies has been both a strength and a weakness: a strength in that it allowed him to modify his government's strategy when necessary, as in 2000 over public services; and a weakness in that he appeared, often falsely, to lack a sense of direction, to be a creature of the latest shifts of public opinion.

Yet for all his caution, Blair has retained a focus on the big issues, even if he has not always been successful in pursuing them. He and his senior ministers – particularly Gordon Brown – have concentrated on economic stability, on improving public services and on tackling crime and anti-social behaviour. Even though his government has been active – arguably too active – over a wide range of issues, his own focus has been narrower. His priorities have been refined by the evidence of polls and focus groups of swing voters. Hence, while his government has introduced many far-reaching constitutional measures, he has paid little attention to them since he has believed, probably rightly, that most voters are not interested in these issues.

Unlike many of the other political leaders discussed above, Blair had a less secure base in his own party despite his electoral success. Even just after he was elected leader in July 1994, he was respected rather than liked within Labour ranks. He and many of his close allies were seen as being outside the main tradition of the party. Blair's authority has rested on the promise, and achievement, of electoral success, not on affection. Indeed, the tactic of triangulation – setting up New Labour in opposition not just to the Conservatives but also particularly to Old Labour – was effective in helping to capture the centre ground, but it alienated many traditional Labour supporters. Gordon Brown and his allies became increasingly critical of triangulation because they believed it antagonised and demoralised traditional Labour supporters. The Brown camp argued that the government needed to work far more with, rather than against, the Labour Party. So when the going got tougher, particularly over the Iraq war, Blair had fewer instinctive layers of loyalty on which to draw. That was particularly true of Labour MPs, who became increasingly rebellious in the Commons, and of local activists, especially in London and in seats with universities. But this was less true in traditional working-class areas where voters were less worried by Iraq. While Blair can fairly argue that Labour is unlikely to return to the high-spending and high-tax days of the 1970s – and he claimed during the 2005 campaign that New Labour was entrenched and would survive under his successor – he had failed to convert his party to Blairism. Its instincts and attitudes have only partly changed. Gordon Brown is widely seen as much closer to the outlook of Labour MPs and activists. The absence of a secure Blairite political base has mattered not only electorally but also at Westminster, where the prime minister was seen as increasingly isolated from 2003 onwards, in ways that previous left-of-centre leaders were not.

Moreover, this weakness has been compounded by Blair's ambiguous, and increasingly strained, relationship with Brown. Blair has never been fully in command, presidential in the way that his image makers and critics have imagined. Effective leadership was shared right from the start. Whatever may have been said by Blair at the famous dinner at the Granita restaurant in June 1994 about Brown's future leadership chances – or, rather, whatever ambiguous hopes may have been left dangling in the air – there is no doubt that Blair formally ceded big areas of economic policy to Brown. There were 'Tony's areas' and 'Gordon's areas'.

These changed over time. But no one had any doubt of Brown's power not only over traditional macroeconomic policy but also over wide areas of industrial and social policy. After the Bank of England took over responsibility for setting interest rates, the Treasury became the lead department in welfare-to-work, anti-poverty and industrial policy with its own initiatives. Moreover, after the Treasury was formally made the assessor, and later self-styled guardian, of the five tests for entry into the euro, Blair had effectively accepted Brown's veto over one of his central political aims. The power of the Treasury, and Brown, were unprecedented. There had been powerful Chancellors before – Lloyd George under Asquith, Stafford Cripps under Attlee, Nigel Lawson under Thatcher – but they had great influence for only part of these periods, not the whole time as Brown did, and their overall power was less than his. When you add in the lingering resentments which Brown felt over not being prime minister himself, which grew as Blair stayed on into a third term, then it is clear why Blair never felt he had a free hand. He always had to consider what 'Gordon would think'. There was a mood of tension for much of the time, particularly over public service reform during the second term. This had a significant effect on the development of government policy. The Blairites argued that Brown's desire to be a few degrees to the 'left' of them frustrated their desire to reform public services, while the Brownites criticised the practicality of some of the Blairites' plans.

Of course, previous governments had had tensions and arguments, but seldom between the same two leading figures for as long. Lloyd George did not really begin to clash with Asquith until after the completion of the main social reform legislation in 1911, while Lawson's relations with Thatcher only began to deteriorate significantly after the 1987 election. Yet stories about Blair–Brown tensions, even if at times exaggerated, were a consistent, and major, theme of these years.

By the time of his third election victory in May 2005, Blair also had to confront the last two aspects of long-serving leaders. He has already passed the eight-year mark when many previous leaders had started to go into decline. In a sense the turning point in his fortunes came after six years with the Iraq war. Nothing was the same afterwards, and there was a sense of the end approaching – even if it might still be years away. His departure was increasingly demanded by some aggrieved former Labour ministers and backbench critics. As one European ambassador headed his farewell despatch when leaving London in summer 2004, it was 'The long goodbye'. But unlike many earlier leaders, Blair was under no illusion that the premiership was a freehold. He knew that he could not remain for ever. Several times he referred to the experience of Margaret Thatcher, who talked, at the time of her third election victory in June 1987, of going 'on and on'. Blair did not want a similar fate. He believed that, while he could and would win a third term, the British public would not accept him seeking a fourth term, and potentially sixteen years in office.

He was aware of his political and personal mortality, notably after heart scares in October 2003 and a year later, requiring hospital treatment. Yet he was also determined to stay on for a third term. This was partly, as we shall see in later chapters, because he believed that much of his first term had been wasted and his reform programme had only got into its stride in the second term after 2001. He wanted a little longer, to extend and entrench these reforms, to achieve a lasting 'settlement' comparable with the post-1945 and post-1979 ones. So he attempted to seize the initiative at the end of the Labour conference in October 2004 by announcing that, while he intended to serve a full term if elected, he would not seek a fourth term. This was partly intended to end speculation about a handover to Brown, whose supporters believed that Blair had promised to stand down in mid-summer 2004. The Brown camp yet again thought that Blair had betrayed the Chancellor. The Blair announcement not only caught Brown by surprise, since he was flying to Washington, but led to a sharp deterioration in personal relations over the winter of 2004–05. The breach was only healed, in public at least, during the election campaign. The date of intended retirement was sufficiently far ahead to discomfort Brown, who feared only having a short period in charge at the tail end of a long Labour period in government, like Balfour after Salisbury, Neville Chamberlain after Baldwin or Eden after Churchill.

Yet Blair's announcement had a double-edged impact. He had admitted his political mortality, becoming the first British prime minister formally to set a term limit on his period in power. While this dampened down leadership speculation ahead of the 2005 general election, it meant that afterwards the political world would start looking to his departure – as indeed happened after the sharp reduction in the Labour majority. So Blair had removed the element of ambiguity essential to the power of previous British prime ministers.

Blair has had many of the qualities of successful, long-serving political leaders. He has been adaptable, flexible, personally resilient, persuasive, focused on the big issues, and, after several years of caution on domestic policy, increasingly willing to take risks. Yet he has lacked instinctive and natural loyalties within his own political party and has faced a long-term personal rivalry with a once close and powerful colleague. Moreover, unlike Asquith, Attlee or Thatcher, Blair has had an uncertain ideological framework. He has operated in the post-Thatcher world, just as Clinton was president in a political world changed by the Reagan administrations. Like Clinton, Blair's early years were dominated by the task of persuading his own party to abandon its failed approach and to adopt some of the policies and priorities of their previously successful opponents. This electorally necessary reinvention of their own parties – under the apt titles of New Democrats and New Labour – complicated the task in government for both Clinton and Blair, who has accepted much of the 'settlement' inherited from Margaret Thatcher and John Major.

Blair's dilemma is whether a pro-market approach to the economy can be reconciled with a universal welfare state. Can you limit the growth of public spending and hold tax rates, while providing public services to the standard that voters expect? Can you be both a social democrat and win the support of the middle classes of Middle England? Can you act centre-left while talking centre-right? The central question is whether Blair, like Clinton, has failed to change the political landscape, and create a 'settlement' of his own.

2

Creating New Labour

'New Labour will be a government of the radical centre ... A modern party, to be successful in the modern world, must be in the centre speaking for the mainstream majority.'

Tony Blair, speaking to the British-American Chamber of Commerce,
12 April 1996.

'There have been few more successful transformations of any organisation than the change from old to new Labour. Why was it so successful? Because, to use the jargon, the "burning platform" was in place. The party knew that the old ways wouldn't do. There was also a single, united goal that linked everyone and created a will to win. Tony was good at opposition. He worked out immediately that it was not about opposing, but being a government in waiting.'

Peter Hyman, Blair speechwriter and strategist, in *1 Out Of 10*, 2005.

New Labour was born out of failure, and fear of failure. For a politician so keen on talking about 'modernisation', and whose election slogan in 2005 was 'Forward Not Back', Tony Blair has been obsessed with the past. His main concern, not just before 1997, but throughout his years in government, has been avoiding any return to the electoral defeats which so marked his formative years in the Labour Party. That meant that Labour adopted a risk-averse approach on policy before the 1997 election.

Winning elections has always come first, governing second. As Blair said on 29 April 1995, at the special conference to approve the rewriting of Clause Four (which enshrined the party's commitment to public ownership), 'I did not come into the Labour Party to join a pressure group. I didn't become Leader of this Party to lead a protest movement ... This is a Party of government and I will lead it as a Party of government.' (The capital letters are in the text of his speech.) At times, it has seemed that his aim has been just to win again, to become the first Labour leader ever to have two full terms, and later three full terms. His priorities were revealed a week before the 1997 election, when I was part of a team from *The Times* who interviewed Blair in his Islington home. Unusually, he was slightly tetchy and irritable, obviously tired from the campaign, wary of saying anything that might jeopardise Labour's victory. When I suggested that Bill Clinton, then three months into his second term, had not achieved much after more than four years in office, Blair replied sharply: 'Well, he got re-elected, didn't he?'

The very process of reinventing Labour in the mid-1990s involved putting electoral factors first, ahead of preparing for government. Not only were policy pledges specifically designed – and market tested – to be voter friendly, but policy thinking was also patchy. With some exceptions, such as Gordon Brown and David Blunkett, New Labour was ill prepared for the challenges of government.

Blair became the first successful British politician of the era of the permanent campaign. Of course, all successful leaders have to be concerned with winning and retaining power. They never forget the voters, or else they will be out of a job. But the balance has shifted. The political adviser and strategist has been a constant presence, not just an expert brought in every four or five years to handle election campaigns. The ultimate in the permanent campaign approach was not in the Clinton era but in the Bush White House, where Karl Rove, the president's longstanding political strategist, has been as important as, and arguably more important than, conventional policy advisers. He has been there to say how a particular initiative or speech will play to this or that key group, or state. In Britain, this role has been played variously by Alastair Campbell, especially after he became less involved in day-to-day press relations from 2001 onwards, and by Philip Gould, who has channelled advice on polls and on focus groups of half a dozen to ten swing voters. Of course, being in government is very different from being in opposition, which is largely about taking positions rather than decisions. And it would be wrong to regard Blair as a slave to opinion advisers: far from it, on foreign policy crises such as Kosovo and especially Iraq, where Blair went against the view of the majority of the electorate. But the underlying assumptions of the permanent campaign era – about being in a constant 24-hour battle to win media headlines, and to retain the support of public opinion – were shared by many of his key advisers, particularly during his first term.

It has not just been a matter of tactics, nor political positioning. It also had far-reaching policy implications. The creation of New Labour inhibited fresh policy thinking and risk-taking. If the priority was not to offend, but to include, then this limited what could be promised. Big tent, inclusionary, politics are also ideologically fuzzy. If you want to maximise your support, you become very sensitive about not offending allies. Blair's watchword in his first term, not heard much in recent years, was the deliberately non-ideological 'what works'.

The one clinching argument with Blair has been to remind him of what made Labour look extreme or cost the party votes during the 1980s, whether it was being seen as favouring high taxes, being anti-business, pro-union, anti-family, anti-Europe or anti-American. He has been determined not to fall into any of these traps, and to appear the opposite when possible: to be nervous about raising taxes, pro-business, cool with the unions, pro-family, pro-European and pro-American. That has made it harder to define a positive policy agenda, as opposed to a reactive, negative one.

All politicians are marked by their early years. For Harold Macmillan, it was the trenches of the First World War and the high unemployment of the interwar period. For Edward Heath, it was the rise of fascism and the destruction of much of continental Europe in the Second World War. For Margaret Thatcher, it was growing up in Grantham in wartime surrounded by American air force bases, and the austerity and controls of postwar Labour Britain. For Tony Blair, it was the fratricidal strife of the Labour Party of the early 1980s, both in north London, where he lived, and then at Westminster after his election as an MP in 1983. For him,

Labour was destructively self-indulgent, and out of touch with the lives and aspirations of ordinary people – particularly their aspirations. That view was reinforced by the contrast with what he saw as the level-headed approach of his constituents in Sedgefield in the north-east.

This reaction did not instantly create New Labour. Rather, its evolution was gradual and collaborative, beginning well before Blair became Labour leader in July 1994. If he instinctively rejected the Labour Party of the early and mid-1980s, the intellectual case for change came much more from Gordon Brown, and was influenced by the increasing links between the two and Peter Mandelson, Labour's head of communications in the second half of the 1980s. All three recognised that Labour had to change. But the birth of New Labour came in several stages: first, the dropping of the more extreme, vote-losing promises after Neil Kinnock became leader in 1983; second, the policy review of the late 1980s changing the approach towards Europe and the unions; and third, after the party's fourth consecutive defeat in 1992. As employment spokesman from 1989 until 1992, Blair had played an important part in the dropping of previous pledges to repeal the Tories' employment legislation, notably on the closed shop. But, as I know from conversations with him at the time, he never really shared the high hopes that Labour would win the 1992 election. He was worried about the impact of the tax pledges, privately joking once in early 1992 about whether he could afford to vote Labour. He believed that the party had not changed enough.

The April 1992 defeat was the key moment in persuading him that Labour needed to change much more. On election night itself, he told his party workers in the Black Bull in Trimdon: 'Reform doesn't stop. We've got to go on. We've got to change' (Seldon 2004, p. 142). He repeated this message over the coming days on television and in the press, telling the BBC on the day after the election that if the party were ever to win again, it had to appeal more to the middle classes. He firmly rejected the 'one more heave' view. This period, immediately after the 1992 defeat, both hardened Blair personally and convinced him of what Labour now had to do. John Rentoul, one of the most perceptive of Blair's biographers, has played down the significance of the manoeuvring after John Smith died in May 1994 and argued:

> Those looking for the explanation of how Blair secured the leadership ought to focus instead on the hours and days after the Labour Party lost its fourth election in a row in 1992. It is in the conversations and calculations of the key players over the weekend from Friday 10 April to Tuesday 14 April that historians will find the answers. (Rentoul 2001, p. 179)

Gordon Brown's failure to stand for the leadership then mattered far more than Blair's decision not to go for the deputy leadership. Blair's emergence as a leadership contender, and winner, two years later can be traced to this period. He was in no doubt what needed to happen, writing in the *Guardian* at the end of June 1992: 'The true reason for our defeat is not complex. It is simple. It has been the same since 1979: Labour has not been trusted to fill the aspirations of the majority.' The boyish smile remained, but now there was also steel. This was shown over the 1992–94 period as he developed populist themes as shadow Home Secretary: the 'tough on crime, tough on the causes of crime' period. (The phrase came from Brown.) His social moralism, while annoying some in the Labour Party, was widely praised outside the party. It was not just a clever repositioning, it reflected his personal views, his ethical outlook, rooted in family, duty and personal responsibility.

Blair's view of how much Labour needed to change was reinforced in November 1992 when Bill Clinton defeated the elder President Bush. Philip Gould, bruised after the April defeat, had spent the last five weeks of the American campaign in the Clinton 'war room' in Little Rock, Arkansas. He was excited by what he saw, and heard and found a ready audience in Blair and Brown, especially after both visited Washington in January 1993 as the Clinton team was taking office and drew clear comparisons with Labour's plight at home. The Gould analysis, as set out in his book, published after the 1997 election but prophetically entitled *The Unfinished Revolution*, was that the Clinton victory pointed the way for Labour (Gould 1998, pp. 170–76). On election night, while awaiting Clinton's acceptance speech, Gould told a BBC reporter that such a victory could happen in Britain: 'When Labour has got rid of high taxes and trade union dominance. When we have changed as the Democrats have changed.' As soon as he got back to Britain, Gould wrote a memorandum arguing for changes both in campaigning techniques ('an effective rapid response and attack capacity') and strategy. Labour, he wrote, was perceived to be looking 'downwards not upwards', and 'backwards not forwards'; it was for 'minorities and not the mainstream' and it was 'not trusted to run the economy properly'. He urged a 'new populism', connecting with the aspirations of 'ordinary working people'. And above all, Labour needed a fresh start: 'A changed Labour Party is the basis of a new relationship of trust with the British electorate.' And this change must be open: 'Labour has not changed until it announces that it has changed.'

That encapsulates the blueprint of New Labour, and many of the themes are still central to its message now. But Gould's analysis, and the enthusiasm of Blair, Brown and their allies for Clinton's success was, at first, rejected by many in the Labour Party. John Smith, the then party leader, disliked the arguments caused by the talk of 'Clintonisation', while others, notably John Prescott, feared how Blair and Brown wanted to change Labour. Little happened at first. The full impact of the Clinton experience was only felt after Smith died in May 1994, and Blair became Labour leader that July. While Blair became much more prominent during the two years of Smith's leadership, he made no secret of his dissatisfaction with the caution of his leader.

Much has been written about the events following Smith's death, and what happened over the following days and weeks had a lasting impact on subsequent relations between Blair, Brown and Mandelson. But the central point was that Blair was elected because he looked like a winner who could appeal to the parts of the country which Labour needed to capture in order to have a Commons majority. It was not because of what he said, or promised. His manifesto for the leadership was a collection of platitudes under the title of 'Change and National Renewal'. It was long on good intentions, short on anything specific. Many of his close supporters during the leadership campaign, such as Mo Mowlam and Peter Kilfoyle, subsequently became disillusioned with him.

However, once elected in July 1994 Blair and his advisers fully understood the importance of demonstrating that Labour had changed, just as Bill Clinton had sought to show that the Democrats had changed in 1992. The renaming of the party as New Labour – in common usage, if not legally – symbolised that change. As Andrew Chadwick and Richard Heffernan have argued:

> The re-branding proclaimed the party as a safe bet for non Labour voters, demonstrating that its previous assumptions were well and truly a thing of the past ... This objective involved the construction of a stereotypical Old Labour. Making clear what Labour was not, and what it did not stand for, was the prime objective. The idea that Labour was in thrall to the trade unions, favoured high levels of taxation, would be profligate with taxpayers' money and 'irresponsible' in its macroeconomic policy – all these had to be banished from popular perception. Thus was the spectre of 'Old' Labour clinically raised to indicate just how fast change was occurring under 'New' Labour. Strangely enough, its target was just as much Jim Callaghan, say, as it was Tony Benn. (Chadwick and Heffernan 2003, pp. 13-14)

Lord Callaghan retained an affectionately ambiguous attitude towards Blair, admiring his daring and his success, but unsure what type of party he was creating. Blair never had an entirely easy relationship with Callaghan's allies on the old Labour right, and was more comfortable with the 'soft' left, former supporters of Neil Kinnock, many of whom achieved prominent positions in his government.

The most significant indicator of change came at the Labour conference in Blackpool in autumn 1994, when, in his first party conference speech, Blair proposed 'a clear, up-to-date statement of the objects and objectives of our party'. He did not specifically refer to Clause Four of the party constitution for fear of provoking open protests, which would spoil the public impact of his speech. But that is precisely what he did mean. He had concluded during the summer that rewriting Clause Four would be the clearest way to highlight that Labour had changed. Previous Labour leaders had failed in the attempt to rewrite it (Gaitskell), not bothered (Wilson), or believed it was impossible or counterproductive politically (Kinnock and Smith). The clause had been adopted in 1918 and very few any longer took literally the reference to the 'common ownership of the means of production, distribution and exchange'. Its retention was an aspiration or symbol, not a target.

In proposing the rewriting of Clause Four, Blair was attacking a cardboard castle – though there were defenders, as was shown when a motion rejecting its replacement (already on the conference agenda) was narrowly approved two days after his dramatic initiative. This was presented in parts of the media as a rebuff to him, but it was more an accident of timing. That defeat and the subsequent anguished debate within the Labour Party over the new wording helped Blair when the new Clause Four was approved with nearly two-thirds support the following April. He was seen to have won a victory against Old Labour and against some major trade unions, even if it was over a piece of paper which everybody then forgot. He won because the case for change had already gained wide acceptance within the party before he launched his initiative; because the case for public ownership had been undermined by privatisation, because no coherent alternative was offered, because of the weakened power of the unions, because he had been able to tap into the changed mood of party members and to mobilise them through ballots, and because he used his own authority as leader to make approval of the change a element key of the party's electoral credibility (see Riddell on Clause IV 1997).

The victory mattered more than the words. It established his own leadership and fortified his claim to be creating a new party. It was a classic exercise in triangulation. Blair himself revealed the importance of the Clause Four debate in impromptu remarks to the Scottish Labour conference in March 1995, when he declared: 'The only thing that stands between us and government is trust. Trust will be gained, not by clinging to icons for fear of thinking anew, but by seizing the spirit without which all thought is barren.' By showing that he had been able to change Labour as a party, Blair hoped to be able to convince voters that Labour could be trusted again in government.

In retrospect, the main criticism of Blair's handling of Labour in the two years between his victory over the rewriting of Clause Four in April 1995 and the general election two years later is that he did not do more to change his party. There was some complacency in the Blair team, as well as an unwillingness to repeat what had been a very draining six-month battle. Moreover, John Prescott, now Blair's deputy, believed that, in return for his public backing for rewriting Clause Four, there would be no further party reforms before the election. As John Rentoul reports (2001, p. 263), Prescott grumbled when the already discussed reduction in the trade unions' share of Labour conference votes was lowered from 70 to 50 per cent, after the trigger point for a review of the share had been reached when party membership rose above 300,000. But there was little appetite for further changes in Labour's relations with the unions, such as moving wholly to a one-member-one-vote party.

One of the many paradoxes of this period is that, while Blair found it much easier to control the party than his predecessors as Labour prime minister like Wilson and Callaghan, he never really changed the party. His power has rested on his personal authority. The shifts in the power balance within the Labour Party as a result of the constitutional and organisational changes, both before Blair became leader and during his years as leader, are complicated, as Meg Russell highlights in her typically thorough book on the subject. The changes in the annual party conference – including the reduction in the ability of ordinary party members to 'exercise voice' in submission of policy resolutions, as well as the creation of the National Policy Forum as a deliberative body to consider new policies – have appeared to strengthen the position of the party leadership. However, Russell notes (2005, pp. 281–2) that the reduction in the unions' dominance, both centrally and locally, has meant that power is more widely distributed. 'Thus leaders cannot afford completely to ignore members' views, and can't rely on negotiating outcomes behind closed doors with loyal trade union leaders, to the exclusion of the wider party. The decline in trade union influence may have freed leaders from one form of constraint, but it has also confronted them with others.' Moreover, as she rightly argues, 'the control that Labour leaders have exercised in recent years results more from cultural change than from any reform of the party's structure.' Party activists wanted to win before 1997, and, while tensions have re-emerged, notably after the Iraq war, they have been containable.

Blair has failed to remake the party in his image. 'His' people have controlled it centrally, but he has failed to place them either in the leadership of the unions, which have become increasingly hostile to the government, or among the new generation of candidates and MPs. Blair's patronage within the Labour Party, as opposed to government, has been limited. His staff in Downing Street have come to realise that he is not good at using the levers of power and influence to secure them parliamentary seats, in contrast to the effectiveness of the Brown camp before the 2005 general election, when three of the Chancellor's closest aides – Ed Balls, Ed Miliband and Ian Austin – were all selected as parliamentary candidates for safe seats. Pat McFadden, Blair's former political secretary, secured a safe

Labour seat in the west Midlands by his own efforts and contacts, not through help from Blair.

During the three opposition years, the Blair team felt they controlled the main levers of power and could do largely what they wanted. Power was centralised around Blair and Brown. While this led to rumblings of complaint from shadow Cabinet colleagues and Labour MPs, no one objected too much because of the absolute priority of winning the general election. Message discipline became the watchword. But it was not just the priority of conveying the impression of unity.

The election strategy also dominated policy-making. If you read the policy documents and speeches of this period of opposition, there is only a vague sense of what New Labour is for, as opposed to what it is against. This was the 'warm words' phase when vague references to 'modernisation' were all. That led to the vacuous claptrap of Blair's second conference speech as leader in October 1995:

> I want us to be a young country again. With a common purpose. With ideals we cherish and live up to. No resting on past glories. Not fighting old battles. Not sitting back, hand on mouth, concealing a yawn of cynicism, but ready for the day's challenge. Ambitious. Idealistic. United. Where people succeed on the basis of what they give to their country, rather than what they take from their country. Saying not 'This was a great country,' but 'Britain can and will be a great country again.'

Such empty rhetoric – and there was plenty more in the speech – showed Blair at his worst, pursuing trendy images without obvious meaning.

The priority was offering reassurance – to voters whom Labour needed to win, to business, and to the markets. Hence, many of Blair's speeches were about what he would not do. He would not repeal the Tories' trade union laws or return to the taxation levels of the late 1970s. This was allied to the assiduous courting of the establishment and of powerful institutions previously strongly opposed to Labour. The classic instance, particularly encouraged by Alastair Campbell, was the attempt to win over, or at least neutralise, the Rupert Murdoch-owned newspaper the *Sun*, in the past one of the strongest backers of Margaret Thatcher. The Blair camp, and later Gordon Brown, were always keen to maintain contact with Rupert

Murdoch on his regular visits to London. Blair even made a short visit to Australia in July 1995 to make a speech at News Corporation's conference for senior executives from around the world. His message then was blunt about the creation of New Labour: 'To become a serious party of government, Labour required a quantum leap.' He talked about 'the long march back from the dark days of the early 1980s when, frankly, we were unelectable'. This trip was seen as a success at a the time and even more when, on the eve of the 1997 election campaign, the *Sun* came out in support of Tony Blair, though in reality its declaration followed a shift by its readers over the previous four years away from the Conservatives towards Labour.

This 'big tent' approach meant that nothing could be done to worry new supporters. That was shown by the leadership's approach to taxation and public spending, which Blair and Brown both believed had been one of the main reasons for Labour's defeats in 1987 and 1992. John Smith's shadow Budget in March 1992 had backfired since it threatened higher taxes for many middle income earners. The problem was not so much the numbers affected or the small size of the tax rises for most as that many more people who aspired to earn such incomes feared that their taxes would rise. So one of the main conclusions that Brown drew was that Labour had to shed its high spending/high tax image. This meant a tight control on commitments, and endlessly repeated statements that a Labour government would not tax and spend for its own sake, but only for specific projects. Regaining an image for economic competence was a pre-condition for regaining the trust of the electorate.

Labour strategists looked for a way of dramatising their new approach. Philip Gould (1998, p. 267) says that focus groups showed that 'people wanted smaller promises they could believe in, not larger ones which seemed incredible. I also found that if we said how the promise would be paid for, the power of the pledge was enhanced enormously. As our policy developed, we tested and re-tested it, with rival manifestos, until gradually the core promises began to emerge.' Peter Hyman, a communications strategist and speech writer for Blair for nine years, came up with the idea of 'an offer', or simple contract. Hyman recalls (2005, pp. 61–2) his view that 'vague promises wouldn't do ... What was Labour offering? The far-away promise of better public services? Stronger communities? The public needed measurable symbolic policies.' The resulting pledge card had deliberate echoes of the 'Contract with America', the series of promises offered by Newt Gingrich and conservative Republicans in the November 1994 mid-term elections, when they captured the House of Representatives for the first time in forty years. The Labour pledges were lengthily discussed by Blair, Brown, Gould and Hyman with members of the shadow Cabinet, and were market-tested exhaustively in focus groups. Gordon Brown and his advisers were determined to be cautious and prudent. But, overall, there was the impression that election tactics drove policy-making.

The result was an effective message, but very patchy policies. The five pledges, unveiled at the launch of the party's draft manifesto in July 1996, promised that in government Labour would:

- cut class sizes to thirty or under for five-, six- and seven-year-olds by using money from the assisted places scheme;
- fast-track punishment for persistent young offenders by halving the time from arrest to sentencing;
- cut NHS waiting lists by treating an extra 100,000 patients as a first step by releasing £100 million saved from NHS red tape;
- remove 250,000 under-25-year-olds from benefit and into work by using money from a windfall levy on the privatised utilities; and
- set tough rules for government spending and borrowing; ensure low inflation; strengthen the economy so that interest rates are as low as possible.

There was a careful emphasis throughout these pledges on new commitments being costed with details about how they would be financed. The first five pledges sounded impressive, but they largely skimmed the surface of policy-making, apart from the broad economic pledge. Promising to reduce waiting lists said nothing about how it would be achieved, or the organisation of the NHS. The health section of the manifesto was headed 'We will save the NHS', with its main emphasis on ending the Tories' internal market and using the savings to treat more patients. Fast-tracking punishment for young offenders was a good idea, but linking the various parts of the criminal justice system together was a very complicated task.

Similarly, reducing class sizes was an admirable objective, but did not explain how standards in schools could be improved.

To be fair, on education at least Labour did work out some detailed policies in opposition. The Labour manifesto stressed that education was the number one priority, but the main emphasis was on making the current system work better. 'Standards more than structures are the key to success ... Our approach will be to intervene where there are problems, not where schools are succeeding.' The focus was on intervention to address failure and a drive to improve literacy and numeracy in primary schools. Ironically, Blair's later slogan, 'Choice and diversity', was the heading for the education section of the Conservative manifesto in 1997, when the party promised more freedom for schools, more specialist schools, and more choice for parents, the themes that Blair picked up after 2000.

But these pledges were only part of the story. Brown believed that tax and spending policies were the key to offering the public reassurance. As William Keegan explains in his critical but sympathetic account of the Brown Chancellorship (2003, pp. 146–9), at the beginning of 1997 'Labour's focus group experts maintained that "fear of Labour" was growing, and that there could be yet another Conservative "Labour Tax Bombshell" scare (on the lines of 1987 and 1992), despite Gordon Brown's prudence with his tax-and-spend promises.' Blair firmly ruled out the suggestion by Brown and Ed Balls that the option of a 50 per cent top rate of income tax (against 40 per cent then, and now) should be left open. So Brown promised to leave the basic and top rates of income tax unchanged and to retain the Tories' existing spending plans for the first two years in office, apart from a specific pledge for a one-off levy on the privatised utilities to pay for the New Deal welfare-to-work programme.

In a typical Brown fashion, he leaked the details in two parts, the spending section to the morning papers, and then the tax pledge on the BBC Radio 4 *Today* programme, before his speech on 'Responsibility in Public Finance' was ever delivered. The point of the promise was less to convince people that a Labour government would not put up taxes – three-fifths still thought they would, according to a MORI poll on the eve of the election – than to bolster the general impression that the party could be trusted in government – 'prudent', in Brown's often repeated word.

But if the need to win the election limited the public promises, was there a clearcut ideology beneath the surface? What did New Labour amount to? For all their 'what works' pragmatism, Blair, and especially his advisers, were always searching for an overarching theory to justify and legitimise their practice. They wanted ideological cover for their electoral strategy. Blair himself talked for a time about 'social-ism', as distinct from socialism, though this amounted to little more than motherhood-and-apple-pie clichés: 'Social-ism is not about class, or trade unions, or capitalism versus socialism. It is about a belief in working together to get things done.' A nursery school teacher could not have put it better. That reflected Blair's interest in communitarianism, an approach developed by Amitai Etzioni, its guru, as well as the ethical socialism he had developed during his Oxford days from the Scottish moral philosopher John Macmurray. Blair's flirtation with 'stakeholding', as publicised by Will Hutton, a voluble journalist/propagandist of the fashionable left, lasted little longer than a holiday romance. Stakeholding was scuppered by suggestions that formally including stakeholders such as workers and consumers on company boards might interfere with managers' right to manage, and directors' to direct, thus raising fears among the new business supporters of New Labour. Then, as close links with Bill Clinton and the New Democrats developed, the 'Third Way' became the mantra which Anthony Giddens, a leading political sociologist and then director of the London School of Economics, developed in a series of books. Giddens, now ennobled, has been for New Labour like Suslov in the Soviet era, its ideologist in good times and bad. He has seen New Labour/the Third Way as a response to globalisation, economic and social changes to traditional family structures and the rise of individualism – in effect a renewal of social democracy which transcends both old-style postwar democratic socialism and neo-liberalism. Even the term, the Third Way, hardly ever used by Gordon Brown, was too loaded for some Continental social democrats. So the blander 'progressive governance' became the umbrella for links between centre-left leaders and policymakers.

This is treacherous ground, on which various political scientists have tried to raise their standards. For some, mainly on the left, New Labour has been merely Thatcherism, the neo-liberal economic model, with a human face. Before 1997 many on the left, for example, condemned the abandonment of a formal commitment to full employment, even though the unemployment and employment record of the Blair government has turned out to be better than most previous administrations that professed full employment as a goal. A more sophisticated version is that Margaret Thatcher established a new consensus about the role of the state, and the creation of New Labour is the proof of her success. For others, New Labour has been an updated version of democratic socialism, showing considerable continuities with previous Labour governments, despite all the rhetorical distancing from 'Old Labour'. On this view, Old Labour and New Labour have a lot in common. Others see a synthesis, defining New Labour as post-Thatcherism. The rival interpretations of the meaning of New Labour are discussed in the final chapter, when I attempt to put Blair and his record into historical perspective.

Blair and his advisers deliberately sought to confuse the debate. The ambiguity over ideology was not an accident. Triangulation by definition means distancing from the recent past, whether of your own party, or your opponents. Rereading the speeches of the period leaves an impression not only of naïve optimism, but also an underlying concern with escaping the recent past. The language is all about newness, dynamism, renewal and modernity. For Blair, the key was to be different because the recent past meant failure. In opposition, his consistent theme was to demonstrate that Labour had changed and could therefore be trusted in government. In a campaign speech in January 1996 he argued: 'The Tories would love to be fighting the Labour Party of the late Seventies and early Eighties. They are not. The public see the same old Tory Party, and a new Labour Party ... A party in the centre ground of British politics that will govern in the centre ground too.' However, to show that New Labour really was Labour at heart, Blair invoked the spirit and values of past Labour governments, but mainly those in the distant past like the postwar Attlee administration, rather than more recent examples from the Wilson and Callaghan era, or the opposition period of the 1980s. Otherwise, New Labour has sought to draw a veil over this more recent past for electoral reasons, even though the origins of Blairism lay in the arguments and policy shifts of the Kinnock and Smith years. Most of the key organisational changes, apart from the re-writing of Clause Four, and much of the clearing away of previous unpopular policies, had occurred under Blair's predecessors. So the break with the

recent Labour past was exaggerated. Yet at the same time, in order to differentiate itself, New Labour both strongly attacked the record of the Major
government and accepted many of the changes introduced by the Tories
during the 1980s. The implicit theme was that New Labour accepted much
of Thatcherism, and even Majorism, but not Thatcher or Major.

However, it is an oversimplification to see the Blair and Brown approach
as merely a continuation of Thatcherism. There have been continuities,
notably in economic policy. But there have been differences in values and
priorities. New Labour was more concerned with helping the least well off
– redistribution by stealth – and improving public services. There has been
a commitment to an active state. Moreover, at least in its aspirations, Blair
promised to be more internationalist and pro-European, while New
Labour's constitutional reform agenda put it apart from the Conservatives
of the Thatcher and Major era.

The distinctive feature of the Blair and Brown approach – by contrast
with the failed policies of the 1970s and the Labour fantasies of the 1980s –
has been its acceptance that Britain cannot isolate itself from the pressures
of globalisation. A consistent theme has been the need to be internationally
competitive, hence accepting a stable fiscal and monetary framework, and
flexible labour and product markets. In contrast with much of the
Continent, or rather the older western European democracies, the
Blair/Brown approach has stressed job creation rather than job protection,
seeing the traditional European social model as an impediment to competitiveness and economic growth. So far, this looks superficially like a classic
neo-liberal case. But New Labour has believed that the state needed to be
active in preparing workers for this more insecure economic environment,
by training and assisting the unemployed into work, and above all by
improving education. Under the much-used vogue word 'empowerment',
the state therefore had to be active in helping people, as well as in extending
the rights of women, parents and others.

The classic statement of this position was in the Commission on Social
Justice, which was set up by John Smith and chaired by Lord Borrie. Its
report was published in 1994. Two of its key members were Patricia Hewitt
and David Miliband, its secretary, both future Cabinet ministers. The
report sought to move beyond traditional Labour thinking on welfare,
which focused on class divisions in society, as reflected in the unequal

distribution of property, wealth and income. The commission took a different view, defining social justice as the pursuit of wider, and more equal, life chances, created particularly by levels of individual skills. This involved a changed role for the state: not managing levels of demand to boost employment, but providing labour with the skills and support needed for better-paid jobs in a global economy. This also meant recognising that the familiar pattern of mainly male full-time, lifelong working was no longer predominant. Social policy had to be more flexible to take account of more part-time female workers and the demands of two-earner households. So there would have to be looser patterns of employment, especially to meet the demands of child care. Similarly, pension arrangements would have to be adapted to respond to needs and costs of the increasing numbers of older people. So government should promote welfare-to-work policies, reform of the tax and benefits system to take account of these social changes, and lifelong learning. The commission portrayed the welfare state as assisting economic development. Starting with welfare-to-work, the commission's ideas have proved to be influential in the development of the Blair government's policies.

In practical terms, Blair was very cautious about commitments beyond the formal five pledges. The main emphasis was on grand-sounding promises of change, linked to sweeping anti-Tory statements. The 1997 manifesto was full of caveats about the party's pledges, for instance, 'more spending on education as the cost of unemployment falls'. There were some exceptions. Blair had inherited from the John Smith era, without enthusiasm, a series of ambitious and specific proposals to change the constitution, notably to introduce elected bodies in Scotland and Wales, a mayor and elected assembly in London, a Human Rights Act, and freedom of information legislation. But these promises were seen by the Blair team as peripheral to his main strategy, and Blair seldom highlighted them publicly. When he did refer to these proposals, it was invariably under the label of 'modernisation' rather than pluralism, a deliberate sharing of power.

Gordon Brown had developed his own agenda for the management and reform of the economy. He was helped particularly by Ed Balls and Ed Miliband (both elected Labour MPs at the 2005 general election) and by a range of advisers recruited from the private sector. (These preparations are discussed in detail in Robinson 2000 and Peston 2005.) The most important was the commitment, secret before the election, to make the Bank of England responsible for setting interest rates and meeting an inflation target laid down by the Chancellor. This was both a reaction to the policy failures of the early 1990s and a further development of the new approach to monetary policy of the mid-1990s. Brown and Balls stressed the vital importance of putting in place a robust rules-based framework for both monetary and fiscal policy to win the key battle of credibility. Prudence had to come first. Brown's team had also prepared plans for a windfall tax on the privatised utilities (justified by their alleged giveaway flotation prices) to finance the welfare-to-work programme to reduce youth and long-term unemployment.

If Brown had a much more detailed and worked-out plan for government than most of his colleagues, there was still plenty of uncertainty about what would and could happen in office. The state was viewed as a generally benign, rather than malign, force. But the implications were fuzzy. Few had thought out the connection between means and ends. Taken literally, Labour seemed to be promising a more active government on the cheap. Moreover, as I discuss in the next chapter, there was little understanding about how government worked, and about the levers of power.

However, there was a clear view that a strong lead had to come from the centre. In many ways the best guide to how Blair would govern came from *The Blair Revolution – Can New Labour Deliver?*, a book published in 1996 by Peter Mandelson, his *éminence grise*, and Roger Liddle, a former Labour special adviser during the Callaghan government who had gone on to become one of the founders of the SDP before rejoining Labour after Blair took over, and who later served in 10 Downing Street. For all the caution of being a semi-official blueprint, the book provides a remarkably prescient guide to the Blair style of leadership, even though it is fawningly adulatory about its hero. The message was clear. Blair would lead from the front. The centre would be strengthened. The Cabinet Office, the authors state, should be more akin to a department of the prime minister and the Cabinet, as it eventually became. Much of their advice about how to handle Whitehall is sensible, and Blair and his fellow ministers could have saved themselves a lot of trouble if they had paid more attention.

Labour went into the 1997 election stronger on the general promise of change than on the detail of how it would achieve it. During the campaign, Blair and other spokesmen talked of 'ten days to save the NHS'. But apart from the ill-thought-out promise to cut waiting lists, there was no hint of how much money might be necessary to 'save' the NHS. That would have to await the 2000 spending review and the Wanless report of five years later. The party promised to scrap the internal market. But there was no indication of how the NHS might serve patients better.

A warning shot came just before polling day in 1997 from Robert Reich, an original American thinker on public policy and President Clinton's first Labor Secretary before he left the administration disillusioned. He argued (1997) that 'A shift to the so-called "center" of the political spectrum is smart politics for Democrats and Labourites alike when conservatives have abandoned the middle ground. But "center" can mean very different things.' Reich contrasted the 'vital center', a liberal vision of individual empowerment and security against 'the more brutal forces of economy and society', and 'a mushy middle'. He said the economic and social divisions and inequalities produced by technological change and global economic integration required more than a 'center' located in moderate Republicanism or watered-down Toryism which could not reverse these trends. So after referring to the pitfalls as well as the successes of the Clinton record, Reich warned Blair: 'Do not take for granted the votes of the working class and the poor. Give them something to believe in, and act on it.'

Labour's endlessly repeated campaign theme, 'Things can only get better', summed up the mood of the time. There was a widespread desire to get rid of the Tories, and a sense of a new beginning, not only among many voters but also in Whitehall and among many journalists. May 1997 was one of those turning point elections, like 1945 and 1979, when the electorate had delivered a decisive verdict. As he responded to the cheers of the carefully orchestrated crowd greeting him and his family on their arrival in Downing Street, Tony Blair had been set, and had set himself, a huge task – much bigger than he realised.

3

Governing as New Labour

'You try getting change in the public sector and the public services. I bear the scars on my back after two years in government and heaven knows what it will be like after a bit longer. People in the public sector were more rooted in the concept that "if it has always been done this way, it must always be done this way" than any group of people I have come across.'

Tony Blair, speech to the Venture Capital Association, 6 July 1999.

'You're either a weak prime minister – in which case they'll knock you for that – or if you appear to have a clear sense of direction, and know what you want, then you are a quasi-dictator. And all this President Blair rubbish, it's just rubbish, absolute rubbish.'

Tony Blair, in an interview with the *Observer*, 5 September 1999.

'This speech does not work because it does not feel authentic. It reads like TB is reacting to criticism that he has dumped the past, rather than saying what he really believes in, that he was elected to take Britain into the future. The result is a speech that makes TB look rather sad, a passive observer of events, not a force for change ... TB pandering, lacking conviction, unable to hold a position for more than a few weeks before he moves on from it, lacking the guts to be able to tough it out.'

Philip Gould in a leaked memorandum commenting on a draft of Tony Blair's speech to the Women's Institute, June 2000.

A flu epidemic, a Labour life peer's elderly mother and a television interview changed the direction of the Blair government. The turning point in its history came not with the Iraq war in spring 2003, but three years earlier, when Tony Blair and Gordon Brown decided both on a substantial increase in spending on the NHS and on far-reaching reforms to its structure. The full implications only became clear later, but the decisions taken in the first half of 2000 both highlighted the shortcomings of the initial approach and defined New Labour's domestic strategy. The political troubles and bad headlines which led to the change of policy are a reminder of how early in its life the Blair government ran into criticism. New Labour's honeymoon was very short, even if the weaknesses of their opponents ensured that Blair and his party could win two further terms in office.

Blair and his ministers took a long time to understand how to use power. The famous 'scars on the back' remarks quoted above summed up his feelings for a large part of his first few years in office. He was impatient for change, but unsure how to translate his broad goals into specific policies and how to achieve them. In retrospect, his decision to call 1999 'the year of delivery' looks absurd, as well as typical of the style of the time. Every subsequent year became 'the year of delivery'.

In Blair's own view, expressed in January 2005 (Riddell 2005), the first term was a period of learning and proving that Labour could again be trusted and competent in government, particularly in managing the economy. But in this later Blair rationalisation, much of the early approach to public services proved to be wrong, with too many media-driven initiatives (endlessly recycled), too little funding (a necessary short-term counterpart of offering reassurance), and too little attention to reform. It was not really until the second term, after 2001, that his government realised what needed to be done to reform public services, and then started to introduce the necessary changes. So Blair looked forward to the 2005 general election as marking the start of his second real term, not his third term. This oversimplified what had happened, since the change of direction occurred three-quarters of the way through the first term, not after 2001. But his retrospective analysis is partly true. Blair's many Labour critics take a different view of what happened in the first two terms. They highlight the government's achievements in its first term, from the ambitious constitutional reform programme to the introduction of a national minimum wage, and contrast them with the divisions of the second term, over Iraq, foundation hospitals and tuition fees for university students. Both views, however, underline the lack of clarity and agreement about what New Labour has been about.

Blair's administration has suffered from three central flaws in the conduct of domestic policy: first, inexperience; second, lack of clarity about both means and ends; and third, and not widely appreciated, confusion about the role of central government. These problems can be traced back to the birth and development of New Labour. The concentration on defining New Labour in negative terms – as being unlike past Labour governments and avoiding fresh spending commitments – prevented clear thinking about what it was positively for. Triangulation has been an effective electoral strategy, but it has not provided a clear blueprint for government. The need to offer reassurance about tax rates and levels of public spending regarded as vital to win the 1997 election made it much harder to develop coherent and sustainable policies.

The first problem was the new government's inexperience. None of the four top ministers (Tony Blair, Gordon Brown, Robin Cook and Jack Straw) had ever served in government before, and only one, Cook, had even been in the Commons when Labour was last in office. Of the Cabinet, only four had had even junior office, and the sole minister with Cabinet experience, John Morris, the Attorney General, was outside the Cabinet. It was the most inexperienced team since Ramsay MacDonald's first administration in 1924, though two of MacDonald's Cabinet had previous experience at that level (Haldane and Henderson). One of Blair's more historically minded advisers suggested that the Cabinet was the least experienced since Rockingham's two short-lived ministries in the second half of the eighteenth century, not a point he apparently made to the prime minister for fear of confusion with Lord Rockingham's Eleven, a rock band of Blair's youth.

Attempts were made to prepare probable Labour ministers for the ways of Whitehall. Seminars were held with former permanent secretaries, special advisers and academics. But these seem to have made little difference at a time when the focus was all on winning the coming election. Jonathan Powell, Blair's chief of staff from early 1995 and a former middle-ranking diplomat, tried to get him accustomed to handling a flow of official papers by putting them in a box for him to consider every evening and weekend, as happens with ministers' red boxes. But these were a poor substitute for the experience of office itself. Talks were also held with Sir Robin Butler, the long-serving Cabinet Secretary, who saw it as his last main function in Whitehall to ensure a smooth transition into power for Labour after the party's eighteen years in opposition. (Lord Butler of Brockwell, as he became, had a final, important role seven years later when he chaired the official inquiry into the intelligence failures before the Iraq war.)

But well intentioned though these efforts were, they could not overcome ingrained habits established during the long years out of office. Blair and Brown were used to working just with small groups of advisers. Their style was bilateral, not collective. They had never run anything and did not understand about organisations. The shadow Cabinet was a necessity, not a preferred forum for taking decisions or holding open-ended discussions. New initiatives were decided jointly by Blair and Brown, often after endless talks between them and their advisers, with little involvement from other shadow spokesmen unless strictly necessary. Their normal method of operation was by pre-emption, selective briefing and bouncing colleagues. The methods were informal and media driven.

Blair and his team saw little reason to change their approach in government. He imported his team into 10 Downing Street, blurring the lines between the political and the official by making Powell his chief of staff in government, as well as in opposition. Powell was given special dispensation under an order in council to give instructions to civil servants, which politically appointed special advisers cannot normally do. This was part of a compromise after Sir Robin Butler successfully resisted making Powell principal private secretary, a role which included handling relations with Buckingham Palace and patronage. Alastair Campbell, as head of communications, was given similar special powers – and the whole media operation was expanded, with the creation of a Strategic Communications Unit to plan presentation and coordinate announcements by departments on a weekly 'grid'. The political was intermingled with the official from the start with a big increase in the number of special advisers in Number 10 and the Treasury. In practice, it is doubtful if these two special dispensations made much difference since Number 10 is an inherently political and partisan place. Permanent civil servants in the private office have in the past routinely acted in a political way in advancing and protecting the interests of the prime minister.

The informal way of reaching decisions also continued. Blair was horrified by stories about the many and often very long meetings of the Callaghan Cabinet in the autumn of 1976 when the government was negotiating with the International Monetary Fund over the terms of a standby loan. Initially, he regarded the weekly meetings of Cabinet as a brief reporting session, seldom long enough for a cup of coffee. Of course, there was nothing new about the Cabinet ceasing to be a decision-making body. Cabinet committees, and informal ad hoc groups (particularly under Margaret Thatcher), had long before become much more important in dealing with government business. But the Cabinet had at least had a role providing an opportunity for ministers to raise the political issues of the day. Even this role was in abeyance for much of Blair's first term, although this changed later, particularly after the Iraq war. There were active Cabinet committees on the constitution in the first two or three years, and later the committee covering domestic affairs chaired by John Prescott, where some of the battles over university tuition fees were fought out between Gordon Brown and Charles Clarke. (These were so vigorous and lengthy that they delayed the meeting of the full Cabinet on one Thursday in January 2003, so that Blair had to send an emissary to find out what was happening.)

But both Blair and Brown preferred to keep control of contentious issues. Even where groups of ministers met, in 10 Downing Street with largely the same membership as the relevant committee, their proceedings were often informal without official papers being circulated to all ministers (the main complaint of the Butler committee about the run-up to the Iraq war). From the Iraq war period onwards, Blair did use the full Cabinet more as a sounding board on the issues of the moment. Each of the main five-year plans for public services were discussed at a Cabinet meeting, revealing some of the rumbling Blair/Brown disagreements on the extent of reform. After the 2005 election, Sir Andrew Turnbull, the Cabinet Secretary, sought to integrate the informal and the formal by advising Blair to set up a series of specialist Cabinet committees covering each of the main public services. These committees, all of which Blair chaired, combined the roles of policy-making and the stocktaking and reviews of progress on delivery which Blair had previously undertaken bilaterally with the relevant ministers and advisers.

Most radical governments have been driven from the centre – in this case a dual centre in 10 Downing Street and the Treasury, working both in tandem and in tension. That was true of the Margaret Thatcher/Nigel Lawson combination at their most harmonious and productive period from 1983 until early 1988, when relations became increasingly frayed over exchange rate policy, and, to a lesser extent, the poll tax. While Thatcher and Lawson generally observed the conventions of the Cabinet system more than Blair and Brown, the differences in practice were smaller than the constitutional purists claimed. Everyone knew where the power lay in both cases.

This dual control also qualifies talk of Blair as president rather than prime minister. Some of Blair's advisers certainly talked about a Blair presidency, and a stronger centre, partly because of the weakness and inexperience of many other ministers. That was a theme of the Mandelson/Liddle book of 1996, the not so hidden Blairite manifesto, as discussed in the last chapter. But even the most zealous Blairites recognised, sometimes unenthusiastically, the sharing of power with Brown and the Treasury. By contrast, some of Brown's allies liked to depict Blair as a non-executive chairman, with Brown as the chief executive. This was a gross oversimplification. Rather, as the next chapter shows, there were 'Gordon's areas' (notably the economy, welfare, industrial policy and international development) and 'Tony's areas' (notably education, health and defence), and areas where they overlapped and often clashed, notably Europe and, increasingly, the direction of public service reform. The boundaries shifted as Blair became more involved in the second term with Africa and with pensions.

The expansion of the 10 Downing Street operation, and the gradual bringing of parts of the Cabinet Office within its control, has created what Peter Hennessy (2000, p. 486) called 'the notion of a Prime Minister's Department that dare not quite speak its name'. Number 10 has a much strengthened domestic and foreign policy capacity, giving the prime minister a much greater influence over decision-making. The number of politically appointed advisers in 10 Downing Street trebled to 24 during the first term (and doubled to 74 in the whole of Whitehall in the period, with a big rise also in the Treasury). However, there is a limit to what even the most assiduous members of the Policy Unit, later the Policy Directorate, can do. They can focus on relatively few issues of direct concern to the prime minister, either pressing 'headline' questions which had blown up or future initiatives. But they, and Blair, cannot run departments. And, increasingly over time as departmental ministers have become more confident and the duds were dropped, advisers have learnt to adopt a more cooperative approach. Nonetheless, ministers often complained of Downing Street's preference for their own proposals over those of departments, a 'not invented here' approach. Downing Street advisers have blamed a lack of originality and drive in some departments.

Foreign policy expertise in Number 10 was greatly expanded. From summer 2001 onwards, a separate senior European adviser was appointed alongside the foreign affairs private secretary, in effect a national security adviser who dealt with Washington and global security problems. Both were also the heads of their respective sections of the Cabinet Office secretariat. Initially, the foreign affairs and European roles were undertaken by Sir David Manning and Sir Stephen Wall respectively, then from 2003 by Sir Nigel Sheinwald and Kim Darroch. Sir David was in charge of Iraq policy in the run-up to the war. These changes gave Blair a much greater personal capacity to lead and develop foreign policy than his predecessors enjoyed, though Charles Powell (now Lord Powell of Bayswater) managed to cover both these areas on behalf of Margaret Thatcher in the second half of the 1980s.

These changes all fuelled charges of presidentialism. That was true in style, and in media management, but in many respects bilateralism is a more accurate term than presidentialism, or rather trilateralism, with Number 10 and the Treasury working with the relevant department. The best description remains that of Lord Lawson (1994, p. 444) of what he has called a 'mutual blackball system ... If a minister wishes to do something within his own field which the prime minister profoundly disapproves of, then the prime minister has a blackball which he or she can cast. He or she may choose not to cast it, but that blackball is there. Equally, however, unless the minister concerned is completely spineless – and that is occasionally the case, but not normally – then if the prime minister wants something done in a particular area, and the minister responsible disagrees with it, then it will not happen because he will effectively veto that idea: he has a blackball, too. And that does limit the power of the prime minister.' The blackball only lasts, as Lord Lawson conceded, until the next ministerial reshuffle.

The New Labour style, highly personalised and reflecting the world of the permanent campaign, clashed with the more formal, structured approach familiar in Whitehall. Sir Richard Wilson, Butler's successor as Cabinet Secretary and Head of the Home Civil Service from January 1998, attempted to reconcile these approaches, what I have called (Riddell 2001) *The West Wing* meets *Yes, Prime Minister*. But Wilson's four-and-a-half-year tenure proved to be bruising. The Blair inner circle saw Wilson as dragging his feet over reform and defending the traditional Civil Service. Wilson did, in practice, push forward changes in the Civil Service, but this was inevitably a gradual process, and the Blair team was impatient. By contrast, many civil servants argued that the Blairites did not really understand how Whitehall could, and should, work, and hence undermined the value of an impartial permanent Civil Service.

Many departmental ministers adopted a similarly informal style. They were suspicious of civil servants, quite wrongly in most cases since most senior officials were, at least initially, enthusiastic about working with fresh political masters after all the divisions of the late Major years. They hoped for a decisive government after an increasingly ineffective one. This was in contrast with the coolness of many senior civil servants about the arrival of the Thatcher government in May 1979. But largely because of unfamiliarity, many new ministers were happier working with the special advisers whom they had known in opposition, and who in most cases were equally ignorant of the workings of Whitehall. This was reinforced by a desire to carry on behaving as in opposition by issuing press releases and staging media events.

The first twelve to eighteen months of the Blair government was marked by 'initiativitis' as proposals were launched, and often relaunched again and again. New ministers wanted to look busy. A classic and widely noted example was in June 2000, when Alistair Darling, the social security secretary and one of the quiet successes of the Blair Cabinet, staged a 'high level' summit to announce the redeployment of a large number of his department's staff. But exactly the same announcement had been made four months earlier. In the same week, Darling also announced plans to cut benefits from British fans attending the Euro 2000 football tournament. This was described at the time as 'gesture politics at its most naked' by Matthew Taylor, previously Labour's head of policy and later in charge of policy coordination in 10 Downing Street. Darling was by no means the worst offender in what Taylor called 'an endless stream of new initiatives, "blitzes" and "czars"' (Taylor 2000).

This phase was partly caused by the tight spending constraints under which most departments had to operate for the first two years after 1997, only gradually relaxed from April 1999 onwards. There was a lot of fatuous talk during this period about extra money not being necessary to produce better services. Money was not the sole or even the main answer, but it was impossible to produce better services when there were shortages of teachers, doctors and nurses, and their pay had lagged behind private sector rates. The full implications are discussed in later chapters. But this period was largely responsible for generating all the fuss about New Labour 'spin' because of the gap between promise and performance. Voters became disillusioned because they did not see any real improvement in the performances of public services, despite all the promises from Blair and other ministers.

Serious mistakes were made. The most spectacular was the Dome, on a bend in the Thames at Greenwich, intended to symbolise the celebration of the Millennium in 2000. The project was launched by Michael Heseltine when President of the Board of Trade in the John Major government, but was taken forward by Tony Blair and Peter Mandelson, despite the scepticism of a majority of the Cabinet at a discussion of June 1997. The Dome embodied all the vacuous trendiness of the 'Cool Britannia' phase of New Labour which so devalued the term 'modernisation'. The project was meant to be a bold demonstration of a new Britain, but in practice was an inherently risky project resting on dubious costing and over-optimistic projections of attendances. While the Dome itself was an architectural success, the contents of the year-long exhibition and entertainment were disappointing and the number of visitors was just half the projected twelve million. The total cost was well over £900 million of money from the National Lottery, which many thought could have been better spent elsewhere. The only beneficial legacy of all this activity was the extension of the Jubilee line on the Underground. The Dome soon became an embarrassing joke, but one that did surprisingly little lasting damage to the Blair government.

Several of the early initiatives proved to be failures, and had to be abandoned or substantially modified. As discussed in Chapter 5, the early pledge (one of the famous five) to reduce hospital waiting lists by 100,000 quickly proved to be flawed because it distorted the allocation of resources. Similarly, many of the early measures created to direct help to disadvantaged areas proved to be overlapping and ineffective, such as education action zones. One of the most revealing failures was the short-lived saga of Individual Learning Accounts to improve people's skills, which began in September 2000 but were withdrawn only fifteen months later. Total expenditure was more than £290 million, against a budget of £199 million, and the scale of alleged fraud and abuse was estimated at £97 million by the National Audit Office, of which fraud was about £67 million. ILAs involved subsidising courses for adults in basic skills and subjects like computing. Students paid a small amount, with course providers claiming the rest of the fee from the government. The aim was to simplify the process, to attract new providers of courses and to increase the number of people being trained. No one disputes that ILAs were a good idea in theory, and they encouraged a much wider range of people to go on schemes. But they were also a magnet to crooks who claimed money for non-existent courses and used people's names to claim money without their knowledge. The whole scheme was rushed. Sir John Bourn of the National Audit Office said: 'The speed with which the department implemented the scheme resulted in corners being cut. Poor planning and weak risk management by the department led to weaknesses in the system which made fraudulent activities possible.' The Public Accounts Committee concluded in its subsequent report (2003, p. 6) that the Education department's 'risk assessment and risk management were not fit for purpose, and were driven more by concerns that the scheme would not attract sufficient new learners. As a result the department did not give enough weight to advice received on the risks of fraud and abuse and about the quality of training.' This was, of course, an extreme example, but it illustrated the problems of inadequate planning and preparation.

The episode illustrated the pitfalls of setting up a new scheme without thinking through its implementation. One of the weaknesses of the Brown Treasury was a lack of understanding of the practical problems of its numerous bright ideas, however well intentioned the objectives. This resulted in very complicated policies.

But it was not just the failure of individual policies. Blair and Brown came to accept that their broader approach was not working, that far more radical changes were necessary. Blair's own drafts then were revealed in the subsequently leaked 'touchstones' memorandum of April 2000. Noting the Government's vulnerabilities, he wanted a greater emphasis on combining '"on your side" issues, with toughness and "standing up for Britain".' Revealingly, he added, 'I should be personally associated with as much of this as possible.' The extent of the soul-searching is evident from a series of private memorandums written by Blair's adviser on public opinion Philip Gould, which were obtained by the *Sunday Times*. Gould has never been known to undersell his views. Everything is in stark colours. But even allowing for his taste for drama, the message was stark. The June 2000 memo, quoted at the beginning of this chapter, was written at a time of turbulence. Citing Labour's private polls, Gould said, 'TB is not believed to be real. He lacks conviction, he is all spin and presentation, he says things to please people, not because he believes them; TB has not delivered.' His verdict, three years into the life of the government, was damning. 'TB promised a new Britain, a transformed NHS and public services, and all we have got is more of the same. Too little change, not too much.' Gould warned: 'We must use the NHS as the principal vehicle for reconnecting the government and TB … It absolutely has to happen' (see Seldon 2005, p. 433).

The story of the NHS over the winter of 1999–2000 symbolised the government's change in direction, as well as the convoluted way that decisions were taken. Before returning to the flu outbreak, the life peer's mother and the television interview, it is necessary to start the previous October when Alan Milburn, an ultra-Blairite, had taken over from Frank Dobson as health secretary. Milburn had been a minister of state at Health before a ten-month stint at Chief Secretary to the Treasury. On his return, he concluded that the NHS was in serious trouble. In his various economic statements since May 1997, Brown had regularly increased NHS funding, but it was clearly not enough. Blair had already raised the issue of extra NHS funding with Brown, but the Chancellor would not agree to an emergency package since he was worried about what would happen to the extra money without a strategy for making the NHS more efficient. For the Treasury, money and reform had to go hand in hand, and he did not want to rush ahead of his spring Budget and the spending review in the summer.

The Chancellor's timetable was upset, first by a serious outbreak of flu before and after Christmas 1999, and second by a partly associated wave of stories about overcrowding in hospitals and patients being moved around the country in the search for beds. For a government that lived by spin and headlines, it was 'a nightmare', as Alastair Campbell was reported to have told Tony Blair. (See Rawnsley 2001, pp. 333–9 for a full account, on which I have drawn.) As so often, the problems were highlighted by the fate of a single patient, and the history of the Blair government could be marked by a succession of harrowing cases. On this occasion, it was not just any 87-year-old lady who suffered a thirteen-hour wait in a casualty department; was eventually found a bed in a mixed-sex ward, which Labour had promised to end; failed to be given drugs when she should have been; and fell out of bed one night, only to develop a leg ulcer. She happened to be the mother of Robert Winston, whose credibility on health matters could not have been higher. He was an eminent fertility specialist, a popular broadcaster and a Labour life peer, a triple whammy which guaranteed him headlines when he delivered a stinging attack on the state of the health service in an interview in the *New Statesman* appearing on Thursday 13 January. Lord Winston said Britain's health service was 'much the worst' in Europe, while the government was not making it any better. Most damning of all, Winston did not think the prime minister knew this. 'I think he is a good man. I don't think he realises.' After pressure from 10 Downing Street, Winston slightly qualified his statement, but his view was rapidly endorsed by other leading doctors. And there was the further widely publicised case of Mavis Skeet, whose cancer operation was cancelled four times in five weeks because of bed shortages and whose condition then became inoperable.

Blair and Milburn agreed that the government had to make specific promises about more money, but Brown was reluctant to commit himself at this stage. The Chancellor certainly believed that more money was necessary, but was not sure how much and, anyway, wanted to make the announcement himself in the March Budget. On the substance, all the ministers were agreed. As Ed Balls, the Chancellor's chief economic adviser, has since said (in comments to the author), the Brown team had underestimated on coming to power in 1997 how much would have to be spent on the NHS. They gradually changed their view over the following few years on the necessary level of spending. But Blair was under pressure to harden his position immediately since he was due to make his usual New Year appearance on the *Breakfast with Frost* programme the following Sunday, 16 January. Alastair Campbell and he knew that the state of the NHS would dominate the interview. Not for the first – or last – time, media pressures forced the pace of policy-making. After lengthy wrangling over the phone on the Saturday between Blair and Brown – their exchanges in private being much more robust and brutal than they have ever admitted – a line was eventually agreed. Blair would give an indication about future increases in spending, but would insist that any extra money was dependent on future levels of economic growth and reform of the NHS. In other words, Blair could be the herald, not the king.

Come the Sunday morning and Blair was immediately confronted over the state of the NHS by Sir David Frost. Reading the transcript now, five and a half years later, the exchanges have a period flavour of forgotten incidents and people, as distant as only the recent past can be. At first, Blair wriggled about 'pretty tight funding' and how many more intensive care beds were in use. But he conceded that improvements would take time. He promised above-inflation pay awards for doctors and nurses. Then, he made the crucial commitment, which pre-judged not only that summer's spending review but also the following one in 2002. He said: 'If we carry on getting real-term rises in the health service of almost five per cent, then at the end of that five years, we will be in a position where our health service spending comes up to the average of the European Union. It's too low at the moment, so we'll bring it up there.' He was quick to emphasise that additional resources must be accompanied by reform and change in the NHS structure.

But his remarks about raising health spending were a political bombshell. Brown had not expected Blair to be so specific and the next day there were the familiar angry exchanges between the two as the

Chancellor accused the prime minister of going beyond their agreement. There was a lot of spinning and counter-spinning between the two camps, with Brown's advisers describing Blair's comments as 'not a commitment, but an aspiration'. There was also argument about what level of EU health spending should be used as a target. But the intention was clear. For once, this was an aspiration that was achieved. In his Budget speech two months later, Brown announced that, from 2000 until 2004, spending on the NHS would grow by 6.1 per cent a year in real, inflation-adjusted terms. The rate of growth was later increased even further after the 2002 spending review. And after a review by a Cabinet committee chaired by Blair, an NHS Plan was published in July 2000 which paved the way for changes leading to increasing diversity of provision and extensions of patient choice. The consequences both for overall levels of spending and for health policy are discussed in the following two chapters.

The episode was highly revealing about how the Blair government worked. A gradually simmering debate about future health funding was brought to the boil by bad headlines and by a long-arranged television interview. (For the historically minded, there were close parallels with an earlier winter health/hospital beds crisis in 1987–88 when Margaret Thatcher decided to set up a review of the structure of the NHS, foreshadowing this in an interview on *Panorama*.) Cabinet ministers, apart from Brown and Milburn, were not consulted ahead of Blair's interview, despite its momentous implications for the level and allocation of future public spending. David Blunkett, then education secretary, was particularly anxious and had to be reassured that 'education, education, education' was still the number one priority. Blair, like all political leaders, has always managed several top priorities, just as American presidents always manage to have several special relationships, depending on which head of government is visiting the White House at the time (Germany, Israel, Canada and Japan as well as Britain). The 2000 spending review and the NHS Plan also marked a big shift in the direction of the Blair government, both in a more social democratic direction on levels of spending and towards a quasi-market model in the running of public services. The tensions between the two have been at the heart of the government's debates ever since then.

The NHS crisis of early 2000 – and it was a crisis in the sense of being a turning point – also showed the ambiguities of 'spin'. Ministers found it hard to persuade the public that their policies were working, largely because of the earlier overclaiming and 'spin'. 'Spin' had by then become a recurrent media story and an easy way to beat the government. Attempts by 10 Downing Street to influence the press and broadcasters were hardly new, nor was 'spin' invented by Alastair Campbell. His aggressive style, including his dislike of the BBC and media inaccuracy, had much in common with that of Sir Bernard Ingham, Margaret Thatcher's long-serving press secretary. Ingham and Campbell were both bullies, though in both cases their bark was usually worse than their bite. Some of the protests about Downing Street manipulation by the media, notably the endless articles and books written by current or former BBC employees, have been naïve. The media are not merely passive recipients of information from on high. Just as government spokesmen have always tried to put over their side of the story, so the media's job is to question and put claims into context. What has happened has been excess by both sides. As spokesmen – spin doctors if you like – have exaggerated and distorted the facts, so much of the media has taken up a strongly adversarial position.

Bernard Ingham furiously denounced Campbell after many of the well-established heads of information were pushed aside or encouraged to retire in the 1997–98 period. Some of the changes introduced after 1997 were overdue and the Government Information Service did need to adjust to the world of 24-hour news and a more demanding media. But fears of politicisation were legitimate. Many new ministers were more used to working through their special advisers in dealing with journalists and did not understand, and deliberately blurred, the long-established demarcation lines between party and government. Of course civil servants, including information officers, serve the government of the day, and it is never easy to differentiate between the objectives of a government and those of the ruling party. That is the argument for having special advisers who can act in a more explicitly partisan way than civil servants. In general, the system has worked well. But under Labour there were some outrageous examples where ministers and special advisers did cross the line, the most notorious being the activities of Jo Moore, adviser to Stephen Byers at the Department of Transport. It was not just her appalling e-mail on the day of the September 11 terrorist attacks about now being 'a good time to bury bad news', but her general approach was seen as defying the proper lines of what special advisers should ask civil servants to do. Blair and his advisers were insensitive to these charges and to questions of what were and were not the right boundaries between politicians and advisers on the one hand and civil servants on the other.

More important than specific incidents, often exaggerated by the government's opponents, was the broader impression of cynicism and exaggeration – that you could not believe what ministers and spokesmen said. That was partly a by-product of the early phase when public spending was held down, and then of the overselling of the spending rises in 1998. Not only did 'spin' itself become a political issue on its own, in part a proxy for other doubts, but criticism of media management made it much harder for the government to 'sell' its achievements at a later stage and to persuade a sceptical public that services were at last improving. This 'spin' gap was shown by the regular finding in Populus polls for *The Times* of a consistent and marked difference between voters' personal experience of various services and their impression of how the service was performing nationally. The former was of course direct and personal, while the latter came through the filter of the national media. The gap was smallest, and narrowed over time, on the NHS, and widest on public transport. Similarly, voters gave a much higher rating to public officials with whom they came into personal contact, such as doctors, teachers and nurses, than more remote ones like ministers and civil servants, whom they generally only learnt about through the media.

Disillusionment with 'spin' convinced Alastair Campbell to detach himself from the day-to-day media battle after the 2001 general election, only to be forced back into it by the new demands after the 9/11 attacks. After 2001, New Labour searched for new ways of conveying its message and overcoming media scepticism. The government's problems were compounded by the controversy over the presentation of the intelligence claims that Saddam's Iraq had weapons of mass destruction, particularly when the Hutton inquiry revealed the central role played by Campbell. Even those who acquitted Blair and his advisers of deliberately lying believed the lines between detached intelligence analysis and assessment and media management had been dangerously blurred. The common

'Bliar' jibe extended beyond Iraq to the government's broader credibility. The government, and particularly Blair, were tarnished by these and several other episodes, such as the tortuous saga over the collapse and rescue of Railtrack, which ended up in court. These rows left a lasting impression of ruthlessness, deceit and slipperiness, as set out in Peter Oborne's polemic *The Rise of Political Lying* (2005), as well as his earlier hostile biography of Alastair Campbell (2004).

Behind the heated battles over 'spin', the Hutton inquiry and other incidents (all fully reported and many exaggerated in the media) was the permanent campaign style of the Blair government. This was not just the use of focus groups to test pledges, or phrases. The government put a high priority on presentation in its decisions, from the most trivial to the handling of the foot and mouth outbreak of spring 2001 and the Iraq war. As significant was the Blairite strategy of triangulation. Blair consistently sought to be different from Labour in the past, especially the recent past. His search for new solutions could appear like rootlessness, with no clear ideological direction. As noted in the previous chapter, there was a constant search for an overarching ideological justification for what the government was doing, or a 'narrative' in New Labourspeak.

The paradox was that a clear 'narrative' or strategy did emerge after 2000, a recognisably social democratic one: the belief that active government backed by rising public spending was necessary to address Britain's problems and to improve public services. The government's policies were directed to assisting disadvantaged groups, but because Blair and his allies seldom presented their approach in this way, partly for fear of worrying their Middle England supporters, voters remained sceptical about what the government was doing, and Labour activists disillusioned. There was much talk in the 2000–01 period about neglect of Labour's core voters in the big industrial cities. Peter Kilfoyle resigned as a junior defence minister in January 2000 because Labour's traditional working-class supporters were being taken for granted. Yet his own Liverpool constituents were the beneficiaries not only of the Treasury's anti-poverty policies but also of the money increasingly coming through to rebuild rundown schools and hospitals. In one sense Kilfoyle was right. Labour supporters were unenthusiastic about a government whose ministers did not talk in ways they could understand: turnout in his Liverpool Walton constituency fell from 59.5 to just 43 per cent at the 2001 general election.

Yet the underlying problem has been less about styles of decision-making and presentation than ambiguity about the role of central government. The New Labour version of active government saw a proliferation of output targets from 1998 onwards, focusing on standards of performance in services on the ground. This was a development of what had happened before and was not wholly new. As part of the new methods of public sector management – and the creation of executive agencies – from the late 1980s onwards there had been a greater emphasis on specific output or outcomes, rather than just the amounts of money spent. This was allied with the publication of league tables of the performance of schools and other services, under the broad umbrella of the Citizen's Charter introduced by the Major administration. The Blair government took this much further, in both the number and the range of targets negotiated between the Treasury and spending departments, known as Public Service Agreements, and in the expansion of league tables to all kinds of public service. The strengths and weaknesses of this approach for public services are discussed in Chapter 5. But the proliferation of targets raised expectations and led ministers to intervene more and more to ensure that the targets were met, since their political reputations were tied to their achievement. The central state was taking responsibility for more outcomes on the ground without having the means to achieve them.

The Blair team asked the Civil Service to change its role, from being primarily policy advisers and administrators to being directly responsible for changing standards of services – in the New Labour jargon, for delivery. This went well beyond the work of the Downing Street Delivery Unit. The senior Civil Service sought to change, to meet the new demands. As Sir Richard Wilson, now Lord Wilson of Dinton, said in 2000: 'The combination of growing consumer power, concentration on delivery of public services, combined with faster communication and rapid developments in information technology represent a great challenge.' Blair and many of his fellow ministers had no real understanding of what this meant since they had never worked in, let alone run, any large organisations. They wanted 'delivery', but were vague about what this meant. They had no feel for management. One close adviser to Blair said the prime minister's eyes glazed over whenever Civil Service reform was mentioned. He could see Blair's attention wandering. When Richard Wilson and a team of his senior permanent secretaries made a presentation on a Civil Service reform package to Blair, he turned to ask the view of David Simon, Lord Simon of Highbury, a former chairman of BP and an industry minister for part of the first term. Simon said the proposals were fine, and the imprimatur of a leading businessman was enough for Blair. Like Gordon Brown, who invited a stream of senior executives to lead inquiries for him, Blair had a big faith in the wisdom of businessmen. Later he put his trust, more controversially, in John Birt, the former Director General of the BBC, for ideas on running Whitehall. Lord Birt, who undertook 'blue-skies thinking' on a range of issues from drugs to education and London, proved to be as unpopular in Whitehall as he had been in the BBC.

Reform was the top priority for Sir Andrew Turnbull, Wilson's successor as Cabinet Secretary and Head of the Home Civil Service from 2002 until 2005. He wrote a manifesto for public service reform, including actions to improve delivery, in his application for the post, and Blair gave him a specific mandate for reform when he took it up. In a speech to a public services conference in February 2005, Sir Andrew highlighted 'the change from civil servants as consiglieri to civil servants as deliverers'. The core jobs of the Civil Service used to be 'providing policy advice and managing government business, but, in addition, there is now delivery.' He gave the example of the Department for Education and Skills. In the old days the department, he said, saw itself as part of the education system, responsible for setting the policy framework and for funding but leaving delivery to local education authorities or the education professionals. But now the department 'sees itself as the leader, the headquarters, of the education service, taking a direct responsibility for achieving certain specified goals.' Whereas in the past senior officials would have been drawn from people recruited and trained in the Civil Service, it now has people with direct experience of schools, further and higher education, and the voluntary sector.

There was a big gap between intentions in Whitehall, let alone in 10 Downing Street, and what happened on the ground. 'Tony wants' may have galvanised Whitehall, but it did not cut waiting times in hospitals, produce clean wards, improve educational standards in secondary schools, or reduce crime and anti-social behaviour. The Blairites talked a lot about joined-up government, and this produced some good analysis in the new Social Exclusion Unit and the Performance and Innovation Unit (later merged with the Forward Strategy Unit to form the Strategy Unit). The Social Exclusion Unit highlighted the horizontal connections between housing, education and youth crime. The vertical implications, implementation from Whitehall downwards, were weaker.

This shift has major consequences for the staffing and skills of the Civil Service. Sir Andrew argued that senior civil servants had been slow to adjust, partly because of concerns of shared leadership with ministers, because the outputs are collective and because so many other organisations are involved. But he said the job of a permanent secretary was much more akin to a chief executive officer than in the past. Just before his retirement, Sir Andrew produced a report on Civil Service reform (June 2005). More outsiders are being brought in as more posts in the senior civil service have been opened up to competition from outside, and one in five of senior civil servants have been appointed from outside Whitehall. There is also a greater emphasis on career development, rather than an automatic progression by seniority, as well as training for the different managerial roles. The report quoted World Bank data for 1996–2004 showing that Britain performs at a very high level across all six governance indicators (government effectiveness, control of corruption, voice and accountability, political stability, regulatory quality and rule of law).

This programme not only challenges the traditional conception of a civil servant but also implies a change in the role of central government. Sir Andrew is rightly proud of the changes occurring in the Civil Service, but behind the management shake-up, are civil servants being asked to do the impossible? Can central government deliver, as opposed to make policy and allocate funds? Can civil servants ever lead change in the way described? In its desire – even impatience – for reform, the Blair view is of government intervening to be the agent of change. In the short term, this can work in some politically sensitive areas, as shown by the work of the Delivery Unit discussed below. In the long term, such a concentration on a few targets is not necessarily sustainable. The Blair government is taking responsibility for more than it can deliver.

A combination of the activist ambitions of politicians and the blame culture of the media have fuelled unrealistic expectations. That has been reflected in the absurd and often distasteful exchanges between the parties over the fate of old ladies who have to wait in an accident and emergency department for a long time, or who have had their operations postponed – which, as noted above, played a part in early 2000 in the government's decision to increase health spending. All the main parties have indulged in such exchanges over individual cases. They win headlines by dramatising a failing in the health service. There is a fine line between saying that a minister cannot be responsible for the treatment of an individual patient of whom he has never heard, and saying that his broader decisions have created the conditions for the delay in treatment. That was highlighted by the controversy during the 2005 election over MRSA, the hospital superbug, which the Tories chose to highlight by making 'Cleaner Hospitals' one of their main pledges. At one level, this was a very micro problem compared with broader questions of the structure of the NHS, waiting lists and times, and levels of mortality. But at another level the government's policy of contracting out cleaning services has blurred lines of responsibility in individual hospitals for dealing with infection. This goes back to the old argument about the dividing lines in ministerial accountability/responsibility between policy and operations. The familiar answer is that, while ministers have to be accountable to Parliament and the public for everything done in their departments, they cannot be held directly responsible for actions of which they know nothing. But that always cloudy distinction is further confused when politicians themselves set detailed targets and central government seeks to influence outcomes.

However, centrally driven initiatives achieved some successes. Standards of literacy and numeracy in primary schools did improve for a time in the late 1990s before remaining on a plateau. This followed a Whitehall-led drive by David Blunkett, Michael Bichard, his then permanent secretary at Education, and Michael Barber, a leading educationalist, and involved close progress-chasing from the centre. That model led to the creation in 2001 of the Delivery Unit, which was headed by Barber and succeeded in bridging the gap between 10 Downing Street and the Treasury. The prime minister himself held stock-takes with the main Secretaries of State every six to eight weeks to monitor progress based on the reports of the Delivery Unit. The unit monitored a limited number of targets and worked closely with departments to achieve them, with some success. Among the targets monitored were failing schools, the numbers waiting for inpatient treatment in hospitals, levels of street crime as measured by recorded robbery in five metropolitan areas, and progress in reaching levels of attainment for eleven- and fourteen-year-olds.

The Delivery Unit was deliberately modelled on the performance management operation of a large business organisation. As the enthusiastic Barber set out in regular Powerpoint presentations, the basic approach involved working with departments on each priority and target set out in a public service agreement: first, to agree a plan to manage delivery and to set out key milestones towards a target, and then a trajectory setting out expectations of the trend in the data towards the target. When the reported data were not on track, action followed. This was not imposed from the centre, but was agreed with departments. Barber talked of several levels of intensity, starting with an adjustment by the department (such as on school leadership); then a problem-solving exercise by the department and the unit (as over bed-blocking of hospital beds by elderly people); then a major exercise involving the commitment of prime ministerial time (as over the drive to reduce asylum applications in the second term); and finally a high-intensity drive led by the prime minister (as in the concerted effort to cut street crime in the summer of 2002). A number of refinements occurred over the years as the unit accepted the need to provide incentives to encourage local managers to meet the targets. The introduction of financial incentives and including accident and emergency performance within the star ratings for hospitals helped, for instance, to ensure that more people attending A&E departments met the four-hour maximum time target. There were, however, complaints from doctors that this target led to hurried treatments and a factory-style approach.

Michael Barber has defended targets as being an essential element of managing any large organisation – as representing real-world outcomes which customers/citizens want to see and enabling the public to hold the government to account. The latter was not always apparent since targets were often changed, and by the time they could be properly monitored, the minister who set them had been moved on. Moreover, in time targets became as much of a bogey as 'spin'. There were increasing complaints from

2000 onwards. In July 2003, the Public Administration Committee of the Commons, chaired by Tony Wright, a keen student of these issues, called for a reform of the system of performance measurement, an independently audited performance report, and a reduction in the number of targets. The MPs applauded the government's aspirations in using targets to promote common standards and to motivate staff. But quoting evidence ranging from primary schools to ambulance services, the committee also suggested that targets and tables could hamper service delivery. It claimed there was a lack of clarity about what the government was trying to achieve, failure to give a clear sense of direction and confused accountability. Wright noted that, while the number of headline targets for central government departments had been reduced (from 366 in 1998 to 123 in 2002), 'the strong impression from the sharp end of services is that the burden of the measurement culture on frontline workers and their managers has increased.'

Perhaps the most damning criticism that central government has been trying to do too much, and being overprescriptive, has come from the ultimate insider, Peter Hyman. He had worked as speechwriter and strategist for Blair for nine years, including six and a half years in 10 Downing Street, before he went to work at Islington Green School at the end of 2003. While remaining a strong supporter of New Labour and of Blair, he concluded:

> Perhaps the biggest eye-opener for me on my journey has been how the approach I had been part of creating, to deal with twenty-four-hour media and to demonstrate a decisive government, was entirely the wrong one for convincing frontline professionals, or indeed for ensuring successful delivery ... What the front line requires is a policy framework and goals, not hundreds of micro-announcements. I am beginning to see how teachers felt like a circus act having random objects hurled at them by a ringmaster, and being expected to catch them all. (Hyman 2005, p. 384)

These doubts about the impact of central intervention and targets on the morale, esteem and self-confidence of providers of public services were highlighted by Onora O'Neill in her much discussed Reith Lectures in 2002. Noting the 'unending stream of new legislation and regulation, memoranda and instructions, guidance and advice' flooding into public sector institutions, she argued that the proper aim of each profession is 'not reducible to meeting set targets following prescribed procedures and requirements'. She was worried that avoiding complaints would become a goal in its own right, producing defensive medicine, teaching and policing. She had a point, but only a partial one. The record of many public services and professionals before 1997 was hardly so wonderful as to believe that a hands-off approach by the centre was helping to produce good results and improved performance. Intervention and targets provided the necessary shake-up to result in higher standards in, for example, primary schools. The question is rather how do you secure a balance between improving standards of performance and necessary freedom of judgement for professionals.

The central question has been how far can management and targets be decentralised. After the 2001 election, there was much talk, from the Treasury and elsewhere, of the 'new localism'. Did this mean that the decisions on allocation of resources and targets would be taken by local representatives? Or was devolution intended to be primarily managerial? Leaders of local councils were worried about a dispersion of accountability with elected boards of foundation hospitals, semi-independent secondary schools and even the idea of elected police authorities. The tensions were recognised, for example, by Wendy Thomson, the prime minister's adviser on public service reform in the Cabinet Office. In a speech in June 2004 to a learning and skills conference, she said a study of the Education department's skills strategy had exposed a conflict between the need to meet both national targets and local demand. Moves to give more power to the frontline – to teachers, GPs and policemen – were the best way to raise standards and efficiency, but national targets still had to be met.

As long as central government provides most of the money for local suppliers of services, demands for accountability are bound to be channelled through ministers. So while Labour ministers talked about rejecting the command-and-control approach of the first term and devolving responsibility, it was always heavily qualified. There were phrases like 'earned autonomy', giving more financial and managerial freedom of manoeuvre to good-performing councils – the definition of 'good', of course, being determined by central government. The centre is reluctant to release its hold.

But the Blair government did not limit its ambitions merely to improving the performance of government; it also sought to change the public's behaviour. It had a view on society, and one of the most distinctive early features of Blairism was a concern with the social and moral state of the country. He made his name, and created the later opportunity to become Labour leader, by his 'tough on crime, tough on the causes of crime' line in a radio interview in January 1993 and his response a month later to the murder of two-year-old James Bulger. Blair showed an intuitive feeling for the public mood, which he later so often displayed as prime minister, notably after the death of Diana, Princess of Wales, just four months after he took office. Blair accepted the changes in the law in the 1960s which helped make Britain a more open and tolerant society, but said, in a speech in July 2004, that people wanted 'rules, order, proper behaviour, a society of respect, a society of responsibility, a community where the decent law-abiding majority are in charge.' This is partly about public disorder and criminalising anti-social behaviour, but it is also about people's ordinary behaviour. This reflects Blair's consistent refrain about rights and responsibilities. People cannot just claim off the state; they also have to play their part by behaving responsibly.

Ministers have had a view on a whole variety of aspects of conduct: smoking, diet and over-eating, drinking, drug-taking, pregnancy (among teenagers), the rearing of infants, homework, the use of firearms, travelling to school, truancy – as well as, more ambiguously, on hunting with dogs. Not only did the government have views, but it also sought to persuade, induce and cajole people into changing their behaviour in line with government targets. This produced protests about the 'nanny state'.

Many of these aspects of behaviour are not simply private, they have public consequences. They contribute not just to personal and family breakdown but also to wider social disintegration. Drug dealers blight many inner-city estates, ruining the lives of local residents, as well as threatening violence. Smoking not only kills smokers – while costing the NHS a great deal of money on the way – but it also damages the health of non-smokers. The taking of most prohibited drugs, including cannabis, both damages health and affects the chance of leading a full life, while being fatal in some cases. Overeating and overdrinking are primarily self-inflicted problems, but by threatening health they can also have wider public costs.

as well as damaging family life. But how far should central government be involved? The state has for long sought to discourage smoking, by the rate of tax levied, by public education campaigns (including prominent health warnings on packets of cigarettes) and by outright bans. The Blair government has sought to take forward each aspect and has moved most controversially into banning smoking in public places, as is now the case with trains, planes and most office buildings. Drinking alcohol is trickier since there is not yet a widespread acceptance of the damaging effects on health of excessive consumption, even though binge drinking by young people is now a growing social and disorder problem in town centres on weekends. However, ministers have faced both ways, deploring excessive drinking but also liberalising opening hours, so enabling some pubs to stay open much longer at night. The biggest problems have arisen where the state has appeared to be intervening in how parents – or, often, a single parent – bring up their children. When does guidance become interference?

Some aspects are, however, relatively uncontroversial and successful, such as the Sure Start scheme. Modelled on the American Head Start programme, the intention has been to help the poorest families with very young children. This was on the basis of evidence showing that neglect in these pre-school years created inequalities in educational performance which were very hard to remedy later on during schooling. In Britain, some 250 Sure Start schemes (later expanded to 500) were established in the areas of the greatest social deprivation to help mothers with toddlers who were often struggling to cope on their own. The schemes' day centres, mother-and-toddler groups and home visits were all intended to bridge the period between visits by midwives and an expanded, universal nursery system for three- and four-year-olds. These locally run schemes started play centres and crèches as more mothers were encouraged to take on jobs and boost their incomes. One scheme I visited in David Blunkett's Sheffield Brightside constituency took advantage of the neighbouring Pennines, as the young and mainly single mothers had responded enthusiastically to growing their own vegetables on nearby allotments, supplementing the inadequate diet from local convenience food stores. This scheme combined paternalism and voluntary effort in the right mixture. This was a first step towards an intended universal system of children's centres throughout the country. By 2005, some 300 centres existed, with a further 2,200 planned by

2008 – a big increase, though still only covering the top third most disadvantaged wards in the country.

However, there were much more elusive targets, such as promising to halve the rate of teenage pregnancies by 2010. The government had no means directly to influence this target. Exhortation often did not reach the girls most likely to become pregnant, while economic influences were largely irrelevant. Sure Start schemes were set up in the most deprived areas where there were most teenage mothers. By 2004, there had been a less than 10 per cent fall in the number of under-eighteen conceptions, compared with the 25 per cent fall needed if the target was to be met. After the 2005 election, Beverley Hughes, the children's minister, conceded the government's inability to affect the level of pregnancies. The dilemma is that a more activist policy of sex education, contraception or even the morning-after pill would be denounced as interference by the state in private lives.

The government has been most active in trying to curb anti-social, borderline criminal behaviour, mainly by young people. There has been a sharp growth in the issue by the courts of anti-social behaviour orders – ASBOs – on applications from the police and local authorities. These orders ban individuals from specific anti-social activities or from entering an area or associating with certain named people for a minimum of two years. Breaches can lead to fines or imprisonment. Four-fifths of the public back the orders, though only two-fifths feel they are effective. But they have been criticised by lawyers, the voluntary sector and some public sector unions for being unjust, disproportionate and ineffective. Louise Casey, the director of the Home Office anti-social behaviour unit, who previously dealt with homelessness, has challenged the civil liberties groups who have argued that ASBOs are too wide-ranging and draconian for 'not necessarily living in the real world'. She has argued (in Ward, 2005) that, while prevention and alternative activities are essential, 'you also sometimes need to say to somebody, "If you don't get your act together … then you face some consequences."'

The greatest controversy has been stirred up by legislation which Blair himself and several other senior ministers, including Jack Straw and David Blunkett, never really wanted: a ban on hunting with dogs. It was a rare case where Labour MPs got their way over the executive. So after years of procrastination and tactical manoeuvring, Blair was reluctantly forced to acquiesce in the use of the Parliament Act to force through the legislation in November 2004 banning fox and similar hunting with dogs. The long battle had roused supporters of fox-hunting – not all hunters or rural residents themselves – to form the Countryside Alliance, which organised a mass demonstration in London in September 2002, the largest ever seen in the capital until the anti-Iraq war protest of February 2003. This march and rally expressed the resentment of mainly Conservative England at the metropolitan prejudices of New Labour. But few of the marchers realised that Blair himself did not want to antagonise them. The advocate of big tent politics would have avoided a confrontation if he could. But the pressure from Labour MPs was eventually too great, especially after his authority was weakened after the Iraq war. This was an inglorious course, but he and his advisers calculated, correctly, that for all the anger of the pro-hunting lobby, the political and electoral consequences were likely to be small. At most, the countryside lobby made the difference in tilting a handful of seats to the Tories in the 2005 general election.

These laws, regulations and attempts to influence behaviour have led to a counter-reaction on the right against an ever encroaching state. It has been a theme that has united Conservatives of all shades of opinion, but it has been easier for them to express general opposition, rather than to identify how and where they want a rollback of the state to occur. The result is 'a new statism of regulation and coercion', according to Martin McElwee of the Centre for Policy Studies and Andrew Tyrie, a Conservative MP, in a pamphlet published in 2002. The problem has been not just increasing taxes and authoritarian measures restricting individual liberty; the size and influence of the state is also being extended through government regulation and coercion. Their pamphlet listed examples of new requirements on companies to handle welfare payments, instructions on how much homework children should do and bans on smoking in offices. 'Rules limiting the freedoms and rights of shareholders and companies are New Labour's twenty-first century substitution for nation-alisation. Central control in the public services is growing, reversing the decentralising measures which had been introduced, often in a piecemeal fashion, during the Conservative years.'

This discussion about the role of the state – about what central government can, and should, do – goes back to the dilemma at the heart of New Labour. Its lack of clear ideological roots, and the Blairites' desire to be as unlike Old Labour as possible, has created a continuing strategic confusion. That was reinforced by its lengthy adjustment to office, learning how to operate the levers of Whitehall, and then its various, only partially successful attempts to achieve change, to deliver. Improvements have occurred in certain public services, as Chapter 5 shows, but only after a big change in approach in 2000.

The Blair government still has fully to resolve two contradictions. First, there was the unwillingness of Blair in particular to take risks, domestically at least, with the coalition of support he built up in 1997. Consequently, tax and spending choices have tended to be fudged or obscured. But Labour has become a recognisably social democratic government that only half-heartedly admits to being so. Second, New Labour has not had a coherent view of what the state should do and how it should do it. Its rhetoric has been sweeping: 'We will save the NHS.' But there is a huge difference between what a prime minister or Cabinet minister wants and what happens on the ground. Its language and aspirations have extended far beyond its ability to deliver. This chapter has looked at broad strategy and how the state operates: the next four chapters will look in detail at the extent to which the government has fulfilled the original hopes, and how far they remain unfulfilled.

4

Prudence and Fairness

'In the Pre-Budget Report, I told the House that Britain was enjoying the longest period of sustained economic growth for more than 100 years. I have to apologise to the House. Having asked the Treasury to investigate in greater historical detail, I can now report that Britain is enjoying its longest period of sustained economic growth for more than 200 years – the longest period of sustained economic growth since the beginning of the Industrial Revolution.'

Gordon Brown, Budget speech, 17 March 2004.

'Britain is today experiencing the longest period of sustained economic growth since records began in 1701.'

Gordon Brown, Budget speech, 16 March 2005.

'Economic management by its very nature leaves only footprints in the sand. The tide of the next Chancellor washes them away.'

Roy Jenkins, *A Life at the Centre*, 1991.

Gordon Brown does not do modesty. His Budget speeches are full of boasts about how wonderful his economic record is and how his critics are always wrong. The superlatives roll off his tongue in his insistent style: the lowest inflation, interest rates and unemployment for thirty or forty years; the longest sustained growth for 100, 200, even 300 years; an end to the stop-go cycles of the past; the best performance in Europe (every year) and in the G7 leading countries (most of the time). It is like the cleverest boy in school telling everyone else about his top marks, as well as hubristic. Moreover, anyone who bases their claims on the economic statistics for 1901, let alone 1801 or 1701, is on pretty uncertain ground in view of the inadequacies of the earlier data. The Chancellor should have a court jester at his shoulder as a medieval king did, reminding him of mortality and the unpredictabilities of fate. The Brown court is the reverse. He is always reminded by his advisers about how good and right he is, and about how the achievements of the Blair government are all his, and nothing to do with Tony Blair.

Some of this self-praise is, however, justified, though Brown is not the only author of this success. His Conservative predecessors also deserve part of the credit. As virtually every independent analyst and international institution has said, the British economic record has been good since 1997, especially by comparison with the rest of Europe. But it has not been flawless. There are a whole series of questions about the sustainability of spending and tax plans, the level of house prices and consumer debt, the funding of pensions, the effectiveness of the various enterprise initiatives, and levels of productivity. This chapter will examine the economic record; look at how far this record reflects decisions taken before 1997, and therefore what was the distinctive contribution of New Labour; consider the implications for levels of taxation and public spending and for traditional social democratic objectives of equity and equality; and then discuss how far Britain's underlying economic position has improved. The central questions are how far the change for better in Britain's performance really dates back to the opening up and liberalisation of the economy in the 1980s; whether the main constraints on inflation are global rather than domestic; how far Labour has mainly entrenched these changes; and whether Brown's belief in state intervention to remove blockages to growth – 'market failures' in producing enough skilled workers or entrepreneurs – has made much difference.

Unlike the other policies examined in later chapters, economic policy has been Gordon Brown's exclusive domain and Tony Blair's role has been relatively small, except on public spending and as a restraining influence on tax proposals which might adversely affect a sensitive business or middle-class group. Whatever else was agreed, or misunderstood, at the famous Granita dinner in 1994 over the future Labour leadership (see Naughtie 2001 for a balanced assessment), there is no doubt that Blair ceded to Brown control over a wide range of economic and industrial policy. This was partly shrewd politics to appease his old friend, but it also reflected Blair's lack of interest in, and of feel for, economic issues. Brown and his close advisers, particularly Ed Balls, prepared in opposition for what they intended to do in power (as discussed in Chapter 2 and in Robinson 2000 and Peston 2005). The Brown team had prepared detailed plans on how to manage the economy and how to improve its performance. For all the vagueness of some of New Labour's policy thinking in the mid-1990s, the economic approach was clear. Brown, Balls and the others were itching to put their ideas into practice.

Moreover, in office Blair was less involved in Treasury issues than any prime minister since Home or Eden, and 10 Downing Street was also deliberately excluded from the Brown camp's discussions. This is not because Blair and Brown were not close. They were, at least until open cracks appeared in the relationship in 2003. They talked daily, often more frequently, but that was mainly about broad political issues, rather than the details of economic policy. A key role was played for over five years by Jeremy Heywood, first as economics private secretary, then principal private secretary, in managing relations with the Treasury. Heywood, and for the first term David Miliband, the head of the Policy Unit, used to have a weekly meeting with Balls and with Brown's principal private secretary of the time in Churchill's, a cheerful but cramped café in Whitehall near the Cenotaph. Little did the tourists who were the main customers know that the four youngish men in the corner were among the most powerful in the country, and that their meetings were vital for the smooth running of the government. Their corner table deserves a place in any gallery of power sites in London.

Derek Scott, Blair's economic adviser until December 2003, has noted (2004, p. 17) that it would 'be misleading to pretend that in opposition or government Tony Blair ever felt much inclination to engage in economics more than was necessary to get by; he could easily be distracted.' Scott notes how Brown wanted 'to run everything on the domestic front', and how Blair went along with this. 'Gordon Brown's attitudes towards any involvement in economic policy from Number 10 became clear soon after the election in 1997. I learnt from some old friends in the Treasury that the Chancellor's office had instructed all officials within the department that any contact they had with me had to be reported, together with the subject discussed.'

Early in Blair's premiership he accepted that Brown and the Treasury would effectively have a veto over one of the key decisions of the government, whether or not to enter the euro. This was conceded when in October 1997 the five tests were announced, since the Treasury was given the key role of assessing them. Moreover, at one point during the long period of frosty relations between the prime minister and the Chancellor from the autumn of 2004 to the spring of 2005, Blair is said to have asked Brown about the Budget at a small meeting of senior ministers, only to have received the terse reply, 'It's on March 16.'

This chapter is therefore mainly about Gordon Brown's performance and policies, rather than Tony Blair's. There is little dispute about the performance. Take, for instance, the assessment of the National Institute for Economic Research produced on the eve of the May 2005 general election: 'Labour's economic record has been very satisfactory. Nothing has gone badly wrong with the economy over the period since 1997. Inflation has been low and stable and output growth has also been stable, at a rate consistent with most views about the trend rate of growth. By contrast with earlier periods, the public finances have been reasonably well controlled and our current position is better than that in both France and in the United States in this respect. Employment conditions have improved markedly continuing earlier trends.' The International Monetary Fund was similarly positive at the same time: 'Macroeconomic performance over the past decade has been strong and steady, owing much to structural reforms and improvements in macroeconomic policies and policy frameworks.' The Organisation for Economic Cooperation and Development (OECD) talked in similar terms in its 2004 survey: 'The performance of the UK economy has been impressive in recent years, underpinned by wide-ranging structural reforms and sound macroeconomic policy frameworks.' There have been worries over the balance of the economy, notably over whether house prices would drop sharply after the big rises in the second half of the 1990s.

Moreover, the expansion of private services in the early years, and then the public sector, offset continuing problems for the industrial base. This was partly because of the high level of sterling, and led to further falls in manufacturing employment. Yet the decline in manufacturing is, in part, a reflection of economic maturity as industrial operations shift elsewhere in the world and newer sectors of the British economy expand faster to sustain the overall rate of growth. The political consequences of big redundancies are now less than in, say, the 1980s, as was shown when the closure of the Longbridge plant in Birmingham in the middle of the 2005 election campaign did not lose Labour seats in the area.

Brown himself claimed in his March 2004 Budget that: 'For decades after 1945, Britain repeatedly relapsed into recession, moving from boom to bust. Since 1997 Britain has sustained growth not just through one economic cycle but through two economic cycles, without suffering the old British disease of stop-go – with overall growth since 2000 almost twice that of Europe and higher even than that of the United States.' This is an exaggeration, based on a favourable selection of years. But his underlying point is right. Britain's growth performance has improved since 1997 and it has also been less volatile than other major economies. According to the National Institute, Britain's growth averaged 2.8 per cent between 1997 and 2004, compared with 3.4 per cent in the USA and 2.4 per cent in France. This is better than in the previous seven years when growth averaged just 1.8 per cent in Britain, only slightly ahead of the French rate of 1.6 per cent in the 1989–96 period, but well below the 2.7 per cent rate in the United States. Since 2001, Britain's growth has averaged 2.3 per cent, against 2.5 per cent in the USA and just 1.5 per cent in France. However, the British performance has not been as good since 1997 as some other 'Anglo-Saxon' economies such as Australia, Canada and New Zealand.

But is Brown right to claim the credit? Did his policies after 1997 really mark a turning point? Or has he really benefited from the tough decisions taken by his Conservative predecessors who reduced inflation to low levels and set the economy on a path of steady growth and falling unemployment? After all, the record period of sustained growth started well before the arrival of Brown in the Treasury in May 1997 and can be traced back four years earlier to 1993. Sir Alan Budd, a former Treasury chief economic adviser and member of the Bank's Monetary Policy Committee, has argued (2005, p. 32), that Britain's unhappy membership of the exchange rate mechanism from October 1990 until September 1992 brought inflation down to levels that we have been able to maintain ever since. Sir Alan makes a persuasive case that the benefits could not have been achieved by other means in the circumstances of the time. Moreover, after Black Wednesday, when sterling was ignominiously forced out of the ERM, 'the policies that were put in place, starting with the system introduced in October 1992 and culminating in the establishment of the Monetary Policy Committee in 1997, allowed the benefits of ERM membership to be sustained.' There was a shift in macroeconomic policy towards inflation-targeting and a more open and transparent method of setting interest rates under first Norman Lamont and then Kenneth Clarke. This saw regular inflation reports from the Bank and the publication of minutes of meetings with the Bank Governor, Eddie (now Lord) George: what became known as the 'Ken and Eddie' show.

However, this view has been challenged by the Brown Treasury. Ed Balls devoted a whole lecture in June 2005 to answering what he called the 'revisionist' case put by Sir Alan Budd and others. Balls, one of Sir Alan's successors as chief economic adviser, was by then a Labour MP. His claim that May 1997 was the turning point was partly based on 'the improved economic performance since that date'. Consumer price inflation had averaged 2.4 per cent a year between 1992 and 1997, but has fallen to 1.4 per cent a year since then. Unemployment had averaged 8.9 per cent in the earlier period, but only 5.5 per cent since 1997. Volatility has also been lower. But this evidence is not by itself conclusive, since the better performance since 1997 could have been largely due to the earlier decisions on monetary policy. But Balls argues that, while the post-1992 monetary arrangements 'did constitute a shift in the right direction ... they did not constitute a credible and sustainable approach.' In particular, he argues that the inflation target of 2.5 per cent or less was 'ambiguous and deflationary'; decision-making remained 'highly personalised'; and the suspicion remained that 'policy was being manipulated for short-term motives.' The Brown Treasury has argued in its official analysis (Balls and O'Donnell 2002, p. 18) that 'this greater transparency was not combined with clear accountability, a well defined target of inflation and separation of responsibilities, and thus failed to lower inflation expectations prior to 1997.'

Both Conservative Chancellors also took painful decisions to reduce public borrowing after it soared in the recession of the early 1990s. The increases in taxes in the mid-1990s and the squeeze on public spending provided a benign economic background to the 1997 general election, and to Labour's inheritance, even though the unpopular tax and spending measures had a malign political influence on the Conservatives' electoral prospects. The Brown camp predictably did not see the inheritance in such favourable terms, arguing that there was little spare capacity in the economy and therefore a risk of rising inflation (though still in low single figures, compared with the much higher, often double figure, rates for most of the previous 25 years). Brown also believed that public borrowing was too high. Some difficult decisions, notably on raising interest rates, were put off before the general election. But the incoming Labour government was distinctly better off than its predecessors in 1945, 1964 or 1974, which faced severe economic difficulties requiring emergency action. What was needed was a small adjustment, not a wholesale change of course, in managing the economy.

The Blair government quickly took a number of decisions which both corrected the inherited problems and put monetary and fiscal policy on a sound footing, the aim being to establish a much clearer long-term framework to achieve both stability and credibility. By far the most important initiative was announced only four days after Brown became Chancellor: to make the Bank of England responsible for setting interest rates to meet an inflation target set by the Treasury. This was accompanied by an immediate rise in interest rates. The plan, later enacted in legislation, closely followed plans prepared in opposition by Brown's advisers, notably Ed Balls (see Peston 2005, pp. 112-30).

Bank independence, via the creation of the Monetary Policy Committee chaired by the Governor, has helped to entrench low inflation and low interest rates. As intended, it has created a more predictable and transparent framework of decision-making. One indicator is that the yield spread between indexed and unindexed government bonds fell by almost one percentage point. Inflation expectations in financial markets ten years ahead have averaged 2.5 per cent since May 1997, compared with 4.6 per cent in the 1992–97 period. This shows the favourable impact of Bank independence. That is why Balls argues that May 1997 was the decisive change.

The previous arrangements still allowed uncertainty, and it was only the creation of a new institutional framework that led to greater predictability, and the revival of trust. 'It was only from 1997 onwards that the evidence suggests that the financial markets and the public started really to trust again in the institutions and commitments made by policymakers working within the new framework.' Moreover, he argues that the new framework has been tested by, and withstood, a series of shocks to the global economic systems, such as the Asian and Russian financial crises of autumn 1998, followed by the hedge fund scare, and then the slowdown in the USA from 2000 onwards. However, these shocks were small by comparison with the inflationary surges of the mid- and late 1970s, and of the late 1980s. So the new framework has not really been tested. Balls argues that the key was that the 2.5 per cent target was symmetric in that inflation below the target is as much to be avoided as inflation above the target. 'It is the key innovation which ensures that monetary policy supports the government's goals for high and stable levels of growth and employment.' He argues that this has enabled Britain to avoid the deflationary bias of other central banks, notably the European Central Bank in managing eurozone interest rates. Bank independence has also permitted greater flexibility and discretion than when interest rates were determined solely by politicians.

Balls is correct that the post-1997 arrangements are superior to what went before, but he overstates his case. It is better to think of a process, rather than a sharp dividing line in May 1997. Bank independence has unquestionably been the most important economic decision taken by the Brown Treasury. But it built on what had happened over the previous four and a half years, and was in many ways the next logical step. It was in that period, from 1992 until 1997, that inflation was reduced to low single figures, and that the period of steady, and sustainable, growth began. But both John Major and Kenneth Clarke had opposed Bank independence, even though it was supported by previous Conservative Chancellors such as Nigel Lawson and Norman Lamont. So Gordon Brown deserves the credit for having the courage to take that step so soon after taking office, however inevitable it now looks and however widely it is now accepted. That is an integral part of any New Labour settlement, strange though it would look to earlier Labour generations, who had fought against the tendency of the Bank to operate as an independent entity even after it was nationalised in 1946.

The other main changes were in fiscal policy. The government committed itself to a formal framework of fiscal rules, invariably described by Brown as 'prudent'. This partly involved the golden rule, to limit borrowing over the economic cycle to no more than investment, and to keep government debt below 40 per cent of gross domestic product. Economists disputed the case for the golden rule, which was in any case elastic, depending both on the definition of public investment and on the length of the economic cycle. The resulting controversies over these definitions and their implications generated more heat than light, since it was clear both that the overall fiscal position deteriorated after 2000 and that the overall macroeconomic environment was more stable than in the past. The problem was partly that the Brown Treasury wanted not just to be acclaimed for doing better than its predecessors (generally true), but it also wanted to be acclaimed as being right all the time (which it was not).

At first, Brown decided to tighten fiscal policy to correct what was seen as an excessive level of public borrowing, though the underlying trend was already more favourable. In his first Budget speech on 2 July 1997 he announced a deficit reduction plan involving a tightening in fiscal policy of around £5 billion a year in both 1996–97 and 1997–98. This reflected a combination of higher taxes and a tight squeeze on overall public spending. So public borrowing over these two years was projected to be roughly £8 billion lower than forecast by the Treasury in November 1996. However, the government never quite stuck to the inherited spending plans as much as is widely believed. The initial £5.2 billion one-off levy on the privatised utilities was used to finance spending on the New Deal programme to reduce youth and long-term unemployment, and for some spending on public services, notably on school buildings. Brown's first Budget in 1997 raised spending on health and education in 1998–99 by £1.2 billion and £1 billion respectively. But this came from within the large reserve already allocated for the year. Nonetheless, contrary to the later popular impression that these services were initially starved of extra money, spending on the NHS was set to rise by 2.3 per cent in real, inflation-adjusted, terms, and current expenditure on schools by 2.7 per cent. These rises were, of course, very small by the standard of later increases. Taking account of the welfare-to-work programme and a slight relaxation of controls on the use by local authorities of their capital receipts, total spending was intended to be between £2.5 and £4 billion higher than previously planned in 1998–99.

However, public spending came in below planned levels and tax receipts proved to be very buoyant. Together with the tax-raising measures, such as the change in the tax treatment of pension funds, there was a marked improvement in the public finances over the first term. Balls has claimed (2005) that 'The two year public spending freeze, tax decisions taken in 1997 and 1998 and, in particular, the decision to use the proceeds from the 3G mobile auction, £22 billion, to repay debt, all helped to establish the credibility of the government's commitment to meeting the fiscal rules, and to strengthen the fiscal position and cut net debt to a lower level than in any other G7 country.' He has argued that this tightening of nearly 4 per cent of national income from 1996–97 to 2000–01 is in contrast to previous periods when the economy grew above its trend rate, as in 1985–86 and 1990–91, when fiscal policy was loosened by nearly 2.5 per cent. In the early and mid-1970s the fiscal stance was loosened by more than 7 per cent, producing severe borrowing problems.

The Treasury was criticised in the early years for being too cautious, but Balls argues that this was deliberate: in the economic jargon, while the monetary target was symmetric, allowing for both undershooting as well as overshooting, the fiscal target was asymmetric, to guard against an unpredictable swing into deficit. 'The reason for building up a margin of error in the early phase of the economic cycle was precisely to guard against an asymmetric fiscal cycle and the kind of upward revision to borrowing that the UK, like other countries, has seen over recent years.' Looked at another way, if the public finances turned out to be better than expected, it would always be possible to correct later via increase in spending or tax cuts. This is what happened, partly because the proceeds from the mobile auction were more than five times what had originally been expected. So there was ample room for manoeuvre when Brown decided to increase public spending.

The IMF has concluded (2005) that the 'the rules-based fiscal framework has served the UK well by underpinning fiscal discipline and assuring scope for automatic stabilisers to operate freely.' This means that, because the rule is over the ups and downs of an economic cycle, there is flexibility. When growth slows down, borrowing is allowed to rise as tax receipts decline and public spending on unemployment and other benefits rises. However, when the economy is strong, above its underlying trend rate of growth, tax receipts are buoyant and spending on benefits slows, thus cutting the level of public borrowing.

In the first spending review in 1998, Brown announced increases in spending for health and education, but there was a big element of double – even treble – counting in the presentation of the changes, as the annual rises over three years were added together to produce a total of £40 billion. This was a gross exaggeration of relatively small real increases in their budgets, and led to disappointment later on. The big rise in spending only came in the 2000 and 2002 spending reviews. By then, as discussed in the previous chapter, Brown and Blair had decided that health spending had to grow much faster than originally planned. This was one of Brown's few admitted changes of view. While the Brown team had a fairly accurate view of what would have to be spent on education, employment policy etc., in 1997 they had underestimated the scale of the extra resources needed for health. As the next chapter shows, the adjustment in health policy came in two stages, first in 2000 and then the Wanless review in 2001–02, and the subsequent tax decisions.

The ability to maintain low inflation, steady growth and low unemployment has also reflected changes in the structure of the economy dating from the Thatcher and Major years. The shake-up in British industry, the deregulation of financial services, the taming of the trade unions and limitation of their legal immunities, and the encouragement of new enterprise combined to make the British economy more flexible and competitive. Most of these changes have been accepted by the Brown Treasury, which has taken forward the broadly pro-enterprise approach, with the addition of a 'fairness agenda' discussed below. Shorn of its responsibility for setting interest rates, the Treasury has undergone a substantial reorganisation, primarily under Sir Andrew Turnbull and Sir Gus O'Donnell, its permanent secretaries from 1998 until 2005. Symbolised by its move from Whitehall to new open-plan offices overlooking St James's Park, there has been a change in what the Treasury does. This has involved the promotion of a number of younger officials in their late thirties and early forties, particularly those who worked closely with Ed Balls and Ed Miliband, Brown's key advisers. Instead of concentrating on macroeconomic management and control of public spending, the Treasury has developed units to look at welfare-to-work policies, at how to improve productivity and how to reduce child poverty, both at home and abroad. At the time of the spring Budget and the late autumn Pre-Budget Report, Brown has made announcements about industrial, employment and welfare policies, as if the departments of Work and Pensions (as it became) and Trade and Industry were wholly-owned subsidiaries of the Treasury, like the Inland Revenue and Customs and Excise before their merger. And the Treasury, for once, became a substantial spending department through Brown's promotion and expansion of tax credits, absorbing billions and billions of pounds. This change is also a potential long-term weakness since it gives the Treasury a specific interest in the allocation of resources, rather than its traditional role of exercising a detached, overall restraint.

The background to this new activism was the Brown Treasury's view (set out in Balls *et al.* 2004) that a sound macroeconomic framework is a necessary but not a sufficient condition for economic success. For all his boasting about the macroeconomic record, Brown has been aware how Britain's competitive position has still lagged behind hits main rivals. He has seen a role for the state in making the market work better in order to raise the sustainable rate of productivity growth. There have been five main themes (Balls *et al.* 2004, pp. 10–11): strengthening the competition regime to encourage innovation and minimising costs; promoting enterprise to help businesses start up and grow; supporting science and the use of new technologies; improving skills through better education for young people and improved training for those already in the workforce; and encouraging investment in the stock of physical capital. As this list implies, the strategy has involved activism across the whole range of government. Tax incentives and new agencies have been created. The rate of corporation tax has been reduced and a lower starting rate has been introduced for smaller businesses. However, much of the impact has been offset for many businesses by the rise in employer, as well as employee, national insurance contributions. The provision of venture capital has been assisted through Venture Capital Trust and the Enterprise Investment Scheme, though sceptics have questioned how much difference these types of initiative have made, as opposed to providing another tax shelter for the already wealthy. The intention has been to maintain a low-rate, broadly based system, one of the arguments against EU attempts to harmonise tax rates. But the Brown Treasury's attempts at simplification have often appeared to introduce more complexity as rules have been repeatedly changed.

On competition, for example, a series of acts have strengthened the authorities' power to tackle anti-competitive practices and alleged abuses of market dominance. Ministers have been removed from decision-making on competition issues to give the Office of Fair Trading and the Competition Commission independence from political interference. Studies have been carried out of markets which may not be working in the customers' interests. Building on the work of the previous Conservative government, Labour has completed the liberalisation of energy markets, and, in this more competitive environment, a substantial number of customers have changed suppliers.

The government has also been very active in the labour market, through welfare-to-work measures to reduce employment, expanding skills training, introducing a national minimum wage, extending parental rights and modifying some of the trade union laws inherited from the Tories. Blair has been firm since his days as shadow employment secretary in the early 1990s about not repealing the key trade union laws of the 1980s on ballots before strikes, against secondary picketing and outlawing the closed shop. But workers have been given a legal right to join a union, and also not to join one. Moreover, unions now get automatic recognition in a firm if more than 50 per cent of workers are members. Despite business worries, the government has not gone nearly as far as the unions would like.

Brown has been very fond of commissioning reviews by businessmen to look at problems. Every Budget and Pre-Budget Report has either launched some new reviews or reported the results of two or three existing ones. We have had, amongst many others, Atkinson (measuring public sector productivity), Barker (housing supply), Clementi (regulation of legal services), Cruickshank (competition in banking), Gershon (efficiency savings in government), Hampton (the burden on business of regulatory inspection and enforcement), Higgs (the role of non-executive directors), Lambert (university organisation and business links), Lyons (local government finance), Miles (the factors limiting the development of a fixed-rate mortgage market in Britain), Pickering (simplification of pensions legislation and regulation), Sandler (long-term retail savings),

Taylor (interaction of the tax and benefits system), Turner (adequacy of future pension provision), and Wanless (funding of the NHS). The list would make a wonderful Gilbert and Sullivan patter song. Brown cites these reports to justify changes he is introducing. However, impressive though most of these reports have been in their analyses, the record of implementation has been patchy. Just look at the problems of first-time house buyers. Some of the attempts to introduce greater labour market flexibility have been undermined by the rapid rate of house price inflation, and in particular the big price differences between the south-east of England and other parts of the country. These have increased shortages of skilled employees, and in particular public sector workers like teachers and NHS staff, shortages only partly offset by an influx of immigrants with the necessary qualifications. Attempts to simplify complicated housing regulations and increase the supply in popular areas in the south-east have proved to be highly controversial.

The independent economic assessments quoted above all pay tribute to the macro and micro policies pursued by the Brown Treasury. They acknowledge the achievements, but then express worries, most of which are publicly unacknowledged or disputed by Brown. The key difference is over fiscal policy. There is no dispute that public sector finances have deteriorated steadily since 2000, from a current surplus of 2 per cent of GDP in 1999–2000 to a deficit of 1.9 per cent in 2003–04, falling to 1.1 per cent in 2004–05. This partly helped to sustain growth in face of a slowdown in the 2001–03 period. However, even after adjusting for the fluctuations of the economic cycle, there has still been a substantial underlying deterioration, from an initial current surplus of 1.9 per cent of GDP in 1999–2000 to deficits of around 1.4 per cent in 2003–04 and just under 1 per cent in mid-2005. While the underlying trend has clearly been adverse, the overall deficit is still low by international standards, less than in most of the eurozone and in the United States.

The Treasury has claimed that borrowing is not only still within its fiscal rules, but will remain so. However, most outside organisations have disagreed about what will happen in future, producing a lively spat between the Treasury and the IMF at the start of the 2005 election campaign. The Treasury argued that slower spending growth and a rebound in tax revenues would reverse past fiscal weakening and ensure that the fiscal rules are met. However, outside forecasters think the Treasury is too optimistic about future growth rates and hence about levels of revenue, particularly from corporate taxes. Their doubts were reinforced by the slowdown in growth to below forecast levels in 2005. While the Treasury thinks there will be a substantial underlying improvement in borrowing over the next four years, the IMF expects only a marginal change. This is not just an arcane argument between economists. It has direct implications for future public spending and taxes. If the Treasury is correct, there may be no need for tax increases. If the outside bodies are correct, then taxes will have to rise further, an admission which the Chancellor was naturally unwilling to make during an election campaign – especially when the Conservatives were talking loudly and often about a £10 billion-plus black hole. Moreover, even on current policies, tax and national insurance receipts are set to rise from 36.3 per cent of national income at present to 38.5 per cent by the end of the decade.

However, in July 2005 Brown suddenly changed his interpretation of the golden rule by announcing that the current economic cycle had begun in 1997, rather than in 1999. This enabled him to include the favourable economic figures of 1998 in his calculations, allowing him to borrow an additional £12 billion and still stay within the limits of the rule (borrow only to invest). At the same time, Brown announced that the usual biannual review of spending plans due in 2006 would not occur, to allow time for a fundamental review of all departmental budgets to take account of 'challenges' such as the ageing population, the terrorist threat, intensified competition from the Far East, technological change and global warming. This would be completed in 2007. The immediate effect has been to reduce the pressure for a tax increase in 2006 – though most economists argued that tricky decisions on tackling the structural deficit had only been deferred. Moreover, by being his own interpreter of the rule, in his own interests, Brown undermined his 'fiscal prudence' reputation. Contrasts were drawn between this fiscal fudging and the openness and independence of monetary policy.

The IMF has called 'for an early start to smooth fiscal adjustment amounting to about 1 per cent of GDP over the next five years'. This dispute has direct relevance to the now deferred review of public spending plans in spring 2007 which will cover the period up to 2010–11, that is beyond the likely date of the next general election. The warnings by the IMF and other forecasters are on the assumption that spending growth 'will taper off as planned' after the end of the current period of above average growth up to 2008. So, on their view, an adjustment will be required even on current plans. This is even taking account of the sizeable efficiency savings which the Treasury is already assuming following the Gershon review. These efficiency gains are supposed to come from improved procurement practices and relocating parts of the Civil Service to lower-cost areas. In his March 2004 Budget speech, the Chancellor said departments would have to achieve annual efficiency savings of 2.5 per cent. This was intended to release funds for 'frontline' delivery of £20 billion a year by 2008. Apart from problems of measuring productivity and efficiency in the public sector, this target was regarded as being very hard to achieve.

Moreover, the government has also faced the dilemma that maintaining the improvement in standards in schools and in the NHS, let alone creating universal child care and reducing poverty, will require total spending to rise faster than the growth of the economy. Since public borrowing is already at its limits, this could only mean higher taxes. The underlying dilemma of the Blair government's approach to public services has been how to balance spending to improve these services while avoiding excessive tax rises.

There is no direct correlation between the relative size of public spending and economic growth. Nor is there any clear or predictable link with competitiveness. The key questions raised by economists are whether the money is being efficiently spent and about the way that services are provided and financed: the balances between taxation and user fees (such as payment for tuition), and between state provision and the involvement of competitive private suppliers in providing taxpayer-funded services. These have been central, and often divisive, questions for the Blair government, which are discussed in the next chapter.

Independent analysts all highlight the looming problem of pensions and low levels of savings in Britain. At the time that Labour came to office in 1997, the new ministers were complacent over pensions provision in Britain. The tone was that we are better off than other European countries – such as Italy, with its large unfunded pension liabilities. Yes, there had been serious problems with the mis-selling of private pension schemes in the mid- and late 1980s, but many British people were well placed because of the strong financial condition of occupational pension schemes. Moreover, the UK's public pension system was, and is, seen as financially sustainable. As a result of one of the earliest decisions of the Thatcher government, the basic state pension is uprated in line with prices, not earnings. The common assumption in the late 1990s was that the balance between public and private sector provision would shift. The state would provide a basic minimum and help the poorest, with the middle class and the better off relying on occupational and private schemes. The belief that everything was essentially fine led to the change announced in the first July 1997 Budget in the tax treatment of dividends received by pension schemes. This effectively took at least £5 billion a year away from funds, amounting to a loss of income of £40 billion over seven years. The government's over-optimism is shown by Brown's comment in his first Budget speech (1997) that 'Many pension funds are in substantial surplus and at present many companies are enjoying pension holidays, so this is the right time to undertake a long-needed reform.'

These attitudes have been shown to be mistaken. The pensions crisis has several causes, many pre-dating 1997, but the Labour government aggravated the problems by this tax change and by new rules affecting their spread of investments. The end of the long stock market boom of the 1990s undermined the value of funds and, combined with the fall in long-term interest rates and inflation expectations, slashed annuity rates and therefore levels of expected income. This created serious funding problems for final-salary occupational pension schemes, especially with people now living much longer after retirement. Many final-salary schemes were closed to new members and some were shut down completely. Such closures created considerable hardship which the government belatedly addressed through the creation of a Pension Protection Fund to protect occupational pension schemes. Meanwhile, the growing numbers in defined contribution schemes, where levels of pensions were related to share price performance and long-term interest rates, faced a fall in their retirement income.

The government was slow to recognise the growing problems over private sector pensions, concentrating on improving public sector pensions for the poorest. There was an early mis-step in 2000, when under the formula linking the annual pension uprating to changes in prices, the annual rise was just 75p – provoking widespread protests from pensioner groups and within the Labour Party. Paradoxically, if inflation had been higher, and the uprating larger, there might perversely have been no protests. Brown refused pleas to restore the link to earnings, rather than prices, arguing that available help should be concentrated on the minority of pensioners in need. However, stung by this episode, he did announce above-inflation increases in the basic pension over the 2000 to 2005 period.

The Treasury's focus was on ensuring an adequate income in retirement. After the initial minimum income guarantee, uprated each year in line with earnings, a pension credit was introduced from 2003 to ensure that no pensioner fell below the poverty threshold. However, at first roughly a third of those entitled to the credit did not claim it, and there were also worries over discouraging private saving (only partly addressed by the savings credit). The very complexity of tax credits created considerable problems as a very high proportion – nearly a half, according to an analysis by the Parliamentary Ombudsman – involved incorrect payments. This was either because of official errors or because families did not report changes in their financial circumstances quickly. Overpayments exceeded underpayments by more than three to one in cash terms.

In addition, a new state second pension was introduced in 2002. This was aimed at carers, the disabled and low-paid people who had failed to accrue pension rights. Brown was not averse, however, to a few populist gestures like a lump sum, untaxed winter fuel payments, and free television licences for the over-75s. These were invariably announced to the cheers of Labour MPs in Commons statements which also included new tax incentives to better-off entrepreneurs. In 2004, in face of protests about council tax bills, the government announced another headline-grabbing across-the-board payment to pensioners to help with their bills.

The debate over the future of state support became tied up with discussion of the future of private pensions. The underlying problem has been the low relative level of savings in Britain coupled with the ageing of the population and the longer life expectancy of people after they have retired. As the IMF noted in its 2005 report, 'a sizeable swathe of the middle class is not saving enough to ensure retirement income that will meet their aspirations.' The government appointed a Pensions Commission under Adair Turner, the former director-general of the Confederation of British Industry, first to examine the scale of the problem and secondly to propose solutions. The first half came in October 2004, with the second, inevitably more contentious, half due in autumn 2005. The interim report of the Turner commission estimated that roughly nine and a half million people (almost half the working-age population over 35) had inadequate savings to meet their likely expectations about retirement incomes. The savings gap, particularly affecting the middle class, was partly because of the difficulty people had in making decisions about long-term saving, and partly because of the complexity and cost of private pensions, as well as doubts created by earlier mis-selling scandals.

As Adair Turner himself admitted, there was little dispute about the solution, a combination of increased saving and greater flexibility in the timing of retirement. This need not necessarily mean a change in the formal state retirement age of 65 (the current age for men and in the process of being equalised for women as well). Rather, the aim is to create a gradual transition from full-time work to retirement, via the creation of more adaptable arrangements so that people in their sixties can work parttime for their employers and receive both pay for the hours worked and part of their pension. All sorts of ideas were in circulation about simplifying pension savings vehicles, though the record with the sales of such standardised, low-cost 'stakeholder' pensions was mixed.

The big decision is how far to increase compulsion in saving beyond what already exists and how much to depend on the state pension system, already one of the least generous among the main industrialised countries. The Turner Commission and most outside experts have recognised the limits to the extension of pension tax credits since these discouraged saving. At the 2005 general election, both the Conservatives and the Liberal Democrats (under two of the most original and intelligent opposition spokesmen, David Willetts and Steve Webb, respectively) had put forward alternative proposals based on raising the basic state pension, so as to reduce means-tested benefits. The Blair government was wary of extending compulsion, because forcing people to save more by deductions from their pay packets would be seen as a form of taxation. During the election campaign, Brown had said that any proposals involving greater compulsion would not be implemented until after a subsequent election. There was scope for strengthening voluntary saving in various ways, such as automatic enrolment in funds, though this was largely compulsion by the back door. David Blunkett, work and pensions secretary after the election, floated the idea of requiring employees to opt out of occupational schemes, rather than opting into them, as now.

But any assessment of the New Labour legacy cannot just look at its claims to economic competence – avoiding the pitfalls that have undermined and often defeated past Labour governments. That is only half the story, albeit a crucially important part. There are two other questions. First, in what sense have Brown's economic policies been social democratic? And second, how far has the government improved Britain's underlying economic performance? Brown has been determined not just to be a competent economic manager. His constant refrain has been 'prudence with a purpose' and he has had very clear social and economic objectives beyond low inflation and steady economic growth.

However, an economic analyst knowing nothing about when Britain had held its general elections, and which party had won, would conclude that the same government had been in charge throughout the second half of the 1990s. But after 2000, there was obviously a change of policy and a more distinctly social democratic approach had been adopted: social democratic in the sense of a commitment to the beneficial role of public spending and a willingness to raise its relative share. Public spending in real, inflation-adjusted terms was flat over Labour's first three years in office, and indeed fell slightly. As a share of national income, total spending fell by 3.4 points to 37.2 per cent between 1996–97 and 1999–2000. This was lower than at any time during the Thatcher era and was the lowest for nearly 40 years, reflecting a combination of a strong rate of economic growth and a much tighter than planned squeeze on spending in the first term. After increasing by just 1 per cent in 1999-2000, total spending expanded by 4 and 6 per cent in real terms annually over the following five years. This was faster than the growth of the economy, leading to a four-point rise in the relative share of public spending to about 41 per cent, with a forecast increase to roughly 42 per cent over the next two years. This is, in effect, back to where Labour started. As noted above, there are now very tough decisions over the future trends of public spending. But in its second term, at least, New Labour has been in the tradition of conventional social democratic administrations.

But it is not just a question of levels of spending or taxation but of where the money goes. Spending on health and education, what New Labour cloyingly used to call 'the people's priorities', has risen substantially in real terms. Spending on these programmes has over the long term grown more rapidly than other budgets. According to a study by the Institute for Fiscal Studies (2004, p. 13), spending on health expanded by 3.7 per cent in real, inflation-adjusted terms every year in the second half of the twentieth century, and education spending by 4 per cent. This compares with a 2.5 per cent annual rate of increase in total spending, more or less in line with the rate of growth of the economy. During the Conservative years in power from 1979 to 1997, the annual rates of growth were 3.1 per cent for health and 1.5 per cent for education. But in the first seven Labour years the annual rates of increase were 5.8 and 4.4 per cent respectively. Moreover, health spending was projected to rise by 7.2 per cent a year up to March 2008, and education spending by 4.3 per cent annually over this period. The share of total national income devoted to the NHS has risen from 5.3 to 6.5 per cent since 1997, and it is heading above 7 per cent towards 8 per cent. The share spent on education has risen from 4.7 to 5.3 per cent, back to the level when the Tories won office in 1979. These figures indicate a substantial shift in the balance of public spending over the past eight years. (The implications for the way that these services are run and for standards of health care and educational performance are discussed in the next chapter.)

By contrast, spending on social security has risen by just 1.8 per cent annually since 1997, or roughly half the rate under the Tories. This largely reflects the sharp rise in unemployment in the 1980s and its decline over the past decade. Indeed, while previous Labour governments would have trumpeted an increase in spending in social security as evidence of their compassion, New Labour has boasted of the decline as a sign that its policies to get more people into work are succeeding. A further apparently unexpected trend is that spending on defence has risen by 0.8 per cent annually under Labour, while it fell by 0.3 per cent a year in the Tory period. This contrast largely reflects the big cutbacks in the size of the armed forces during the early 1990s after the end of the Cold War and the increases in recent years associated with the series of wars of the Blair era, and the commitments to the Balkans, Afghanistan and Iraq.

The tax burden has been flatter than the trend of spending, but is now rising steadily to around 40 per cent during this decade. This is the highest level since the mid-1980s at the start of the Lawson boom, but still less than the average for the whole of the Tory years from 1979 until 1997. The tax picture is complicated, for the tax burden reflects a mixture of influences, such as variations in national income, fiscal drag (increases in tax receipts related to growing earnings and profits), and the impact of past tax changes, as well as new discretionary tax changes. Tax revenues in Britain are slightly higher as a share of national income than in the rest of the G7 countries (largely because of the low shares in the USA and Japan), but lower than in most European countries.

The Conservatives have made much of Labour 'stealth taxes', talking about 66 increases. However, the Institute for Fiscal Studies estimated, before the March 2005 Budget, that there had been 157 tax-raising measures, but also 215 tax-cutting measures. Most are minor and the real point is the total amount raised. The 2005 Green Budget from the IFS (2005) showed that government revenues had risen by about £26 billion over Labour's first two terms. About a third reflected policy announcements by Brown, notably the increase in national insurance contributions. Another third reflected the continuing impact of the tax rises announced before 1997 by the Major government which Labour chose not to reverse, such as the increases in fuel and tobacco excise duties. Of the rest, the economic cycle and fiscal drag boosted revenues by over £23 billion, though this was offset by other factors costing nearly £15 billion, such as the falling profits of financial companies. Overall, government revenues grew by 3.3 per cent in real terms over Labour's first eight years in office, almost twice as rapidly as over the whole eighteen years of Tory rule. However, because the economy has grown more strongly since 1997 than before, national income after deducting tax receipts has risen slightly faster under Labour than the Tories, but the difference is slight, 2.6 per cent a year as against 2.4 per cent.

Moreover, Brown has pursued his own redistributive agenda, even if neither he nor Blair have been keen on using that word. There has been nothing about squeezing the rich. New Labour has been very keen on entrepreneurs, giving a series of tax reliefs for setting up new enterprises, which are mainly of benefit to the already well off. During the 2001 election campaign, when refusing to use the word 'redistribution' during an interview with Jeremy Paxman on the BBC2 *Newsnight* programme, Blair said: 'It's not a burning ambition for me to make sure that David Beckham earns less money.' Blair has wanted to help the poor by helping those most in need, and by increasing opportunities through better schools and improved training, but not by penalising the wealthy, or raising taxes on the better off. Consequently, the top marginal rate of income tax has remained at the 40 per cent level at which it was fixed in 1988, but the starting point for this higher band has not been raised in line with earnings. At present, it applies to earnings of just over £37,000 a year, or 1.6 times the national average wage. The number of higher-rate taxpayers has increased since 1997 by roughly three-quarters to over 3.6 million. However, in terms of wealth, as opposed to income, the super-rich – the top 1 per cent of the population – have increased their share under Labour.

Brown has been passionate about reducing poverty, both at home amongst children and pensioners and overseas by boosting the budget of the Department for International Development to reduce poverty in developing countries, particularly in Africa. Blair has been fully behind this approach, making a commitment in 2000 to abolish 'child poverty for ever'. The tax and benefit changes introduced by Brown since 1997 have largely offset each other in aggregate. The net cost to the Treasury works out at £1.1 billion a year at present (2005–06), according to the IFS estimates. This is the difference between two large sets of changes, one of £57.2 billion and the other of £58.3 billion. In some cases, the offsets are within the same tax. The introduction of the 10 per cent starting rate of income tax and the cut in the basic rate have been more than offset by changes to the married couple's allowances and to other allowances, let alone the increased national insurance contribution rates. Indirect taxes and stamp duty have risen substantially, though revenue from companies from corporation tax has fallen as a result of a series of new reliefs. On the other side, the biggest boost has come from the array of new personal tax credits (for working families, children, disabled people, and pensioners, all of which have been modified during the period), from increases in child benefits, and from a whole range of measures to assist pensioners. There has been a considerable amount of churning, with the state taking in a great deal of money and giving it out again, partly to the same people, creating substantial administrative problems.

The net effect of the tax and benefits adjustments has been equivalent to 0.2 per cent of household disposable incomes, or 84p per household per week on average, though this turns into a loss per household equivalent to £3.62 per week once real increases in council tax are included. However, there have been considerable variations along the income scale. The largest gains have been received by the second poorest tenth of the population, who have gained nearly 11 per cent of their incomes, excluding the impact of council tax rises which are anyway largely covered by council tax benefit for this group. By contrast, the richest tenth have lost 5 per cent of their incomes. Moreover, the redistribution to the poorest groups was greater in the second term than in the first term. The IFS shows how the main gainers have been households with children, both lone parents and non-working families with children, and, to a slightly lesser extent, pensioners. This reflects Brown's focus on reducing child and pensioner poverty and on getting people into work.

The IFS has estimated that tax credits had boosted employment by around 80,000 by 2002, and cut the number of workless families by 100,000. Much of the new assistance has been given through tax credits for children and additional benefits of various kinds for pensioners. Childless workers have done much less well. The counterpart to the reduction of poverty is the imposition of higher marginal rates on growing numbers of people as tax credits are withdrawn at higher levels of income. This worsens incentives.

Overall, the system has become fairer, less because of changes in taxes than because of these new benefits. What the government has sought to do – and to some extent has achieved – has been to reduce the impact of all the economic forces pushing towards greater inequality without under-mining the competitive position of the British economy. It has been trying to combine globalisation with social cohesion. As Polly Toynbee and David Walker conclude (2005, pp. 49–50): 'At best, Labour stopped inequality in the UK getting worse. Its programme of benefits and credits was egalitarian and redistributive. But it served, in the IFS phrase, "just about to halt" growing inequality, not to cut it.'

In terms of the stated objectives of poverty reduction, the government got some way towards its targets. Poverty is, of course, a relative and not an absolute concept. It is not just the amount of money needed to survive or buy necessities, but the definition is related to levels of earnings generally. It is usually measured as a certain percentage, 60 per cent, of median income – not the same as a mean or average, but the middle point where half earn more and half less. Thus it is a moving figure depending on what has been happening to incomes. Two or three decades ago, the poverty line would have much been lower in real terms. Taking poverty as 60 per cent of median income, the percentage of the population in households below this level fell from nearly 25 per cent in 1996–97 to 21 per cent in 2003–04 (after taking account of housing costs), according to a study of poverty and inequality in Britain by the IFS (2005). Before housing costs, the decline was from 18.4 to 16.8 per cent. The government had a formal target to reduce child poverty in 2004–05 by a quarter from its level in 1998–99. This fall was less than some analysts expected, partly because of administrative problems with the new tax credits in 2003 and because of a rise in the number of children living in families where no adult works. There are also ambiguities about the definitions and the figures, but child poverty is now clearly on the decline to its lowest level since the late 1980s. Similarly, poverty amongst pensioners has also fallen sharply, with the number below the poverty line (after taking account of housing costs) down from 28 to 19.7 per cent between 1996–97 and 2003–04. This total was set to fall further as the full impact of pension credit works through. Revealingly, the IFS noted that for the first time since the early 1980s a smaller fraction of pensioners are poor than non-pensioners. There has been little change in poverty among adults without children.

The government has also sought to tackle gender, race and age inequalities. While the above paragraphs have focused on income inequality, there has also been a growing debate about social mobility and life chances: the links between poverty, living in a run-down and crime-ridden estate with high unemployment, health and educational performance. In short, the chances of many children are largely determined by where they were born, by their parents' family circumstances. This has been reinforced by educational and housing inequalities. As Labour's ministerial intellectual David Miliband argued in a speech in March 2005, there is ample evidence that the country remains 'deeply scarred by unequal life-chances', as shown by pay gaps and sharply different educational outcomes, and in social mobility. The chances of the son or daughter of someone in social class V reaching social class I are 32 times lower than the chances of the son or daughter of someone in social class I staying there. In many respects, social divisions had become harder, rather than easier, to overcome: children born in 1958 were more likely to move up their parents' social class and income than those born in 1970. But Miliband pointed to some positive developments, as a result of the New Deal helping 1.2 million people into work, falling waiting lists, improvement in school exam results in inner city areas, and a reversal in the seemingly inexorable rise in child and pensioner poverty.

The main economic, as opposed to social, question about Gordon Brown's record is whether the underlying competitive position has improved: whether his success (partly inherited) in creating stability has helped to enhance Britain's underlying potential to grow and create jobs. The evidence here is mixed. Britain has experienced remarkable macro-economic stability since 1997. It is not just a matter of rates of growth or of inflation, it is also a question of reducing their volatility, now at the lowest levels since records began and the best of all the G7 countries. From being one of the most volatile economies in the G7, Britain is now the most stable. This has been coupled with faster growth per head than the rest of the G7, apart from Canada. Both inflation and inflationary expectations have remained low and have coped with disturbances like the global slowdown and the 9/11 attacks in 2001. Low inflation and low interest rates are obviously a significant help to business. Public finances have also remained healthier than the rest of the G7, both in terms of borrowing and outstanding debt, though there has been some deterioration in the last few years.

The biggest doubts are about the underlying growth potential. Some of the schemes to assist enterprise, improve skills and extend competition have helped, but there has been only a limited overall impact so far. As measured by the National Institute in its survey of the Labour government's economic record (2005, p. 8), productivity has been extremely stable. Looking at output per hour worked, productivity growth in Britain was 2.1 per cent a year over the 1989–96 period, but only fractionally higher at 2.2 per cent a year from 1997 until 2004. There has therefore been little change since the early 1980s. The National Institute concluded that, 'while there has been no obvious improvement since 1997, the United Kingdom is no longer falling behind France (and other European countries) in the way it did for forty years after the Second World

War. At the same time, we are not obviously closing the gap with France and we may have stopped closing the gap with the United States.'

The Treasury itself in its analysis in the 2005 Red Book (Treasury, Budget 2005, p. 43) notes that Britain has narrowed the output-per-worker gap with France to 10 per cent from 22 per cent in 1995. And, despite a slight widening in 2003, the gap with the US has narrowed to 20 per cent from 25 per cent over the same period. But on an output-per-hour basis, Britain has further to catch up. The Treasury argues that 'the UK performs relatively well in terms of output per person of working age,' a measure which reflects both employment and productivity performance. This is intended to show how well an economy is using all of its potential labour resources. Britain is over 12 per cent higher than Germany, and similar to France. But it still lags well behind the US, which combines high labour productivity with high employment.

The OECD concluded in its 2004 survey of the UK that the economy has 'achieved a commendable rate of potential growth, which is above the European average. As a consequence the GDP per capita gap with the major continental European countries has nearly closed. However, the gap with the best performing OECD countries – such as the United States, Canada, and Australia – has hardly diminished and stems mainly from weaker levels of productivity.' The OECD concedes that the government has introduced structural reforms to address these weaknesses. The most important are raising skills throughout the workforce, increased government infrastructure investment, and increasing competition. Britain still compares poorly with its main competitors on basic literacy and vocational skills. (Fresh initiatives in this area are discussed in the following chapter.) This explains why productivity growth has been stable despite the big increase in investment in information technology. Britain does not yet have enough skilled workers to exploit this investment. Improvements in education have also been slow, with too many leaving school and relatively few getting apprenticeships. These failures are routinely deplored by education ministers, but their efforts to remedy these failures have been tardy, and so far insufficient.

Public investment has belatedly been increased, particularly after the 2000 and 2002 spending reviews. But, the OECD notes, plans to double the share to just over 2 per cent of national income would still leave government investment at lower levels than in most other countries, particularly in transport.

Competitive pressures are also relatively strong in Britain, with economic and administrative regulations holding back competition and barriers to trade and new businesses among the lowest in industrialised countries, according to the OECD. The semi-independent Competition Commission, very much a Brown initiative, has been active, but there is still a long way to go to open up the retail and professional services sector to more competition.

Moreover, there are still serious problems in the labour market. While unemployment has declined substantially from the levels of the 1980s and 1990s, there has been almost no increase in the level of economic activity: that is, the percentage of an age group participating in the labour market have shown virtually no increase. The National Institute argues, however, that the current activity rates are sustainable, while in the late 1980s they were associated with accelerating inflation. The improvement in employment rates for both men and women aged between 25 and 54 started to occur well before 1997 and are now higher than in either the United States or France. Employment rates for people between 55 and the state retirement age (currently 62 for women and 65 for men) have tended to pick up in the past decade. Youth unemployment has also fallen. How much of this is due to the various government welfare-to-work initiatives to 'make work pay' is uncertain. Such initiatives not only involve help and advice for people to join or rejoin the labour forces, but also tax credits to reduce financial disincentives for people moving into employment. The National Institute concludes (2005, p. 8) that despite disincentive effects of the long tapering off of benefits in the various tax credits, 'a reasonable judgement is that the current structure promotes employment more effec- tively than does its predecessor.' This has particularly helped lone parents and unemployed couples with children. The national minimum wage has helped the working poor, and does not appear to have any significant negative effect so far on levels of employment.

The other side of the picture, however, is the increasing burden of regu- lation on business, in part the result of various new government initiatives listed above. The Confederation of British Industry and other business bodies have increasingly complained about the weight of new regulations, from both Whitehall and Brussels. They have cited the amount of form-filling, the disincentives to hiring, and the additional costs they face. However, international comparisons show that Britain is among the most lightly regulated business environments in the main industrialised countries, near the bottom of the OECD's index of product market regulation – and, as in most countries, the amount of regulation has fallen in recent years. A similar picture is shown for labour market and employment protection legislation. However, businesses argue that employment regulations are increasing rather than falling, with employees being given new rights to maternity and paternity leave, as well as the threat of being taken to employment tribunals for alleged discrimination. In his economic statements in 2004 and 2005, Gordon Brown sought to address these worries by announcing a review of the cost of compliance and a big cutback in regulations affecting business.

Business has also complained about a rise in taxes, notably the increase in national insurance contributions which came into force in 2003. Otherwise, the abolition of dividend tax credits to pensions funds has been mainly offset by a cut in the rate of corporation tax (from 33 to 30 per cent in two stages) and new reliefs such as the research and development tax credit. But some other countries have cut their company taxes even more in recent years. The windfall tax on the privatised utilities was a one-off levy and changes in the timing of payment of corporation tax have largely worked their way through the system. But the contribution of taxes on business to the public finances is expected to rise sharply over the next few years, largely because the Treasury expects a big recovery in corporate profits.

Britain has been a pretty good performer in the league tables of global competitiveness compiled by the World Economic Forum – though its ranking has slipped from being in the top eight out of 50 to 60 in the late 1990s to between tenth and fifteenth out of more than a hundred by 2004–05. These fluctuations from year to year have been seized upon by both politicians and the press to claim that competitiveness has declined. But the underlying picture is still not bad, with Britain rated well for management of the economy and the general business environment, but poorly for public infrastructure.

The overall performance has been good, but it hardly rates as a miracle. The economic position in 1997 was a more favourable one than any previous Labour government had inherited. But unlike its predecessors the Blair government did not squander its legacy. The Brown Treasury built on the new monetary framework created in the mid-1990s, remedying defects and taking the bold step to make the Bank of England independent. That decision alone has singled Gordon Brown out as a path-breaking Chancellor. The result has been to entrench a period of low inflation and steady growth, avoiding the volatility of the past, and to have got that largely right is a considerable achievement. There are now major questions about the sustainability of current spending plans and borrowing levels and whether – or perhaps how much – taxes will have to be raised. Brown's margin of manoeuvre has been underlined by the slowing of the economy during 2005. Politically awkward though these decisions will be, we are not talking about a crisis of confidence or adjustment remotely comparable with the tough fiscal packages introduced by past Labour governments in the 1966–69 period and in 1975–76. There are also major questions, discussed in the next chapter, about whether and how far the big increase in spending has improved the underlying results of public services, as opposed to raising the numbers and pay of public sector workers. Could the money have been better spent? Moreover, it is still too early to judge all the various initiatives to improve the productivity performance of the economy. Many of these measures are in the right direction, though there are legitimate business worries about the dangers of excessive regulation. Gordon Brown and his team have managed the economy well, creating a sensible framework and avoiding the errors of the past, but they cannot claim to have transformed the position of the British economy. That is beyond any government, and Chancellor.

5

Struggling to Deliver

'The myth that the solution to every problem is increased spending has been comprehensively dispelled in recent years. How effectively money is spent counts for much more than how much money is spent.'

Treasuty Financial Statement and Budget Report, Budget, July 1997.

'After decades of under-investment, investment in schools is doubling, in policing doubling, in transport doubling, in housing doubling, and instead of £40 billion spent on the NHS in 1997, by 2008 £110 billion for the NHS.'

Gordon Brown, speech to the Labour Party conference, Brighton, 27 September 2004.

'We are completing the re-casting of the 1945 welfare state to end entirely the era of "one size fits all" services and put in their place modern services which maintain at their core the values of equality of access and opportunity for all; base the service round the user, a personalised service with real choice, greater individual responsibility and high standards; and ensure in so doing that we keep our public services universal, for the middle class as well as those on lower incomes, both of whom expect and demand services of quality.'

Tony Blair, speech at St Thomas's Hospital, London, 23 June 2004.

Public services are the heart of Tony Blair's claims to be able to leave a substantial legacy. When he has faced difficulties in other areas, such as Europe or Iraq, Blair has always turned to reform of public services to claim that the government is making a difference. When asked during the run-up to the 2005 election what he hoped to be remembered for, his reply was invariably 'modernising public services': bringing the postwar welfare state up to date, making it less centralised and more tailored to the individual needs of the public. His focus on education and health led one critical ex-Cabinet minister to remark privately that 'when he is not being a world leader, Tony just wants to be education and health secretary.' In his days as a journalist, Andrew Adonis, later one of Blair's main policy advisers and then an education minister in the Lords, had written an article in the *Observer* in December 1996 urging Mr Blair to combine the posts of prime minister and education secretary, 'in order to make the plight of the nation's youth a prime Whitehall concern for the first time'. Blair often talked of 'education, education, education' being his priority and passion.

Yet there has been frequent confusion about both ends and means. With the exception of primary education and youth justice, Labour came to office in May 1997 with a muddled package of good intentions on public services and a determination to reverse many inherited Conservative policies. These were all within the tight spending straitjacket imposed by Gordon Brown. Yet eight years later spending on health and education has been increased considerably, while a reform programme has been adopted which differs substantially from the initial policies and in many ways resembles the approach of the Major government. In this chapter, I examine the shortcomings of the original approach to public services, and the debates over extending choice and breaking up monopoly state provision. Then I will look at the policies and performance in each of the main public services: health, education, law and order, transport and welfare.

As I discussed in Chapter 2, New Labour's priority in the 1994–97 period was winning the next election. All pledges were tailored to that overriding aim, avoiding any hint of the long list of expensive promises that had cost Labour so much in previous elections. The key constraint was financial. All specific commitments had to be costed and within inherited spending plans, apart from those funded by the windfall levy on the privatised utilities. This had two bad results, matched in many respects by the flaws in the Conservative election pledges in 2005. First, the precise commitments were selected for their eye-catching appeal and, particularly in the public services, did not form part of a coherent strategy. For instance, the promise to cut waiting lists by 100,000 was widely regarded by health professionals as bad policy even before the 1997 election. It was seen as not being justified on clinical grounds and likely to lead to distortions in clinical priorities in the handling of cases, as hospitals sought to meet the targets. The Blair team, and Harriet Harman, the shadow health secretary, had to be persuaded not to promise an even larger reduction in waiting lists. Second, the tight spending constraints meant that the real choices facing these services could not be addressed. There was little dispute that spending, particularly capital investment, had been insufficient during the Tory years. The damage done to health and schools by the Conservatives was one of the main Labour election themes. But Labour was unable to promise to do much about these problems in the short term.

Consequently Labour ministers arrived in office with little freedom of manoeuvre, and in most cases no clear strategy. Most of their promises were negative, reversing changes introduced by the Tories, such as limiting the freedoms and advantages enjoyed by grant-maintained schools and ending the internal NHS market. Otherwise there was the endless repackaging of small-scale schemes to give the impression of activity.

Moreover, since there was not much extra money around, ministers tried to play down its significance, and every keen, aspiring Blairite minister would say that money was not the answer. That phase is perfectly caught by the quotation from the Treasury's July 1997 Budget Red Book at the start of this chapter. Of course it is true that extra money alone was not, and is not, the answer, and how the money is spent is crucial. But extra money is part of the answer if the state is going to rebuild rundown schools and hospitals and if more teachers, doctors and nurses are to be recruited.

This early phase from 1997 to 2000 had three controversial features, all resulting from the spending constraint. First, the mantra was 'standards not structures', a phrase from the government's first education White Paper in 1997. This meant that there was no need to alter the existing framework of state provision and move towards a quasi-market structure, as the Tories had been doing. Indeed, the government initially went in the opposite direction by abolishing the Conservative-introduced internal market, and replaced GP fundholders, which had their own budgets, with primary care groups then trusts, which placed GPs at the forefront of commissioning services for their patients. Labour also ended the assisted places scheme, supporting less well-off parents to take places in the private sector, and cut back the financial advantages of grant-maintained schools. The latter change, in particular, was regretted by some Blairites.

Second, to ensure that the available money was used properly, a series of centrally imposed targets were introduced, notably under public service agreements brought in after the 1998 spending review between the Treasury and departments. As discussed in Chapter 3, this proliferation of targets led, before long, to strong protests against overcentralism and complaints about overprescriptive and burdensome instructions from doctors, teachers and other local providers. The number of the PSAs was substantially reduced over time.

Third, since 1997 the Treasury has greatly expanded the Private Finance Initiative to raise capital from the private sector for public projects such as new hospitals, schools, roads and even prisons. PFI is a form of leaseback arrangement under which a private group raises the capital and builds and manages an infrastructure project for a number of years. This entails transferring the risks associated with public service projects to the private sector contractor. PFI also gets round the Treasury's tight spending and borrowing limits, though the taxpayer has been saddled with a sizeable stream of payments to the contractor for one or two decades, or longer. The hope has been that the private sector will both build and manage these projects at a lower cost than government had on its own in the past. PFI has proved to be highly controversial, both on grounds of the longer-term costs to the taxpayer of making payments to the private sector – estimated at around £7 billion a year for the next decade – and because of fears in public sector unions that workers employed by the contractor will have poorer terms and conditions. Various assurances have been given by the government that workers transferred from, say, the NHS to a private contractor will not suffer in this way, that there will not be two-tier work-forces. There have also been questions as to how far the capital investment financed by PFI has been additional to, or a substitute for, taxpayer-funded expenditure.

PFI has made a huge contribution to public sector projects, with contracts signed of well over £40 billion. Half of that expenditure has involved the Transport department – both roads and the big contracts to run and improve the infrastructure of the London Underground. Next has come the Health department as PFI has been used extensively to build and rebuild hospitals. The biggest contract was for the redevelopment in London of the University College Hospitals group on the Euston Road, also including the Middlesex Hospital and the Hospital for Tropical Diseases. Within three weeks of being opened in early summer 2005, the brand new hospital was tested to the full by handling some of the victims of the 7 July terrorist attacks, two of which had happened nearby.

The evidence is that PFI has worked best on capital projects like roads and, to some extent, prisons (both new and existing), where the involvement of the private sector has led to improvements in previously antiquated management techniques. However, the record has been more mixed in hospitals and schools where delivery of the contract depends not just on the efficiency of the construction work but on the subsequent management of the new building. And big computer projects have faced the same cost overruns as have bedevilled most big information technology projects in the public sector.

This early approach gradually came to be questioned during the first term. First, it became obvious that more money was needed to remedy the problems in the main public services, and, as noted in the previous chapter, spending was increased substantially on health and education in the 2000 and 2002 reviews. This shift reflected both the increasing realisation at the top of the government – that is in 10 Downing Street and the Treasury – about the scale of underfunding, especially in health. As I discussed in Chapter 3, a combination of external and partly media-driven pressures in the flu/beds flap of early 2000 forced a rethink and a commitment to much more rapid rates of growth in spending, first in health and then in education. The change took place over three years, with first the big increase in spending in the 2000 review, then the Wanless review in two stages over the winter and spring of 2001–02, and finally the announcement of the rise in national insurance contributions in April 2002, to back up the big expansion of spending announced in the 2002 review.

Second, while there were successes in some areas, such as literacy and numeracy standards in primary education, the existing structures did not appear to be delivering the hoped-for results. This was partly the problem of the Blair team adjusting to the realities and constraints of government. But there was also an increasing debate about whether the traditional structure of monopoly provision could produce better services, which was related to a debate about what 'better' meant. Blair was particularly sensitive to the frustrations of middle-class people, notably in London. It was in this period that Blair's advisers, particularly David Miliband in the Policy Unit, were persuaded that the government needed to concentrate more on the practicalities of delivering on their targets, rather than an endless stream of new initiatives. This led to the creation of the Delivery Unit in the following year.

Insiders regard 2000 as the key year, not just for funding, but also for reform. Blair and his advisers began to realise how much more needed to be done, so the emphasis began to change. Blair himself said in a speech in February 2001 that 'after years of intervention centrally, necessary to get the foundations right and basic standards in place, I want power devolved down in our public services, so that the creative energy of our teachers, doctors, nurses, police officers, is incentivised and released.' This begged a lot of questions. Was there to be decentralisation within existing structures? Or were these structures themselves part of the problem, which needed to be changed? This would involve reversing the initial mantra about 'standards not structures'. Blair later explicitly accepted (in Riddell 2005) that this initial mantra was mistaken, and that the pursuit of higher standards was dependent upon reform of structures. Change came gradually, at different times in different areas, as I will discuss later in the chapter. The increased diversity of provision came mainly from 2002 onwards. But a shift of approach became increasingly evident from 2000–01 onwards.

The commitment to spend more came first. As the last chapter showed, there was a marked change of trend from the 2000 review onwards, implemented mainly from April 2001, a couple of months before that year's general election. Over five years, the government was planning to increase spending on the NHS by a third overall in real terms. The public finances were so strong at this stage that it was largely a question of using existing surpluses to finance an increase in spending at well above the rate of growth of the economy. Admittedly, there were what became known as 'stealth' taxes during the first term. But Labour was able to go into the 2001 election sticking to its previous pledge of not increasing the basic and higher rates of income tax (the basic rate had been cut by one percentage point) and broadly maintaining the existing VAT base. But both Brown and Blair were evasive during the campaign about whether other taxes would have to be raised. There were no plans to do so, ministers repeated, in face of warnings by outside economists that tax increases would be necessary to finance promised rises in public spending, particularly on health.

The Treasury already accepted that more would have to be spent on health: that the faster growth in the health budget announced in the 2000 spending review was only a first step. In classic fashion, Brown set up a review to establish the evidence and to provide independent backing for the political case for what he already wanted and intended to do. Always careful to stress that money and reform must be linked, he announced the review into long-term health needs and costs in Britain in March 2001, that is before that year's election. The review had very specific terms of reference: 'To examine the technological, demographic and medical trends over the next two decades that may affect the health service; and, then, to identify the key factors which will determine the financial and other resources required to ensure that the NHS can provide a publicly funded, comprehensive, high quality service available on the basis of clinical need and not ability to pay'. The review was told to report to the Chancellor by April 2002, 'to allow him to consider the possible implications of this analysis for the government's wider fiscal and economic strategies in the medium term; and to inform decisions in the next public spending review in 2002'. In short, to provide cover for both a big rise in public spending and possible increases in taxes. The review, by former senior bank executive Sir Derek Wanless, was carefully planned in two stages. The first, interim report in November 2001 showed the funding gap, and the second, final report in April 2002 examined and dismissed alternatives to funding via a taxpayer-financed system. The Wanless estimates of future resources took account of commitments already made to reduce waiting times and to guarantee times for specific treatments, such as cancer; changes in patient and public expectations; advances in medical technologies, including the availability of new drugs to treat chronic conditions; changing health needs, balancing improvements in public health and the increased numbers of old people; faster relative increases in health costs; and uncertainties over the level of productivity improvement.

The final report stated: 'If our health services are to meet people's expectations and deliver high standards over the next twenty years, we need to devote a significantly larger share of our national income to health care. But money on its own is not enough and provides no guarantee of success – it is essential that resources are efficiently and effectively used.' Nonetheless the money was substantial. The Wanless projections showed a rise in the share of national income spent on health care from 7.7 per cent to between 10.6 and 12.5 per cent by 2022–23. These estimates covered both public and private health care, but the former would continue to dominate, and the relative share of private health care was assumed to remain constant at around 1.2 per cent of national income. The projections implied average annual growth in NHS spending in real terms of between 4.2 and 5.1 per cent a year over a twenty-year period. There would be particularly rapid growth at first, of between 7.1 and 7.3 per cent annually over the first five years, to allow the NHS to catch up to standards elsewhere and to create the capacity essential to expand choice in future. These figures were two to three times the Treasury's assessment of the potential underlying growth of the economy. So the Wanless report had big implications for future levels of taxation.

Moreover, Wanless noted: 'On funding, the majority of those expressing views agreed that the current method of funding the NHS through taxation is relatively efficient and equitable … The need for equity and to avoid any disruptive change when such a huge process of change is already underway seem to me very persuasive arguments.' He said it would be 'inappropriate to extend out-of-pocket payments for clinical services', though, he suggested, there might be some scope to extend charges for clinical services. Wanless provided powerful ammunition for the Treasury, as there had been a lengthy public debate about alternatives to taxpayer funding – such as private health insurance as in the United States, which few supported, or compulsory insurance on the Continental model with a much wider choice of treatment in private, voluntary and state-run hospitals.

Brown cited Wanless repeatedly in his April 2002 Budget speech to justify both the retention of the existing system of taxpayer funding and an increase of one point in both employee and employer national insurance contributions. This raised far more than, say, a one-point rise in the basic rate of income tax would have done, but these increases were treated as a special case, to allow a once-and-for-all catch-up in spending on health and remedy previous underfunding. It was a very skilful exercise since there was widespread public support for both the increase in spending on health (not surprisingly) and no backlash over the rise in contributions (less predictably). But there was also a sleight of hand since by informally earmarking the rise in national insurance contributions for health, it permitted the rise in other tax receipts to be allocated to other areas, notably education.

The increases in spending were linked to reforms in the way public services were run, and the more controversial decisions were over the structure of health and education. The replacement of Frank Dobson as Health Secretary by Alan Milburn in October 1999 and the flu crisis of the following January led to a great debate about the future of the NHS – in practice a long series of meetings chaired by Blair himself – and the publication of the Ten Year Plan in July 2000. That opened the way not only for big increases in capacity and new targets to reduce waiting times, but also the much greater involvement of the private sector. The plan set a whole series of ambitious pledges: 7,000 additional beds, 7,500 new consultants, 2,000 more GPs, 20,000 more nurses, etc. Every possible item in an NHS wish list was included, as well as some specific targets such as reducing the maximum waiting time for an operation from eighteen to six months by 2005, and to three months by 2008, when 75 per cent of operations will be day cases; reducing the maximum waiting time for an outpatient appointment to three months by 2005; cutting the maximum waiting time for accident and emergency cases to four hours by 2004 (with the average down to 75 minutes); and reducing the maximum waiting time for a GP appointment to just 48 hours by 2004. Obviously the extra money for more doctors, nurses and so on was essential, but critics were sceptical whether such a central plan could deliver its targets without more change.

In education, David Blunkett had operated an interventionist model. If local education authorities failed to come up to standard, or schools did not perform, then Whitehall would step in with the 'naming and shaming' phase. Schools which failed inspections were subjected to 'special measures'. This was linked to a centrally imposed drive to improve reading and mathematical skills, via first the literacy hour and then the numeracy hour. These had a sizeable initial impact, and though the move might have been centralist, it worked. Teachers complained at the extra workload and at the decline in their relative pay, but when more money began to come through they benefited, though increased pay was tied to performance. The government was slower to address poor performance in secondary schools, though Blunkett created scope for failing schools to be replaced by city academies, semi-independent schools operating within the state system but free of local authority control, which later became an important part of the Blairite agenda.

After 2001 these plans were expanded into what became known as the 'choice and diversity' agenda. The basic argument was that expanding the number of providers would both increase efficiency and offer consumers of services a greater choice. Blair explained the change in a speech to a Fabian Society conference in June 2003. The first term, he said, was about 'introducing proper means of inspection and accountability for public services and about intervention where there was failure. Inevitably, it was driven from the centre.' But that, he conceded, 'only takes us so far'. So a new phase was needed: 'Reform means putting power in the hands of the parent or patient so that the system works for them, not for itself. Our aim is to open up the system, to end the one-size-fits-all model of public service, which too often meant one supplier fits all, with little diversity, irrespective of how good new suppliers – from elsewhere in the public sector, and from the voluntary and private sectors – might be.' This involved moving beyond the target-dominated regime.

But the changes were not easy, and the 2001 manifesto was a messy document, partly put together at the last minute. Ideas floated during that general election campaign for greater private involvement in the provision of services stirred up considerable opposition within the Labour Party and the trade unions. Indeed, it is often forgotten that Blair went to Brighton for the TUC's annual congress on the afternoon of 11 September 2001 facing a very tricky task of trying to convince and placate the unions. He also faced strong criticism at the Labour conference a few weeks later. In the event, of course, he never delivered the planned speech. The issue was obviously eclipsed that autumn, though it returned to produce a rare defeat for the Labour leadership a year later at the party's conference over the question of the extension of PFI – though this had no impact on what happened.

In some cases, the new approach involved picking up the thread of some of the Conservatives' thinking before 1997 and taking it further. The Tories had introduced the principle of money following the patient in the NHS, per-pupil funding in schools, and private suppliers challenging public monopolies in local government, via compulsory competitive tendering and contracting out (working well in refuse collection, but not in the cleaning of hospital wards). But Labour sought to go even further in the market direction with private firms carrying out an increasing number of operations for the NHS, with fixed payments per case for specific treatments by NHS hospitals. Treatment centres, which made a big impact on waiting lists and times, were not even mentioned in the 2000 NHS Plan. In higher education, discussed below, a concentration of funding on elite research bodies encouraged universities to compete not only for top-name academics but also students.

This approach ran into a series of objections, some based on principle, some on self-interest, and some on prejudice. These arguments tend to be wrapped together. Public sector unions have argued that diversity of provision is wrong because it threatens the disinterested public service ethos by introducing the profit motive. There has been a lot of grand talk about public space and the public domain. Some critics of Blair like Neal Lawson (see Lawson and Leighton 2004) have argued that social democracy 'at its best created non-market spaces where the values of liberty, equality and community could thrive', such as the NHS and the Open University. Similarly, David Marquand has argued (2004) that 'New Labour has pushed marketisation and privatisation forward at least as zealously as the Conservatives did. The new regime is no more friendly to professionals than the old one was. Ministerial rhetoric is saturated with the language of consumerism.' The danger, in Marquand's view, is a loss of trust, so that ideals of service, equity and civic duty are all but gone.

Much of this talk is muddled and is really about preserving the existing terms and conditions of producers, whether highly educated professionals or manual workers in trade unions. There is no reason why the private sector cannot provide a service more attuned to consumer needs than the public sector. Also, there has been a confusion of provision and funding, via the introduction of the deliberately pejorative term – in some Labour and union eyes at least – of *privatisation*. But there is a big distinction between allowing private and voluntary groups to provide services within the state/taxpayer-funded sector and allowing a mixture of private and taxpayer funding via subsidies to those opting out of the NHS, as the Conservatives proposed at the 2005 election. The fear of those opposed to change is that even diversity of provision will result in a two-tier service with the reintroduction, for example, of selection in secondary schools. But this ignores the fact that there have anyway been several tiers of standards in most services, and that many of the new initiatives, such as city academies (now just academies), are targeted at the most rundown and deprived areas.

Public sector employees and executives can be as self-interested as those in the private sector, hence the widely misunderstood title of Julian Le Grand's book on the subject: *Motivation, Agency and Public Policy: Of Knights and Knaves, Pawns and Queens* (2003). His argument is that the conventional assumption that public sector professionals are public-spirited altruists, or knights, is misplaced, but so is the alternative view that they are all knaves, or self-interested egotists. Similarly, individual citizens are not just passive recipients of services (pawns), but nor can they be untrammelled sovereigns with unrestricted choice over services and resources (queens). Professor Le Grand – later an adviser in 10 Downing Street for the latter part of the Blair second term – argues, for example, that it is possible to design policies for publicly funded health care that offer robust incentives for medical professionals and that go some way towards empowering patients, but that avoid the problems of unfettered patient choice. He gives the example of devices such as allowing budget-holding professionals to keep surpluses on their budget, providing those surpluses are spent in a way that improves patient care, or paying professionals fee-for-service at a rate that incorporates some sacrifice compared with alternatives. This applied with the GP fundholding scheme introduced by the Conservatives when they were in office. In education, he points out that the introduction of a quasi-market by the Major government, via the publication of detailed, comparable results between schools in a local authority area and limited parental choice, had been followed by an improvement in results. Moreover, the relative efficiency of schools, in terms of exam performance and attendance rates, is directly related to the extent of competition, as measured by the number of schools of different types in an area. Competition also encourages changes in efficiency over time: the greater the competition, the faster the rate of change.

Politically, the most important contribution came from Gordon Brown, in a speech to the Social Market Foundation in February 2003 while most attention was focused on the approaching war in Iraq. Brown's main theme was the relationship between the state and markets. He began by high-lighting where markets were in the public interest - 'not just a new pro-competition policy, but also a new industrial policy whose aim was not to second guess, relegate or replace markets but to enable markets to work better'. He emphasised not just challenges to monopolies and cartels but also free trade rather than protectionism. Moreover, 'instead of thinking of employment policy as maintaining people in old jobs even when techno-logical and other change is inevitable, it is by combining flexibility – helping people move from one job to another – with active intervention to provide skills, information and income support that is the best route to full employment.'

So far, so New Labour. But having established his reformist credentials, Brown then went on to discuss the limits to markets, where 'market failures cannot be corrected through market-based government intervention to make the price mechanism work.' In particular, in health care, 'we know that the consumer is not sovereign: use of health care is unpredictable and can never be planned by the consumer in the way that, for example, food consumption can.' He argued that a market system could not apply in health because of 'chronically imperfect and asymmetric information' – that is, doctors and hospitals will always know more than patients. This imbalance is reinforced by 'the potentially catastrophic and irreversible outcome' of health care decisions based on that information and the necessity of local clusters of medical and surgical specialisms. He noted that half of hospital admissions, and three-quarters of hospital beds, were taken up by emergency, urgent or maternity cases – 'non-elective' in the jargon – where patients are generally unable to shop around. The need for guaranteed security of supply meant that a hospital could not be allowed to go out of business, while there were economies of scale.

Brown's fear was that market solutions, and 'a policy that put profit maximisation by hospitals at the centre of health care' would put patients at the risk of being overcharged and of not receiving the care they need, as financial reasons overrode clinical need. He argued that public provision was likely to achieve more at less cost to efficiency, and 'without putting at risk the gains from the ethic of public service'. So not only should health care be publicly funded – rather than through private insurance – on efficiency as well as equity grounds, but it should be mainly publicly provided. The latter was the most controversial point.

Brown's speech coincided with intense arguments about the creation of foundation hospitals, which were given managerial independence and greater flexibility in setting pay scales. However, after a lengthy dispute between the Treasury and Alan Milburn, tight limits were imposed on foundation hospitals' borrowing powers and on the number of private patients they could treat. Brown regarded the row over foundation hospitals as a damaging distraction which stirred up unnecessary opposition to reform. His view of reform rested on devolution within the existing framework, so that local primary care (GPs) and hospital trusts would have greater flexibility and multi-year budgets. Choice would mainly involve booked appointments for treatment and direct walk-in centres for speed and convenience. The Treasury believes efficiency can be driven by centrally driven initiatives like the Gershon review to cut waste and bureaucracy, but the flaws in the Brown approach have been highlighted by the economist John Kay (2003). He argues that national standards and local autonomy are incompatible. 'There is a conflict between traditional social democracy – in which legitimacy is conferred from the top down through the blessing of elected politicians and their officials – and a market-based economy in which legitimacy in economic matters is earned from the bottom up through success in meeting consumers' needs. There is no fudging the distinction: it is the difference between social democracy and a market society.'

The scope for market solutions and for choice is limited by the availability of alternative suppliers – the number of local hospitals or schools. Hence the often heard claim that what people want is a good local school or hospital, not to have to travel a long way to exercise choice. That is true, but it ignores the fact that the way to ensure that the local school or hospital has high standards is to put it under competitive pressure by offering choice to parents and patients and by allowing alternative providers to challenge existing ones ('contestability'). The only way that theory can be turned into a reality is by increasing capacity, partly by expanding the state sector and partly by allowing in private and voluntary sector providers. So additional spending to expand capacity goes hand in hand with the reform programme. But there are big questions about how choice could be exercised in health care: whether collectively by primary care trusts (the Brownite view) or individually by patients (the Blairite one).

A study by the National Audit Office for an inquiry into choice by the Public Administration Committee showed that, nationally, 85 per cent of parents are offered a place for their child in the school they most wanted to attend, with 96 per cent receiving an offer in a school for which they had expressed at least some preference. In London, just 68 per cent received a place at their favourite school. The choice of a GP is limited by the local availability of primary medical service providers. There are huge inequalities, with 50 per cent more GPs *per capita* in 2000 in Kingston-upon-Thames and Richmond, or Oxfordshire, than in Barnsley or Sunderland. But there has been a big expansion of choice for hospital care exercised by a GP on behalf of a patient. For example, all patients who had been waiting six months or more for elective surgery would be able to choose the location and, by using patient pre-booking systems, the timing of their treatments. This is a step towards giving such patients a choice of four to five hospitals once a GP has decided that a referral is required.

The controversy over the use of markets in public services has continued, and proved to be a rallying point for critics of Blair. A surprising critic emerged in January 2005 in Lord Browne, the chief executive of BP and one of Britain's most respected businessmen. In a speech to the World Economic Forum in Davos, he said the use of internal markets was 'damaging professional people who probably should not be subject to these pseudo-markets'. He warned that the use of markets in the public sector was turning people against business in general. His comments fuelled an intense controversy (as reported by Nicholas Timmins in the *Financial Times* in January 2005). Lord Browne was strongly supported by left-wing union leaders, but criticised by a number of academics, who argued that while quasi-markets could be making life more difficult for some profes-sionals, they were benefiting consumers. Diversity of provision allowed competition to raise standards while keeping the NHS free at the point of use. Similarly, as noted above, competition had improved results in some of the best-performing schools. Stressing the benefits of quasi-markets, Professor Howard Glennerster of the London School of Economics argued: 'The alternative is central government regulation and hundreds of performance targets which carries its own price for professionals in form filling, distortion of services and perverse incentives' (quoted in Timmins and Turner 2005).

Much of the debate has turned on the balance between choice and voice: between a consumer and a political means of ensuring satisfactory public services and raising standards. Is a consumer view of public services compatible with democratic accountability? Choice has been discussed above. Voice covers everything from expressing a political preference in the ballot box about the running of services to complaints as a formal means of improving services and obtaining redress. The latter has proved to be an unequal and often far from perfect means. Voice also means the direct involvement of users in school governing bodies, the boards of foundation trusts running hospitals and tenants' bodies. In practice, the two are inter-linked: choice will not work without voice, politically accountable for setting a framework for a service and determining its funding, while voice on its own is insufficiently responsive to the wishes of consumers of services which are expressed through choice. Moreover, there can be choice within institutions, like schools, as well as between them.

Free market critics, however, said the government's reforms did not go far enough since the state remained the monopoly buyer of services. The supply side reform of opening a wider range of providers was insufficient. The demand side must be opened up by giving consumers direct power. This could involve charging for services in whole or part, or the use of vouchers, financed by taxpayers. Much would depend on how the vouchers were structured: would wealthier people be allowed to top them up, in effect creating a taxpayer subsidy for parents and patients using private services? Blair was cautious about charging, not least to preserve a clear dividing line with the Conservative approach. During an appearance before the Liaison Committee of the Commons in February 2004, he hinted at the possibility of co-payment for some services, a form of partial charging alongside taxpayer funding of services. Blair told MPs that schools and the NHS would continue to be funded by general taxation, but user fees could make an increasing contribution in the case of tuition fees and congestion charging. 'I think there is an issue for the long term about how – not for core public services which traditionally have been funded out of general taxation, but for other issues, like skills, we look at co-payment.' The focus is on new, rather than existing, services. Apart from tuition fees, other possibilities include extending road pricing (see below), lifelong learning schemes where workers upgrade their skills, and some premium services for the elderly. The whole idea of co-payment has proved to be highly controversial and references were toned down in Labour's 2005 manifesto. However, the plan to establish universal child care will not be all taxpayer financed and will involve payments by the better off.

The public's own views were, as often, ambiguous. A MORI poll undertaken in July 2004 for the BBC *Today* programme showed that there is overwhelming public support for the principle of health and education services funded from taxation and free to all. However, most voters also believe that public services need to learn from the private sector about how to treat users as customers. By a narrow margin, 42 to 36 per cent, the public agreed that private companies should be involved in providing public services. A majority also accepted that offering a wider choice would help push up standards for everyone, not just mostly benefit the better off and better educated. A Populus poll for *The Times* at the same time showed that 58 per cent believed that a wider choice of hospitals and schools would improve the quality of those services.

Two of the most controversial reforms have been in education: the creation of city academies and tuition fees in higher education. Academies have been criticised for being elitist and divisive, but their aim is the opposite, to revive secondary schooling in areas of low performance and deprivation. They are very similar to the fifteen city technology colleges set up by the Conservative government in the late 1980s and early 1990s, which were privately sponsored and independent of local education authority control. Several also replaced failing schools in rundown areas. By 2004, eleven of the fifteen CTCs had more than 75 per cent of their pupils achieving five or more high GCSE passes, compared with a national average of 53 per cent. That was the aim of academies as well, which were sponsored by a private sector company, individual or charitable organisation, who were expected to put £2 million towards the initial capital cost with the Education department putting in an additional £23 million. They are not bound by the national curriculum and are not required to adhere to national pay scales for teachers. But, like specialist schools, they can only select 10 per cent of their intake according to their aptitude in a particular specialism and they cannot expand in response to parental demand. The academies have created public argument out of all proportion to their number – seventeen by mid-2005, with a target of 200 by 2010 – compared with 3,400 secondary schools in England. This is partly because of the controversial nature of some of their sponsors, with strong religious views. But in most other cases the sponsors were philanthropic, often Tory-supporting, businessmen. For example, Lord Harris of Peckham, a former Conservative Party treasurer, was not only a sponsor of a successful CTC in south London, but is also sponsoring three academies – as is the Corporation of London in Southwark. The critics also fear that the academies will spearhead a break-up of state provision. There has been a big focus on their mixed results so far – particularly the problems of the Unity City Academy in Middlesbrough – but most of the academies have only been going for a very short time and they have replaced failing schools. So the fair comparison at present is not with the average of all schools but on a year-on-year basis against the predecessor schools. On this basis, there is evidence of marked improvement – as would be hoped, given the amount of money put in. In the eleven academies reporting results in 2004, 30 per cent of pupils achieved five A to C grades in GCSEs, compared with an average of 16 per cent in the predecessor schools. There was also a marked improvement in test results for fourteen-year-olds, Key Stage 3.

Academies are only part of the government's strategy for secondary schools, and they are concentrated in inner city areas. But there has been a great deal of activity elsewhere: in rebuilding and renovating many secondary schools; in turning many more into specialist schools with a much wider range of specialisms; and in giving head teachers more flexibility with three-year budgets; and there are also three-yearly rather than six-yearly inspections. The curriculum is also being changed to stretch and interest the less academic fourteen- to nineteen-year-olds, though this has taken a long time and is some way from implementation. Teachers are being better paid and trained, with performance assessments linked to career moves and pay increases.

The government faced its toughest parliamentary battle over the introduction of flexible tuition fees for university students. The problem was straightforward: how to fund a commitment to mass higher education while providing universities with an assurance that they will receive the longer-term funding they need. The principle that the taxpayer funded all higher education had ended long ago as, with the increase in numbers, students took out loans to pay for their time at university. The argument was further blurred by the merger of the universities and polytechnics in the 1990s. These were publicly treated as the same, even though they were very different. The government began to encourage two-year, more vocational foundation degrees on the one hand, and the concentration of research funding on highly rated departments in elite universities on the other hand.

The key was student funding. In the first term of the Labour government, David Blunkett had inherited a review by Lord Dearing but rejected its proposals by abolishing grants for students' living costs and introducing loans for all, with students also having to pay £1,000 a year towards the cost of tuition (though, under means testing, only a half would actually do so). But this did not really deal with the universities' funding problems, especially with a commitment that 50 per cent of the age group would go through higher education – up from around 40 per cent when Labour came to office, 45 per cent in 2004 and a mere 6 per cent in the 1960s when many MPs and ministers were going through university. The argument was about both how much the taxpayer should contribute and how much differentiation there should be between different institutions. There is a strong case that those who benefit from higher education should contribute since, over their careers, they will earn much more than those who do not go to a university. But how? There was a fierce debate between 10 Downing Street and the Treasury over the proposal to allow universities to charge variable tuition fees up to a maximum of £3,000 a year. This limit would not be increased until after the 2009–2010 general election and only after a vote by Parliament. Tuition fees would be funded by loans repayable after graduation, but over a long period and only when a graduate's earnings rose to more than £15,000 a year. In addition, the non-repayable maintenance, abolished in Labour's first term, was brought back, worth up to £3,000 a year for low-income students (with a contribution from universities). The alternative, floated by the Treasury, was a graduate tax, but this would mean making individuals' payments separate from the costs of their studies, while leaving universities still dependent on the state. Critics argued that the very limited flexible element risked creating a two-tier structure, as if this did not already exist, while fees would discourage poorer students from applying to universities which charged higher fees. But this ignored the substantial help to poorer students, while a new regulator was appointed to ensure that universities had procedures to ensure fair and equal access to students from all backgrounds. In the event, the Bill was approved on second reading in January 2004 by a majority of just five, the closest Commons margin in the history of the Blair government. Its subsequent passage was trouble free, though tuition fees, along with the Iraq war, were a factor in Labour's loss of several university-dominated constituencies to the Liberal Democrats in the May 2005 general election.

The change, while very limited, offered the universities the hope of an increase in funding in the long term as well as greater independence. The OECD concluded in its 2004 survey of the UK: 'Letting graduates pay a share of the study costs would be both fair and economically efficient, and the government's plan to introduce a graduate contribution scheme is both innovative and welcome. Expanding higher education based on income-contingent graduate contributions while maintaining large publicly funded improvements made in early childhood and compulsory schooling is the most direct way to achieve equity in access to higher education and economic outcomes more generally.' So contrary to the fierce criticism of Labour MPs, the government's plan was arguably the most social democratic.

By 2005, many of these changes were being implemented, or had been enacted, but their measurable impact was limited. The Blairites were determined to avoid the ambiguities of the 2001 manifesto and the fierce arguments of the second term. The prime minister therefore decided that all the key departments should produce five-year plans, which would form the heart of Labour's domestic commitments in the 2005 election. This was linked with a lengthy consultation exercise within the Labour Party called 'The Big Conversation', coordinated by Matthew Taylor and launched after the Iraq war both as a healing initiative and to prepare the way for the 2005 manifesto. In contrast to the past, Blair fully involved the cabinet in the discussion of these five-year plans, as each of the main ministers made a presentation. Although some doubted the value of these presentations, questions were raised by (among others) Gordon Brown and John Prescott about the proposals to extend private involvement in both health and education. However, Blair and his allies like John Reid, then at Health, and more ambiguously Charles Clarke, first at Education and then the Home Office, won the day. In health and education, the aim is to expand the existing choice and diversity programmes. For instance, in health a further wave of procurements of an extra 250,000 elective (that is non-emergency) procedures each year has been planned. Consequently, nearly 10 per cent of procedures will be undertaken in the independent sector, though financed by the taxpayer. Choice is being extended to cover all elective procedures by 2008. In education, specialist schools will become near universal, while the neglected vocational link from school into apprenticeships and further education will be strengthened. Ruth Kelly, who took over from Clarke at Education in December 2004, quickly emphasised her commitment to parental choice and diversity of providers. On law and order, community/neighbourhood policing is being strengthened with both record police numbers and community support officers and street wardens.

Consequently, the Labour manifesto in April 2005 had some ambitious commitments:

- Every secondary school to be an independent specialist school.
- At least 200 academies to be established by 2010, up from seventeen in spring 2005, with 50 more in the pipeline.
- Extended opportunities for independent providers, including church and other faith schools, within the state system, subject to parental demand, fair funding and fair admissions.
- Every sixteen-year-old to be offered school, college, training or apprenticeship.
- By the end of 2008, no NHS patient will have to wait longer than a maximum of eighteen weeks from the time of being referred for a hospital operation by their GP until the time of the operation. This should mean an average wait of nine to ten weeks.

- By the end of 2008, patients referred by their GPs for an operation will be able to choose any hospital that can provide the operation to NHS medical and financial standards, with a choice of time and place for non-urgent operations.
- Universal, affordable childcare for three- to fourteen-year-olds and a Sure Starts Children's Centre in every community.

This is a mere sample of over 300 promises, big and small. But after eight years in office, promise has to be judged against performance so far. The rest of the chapter looks at the record in the four main areas of health, education, transport and criminal justice. In each case, there has been a substantial shift in the direction of policy compared with the first two years – towards more choice, the application of quasi-markets and, in some cases, charging and a breakdown of previous monopoly state provision. There are various ways of assessing performance. First, you can look at the five pledges first announced in 1996, and then included in the 1997 manifesto:

- **Cut class sizes to thirty or under for five-, six- and seven-year-olds by using money from the assisted places scheme.** Pledge met for most classrooms, though problems in small schools, and still classes of 28 for older primary school children.
- **Fast-track punishment for persistent young offenders by halving the time from arrest to sentencing.** Achieved in five years, not four.
- **Cut NHS waiting lists by treating an extra 100,000 patients as a first step by releasing £100 million saved from NHS red tape.** Pledge met, though with disruption to hospitals, and change in target to waiting times, which are of more concern to patients.
- **Remove 250,000 under 25-year-olds from benefit and into work by using money from a windfall levy on the privatised utilities.** Nearly twice as many young people have found jobs, though critics argue most would have work anyway in view of the strength of the economy.
- **Set tough rules for government spending and borrowing; ensure low inflation; strengthen the economy so that interest rates are as low as possible.** Pledge met – one of government's big successes.

But as is clear from the above discussion, these five promises, with the exception of the economic pledge, only skimmed the surface. It is better to look at the various public service agreement targets agreed between the Treasury and the main departments, some of which are monitored by the Delivery Unit.

In health, these targets showed a sharp rise in the number of nurses, and a steady growth in the number of doctors. Additionally, heart disease mortality is on the decline, ahead of the trajectory to meeting the target of a 40 per cent reduction by 2010, while cancer mortality is on target for a 20 per cent reduction by 2010. (However, Patricia Hewitt, health secretary after May 2005, acknowledged that progress towards the target set in 2000 for cancer patients to have to wait only two months from referral to diagnosis, and a month from diagnosis to treatment, was slow. Waiting times for bowel cancer patients have risen sharply.)

Nonetheless, looking at health overall, Sir Michael Barber was able to claim in his July 2004 report to the Cabinet that health reform was working, with a rapid build-up of capacity, and 'increasingly effective, radical reform of the whole system (choice, incentives, alternative providers) is making the difference.'

There has been a substantial increase in the number of doctors and nurses, with a sharp rise also in the number of medical students. The number of hospital doctors rose by nearly 29 per cent between 1997 and 2004, consultants by 43 per cent, total qualified nurses by 23 per cent and GPs by 11 per cent, though management was up by 68 per cent. Over 60 NHS walk-in centres are now open, with a further twenty in development, while 28 NHS treatment centres are operating, with a further eighteen in development. The number of beds available in NHS hospitals has declined by roughly 5 per cent since 1997, while the number of hospital treatments, known as 'finished consultant episodes', has also been rising.

The impact of the combination of extra money and the diversity programme, providing more capacity from the independent and private sector, can be seen in the fall in waiting times. This is a far more significant indicator than the original 1997 target of waiting lists. Labour has introduced seventeen targets for waiting lists and times since 1997, which alone accounts for much of the frustration of doctors and those running hospitals. This is a very contentious area, depending on when a patient is placed on an outpatient waiting list, and then on an inpatient list after seeing a consultant. There are a number of tricks – such as hospitals cleaning up waiting lists, changes in priorities within a list and alterations in the way that figures are recorded. While this is a murky area, the trends are undoubtedly in the right direction. Some 820,000 people were waiting for inpatient admission to NHS hospitals at the end of March 2005, 330,000 fewer than in March 1997. Moreover, in the key indicator, the number waiting more than six months has fallen from 25 per cent to just 5 per cent. The public service agreement targets reveal an upward trend in the numbers of people waiting no more than four hours for accident and emergency treatment (96 per cent), and able to see a GP within two working days (99 per cent).

The government argues that the new treatment centres have had a big impact. However, critics such as Professor Allyson Pollock of University College, London have argued (2005) that the incentives have had perverse effects. 'There have been reductions in waiting times for cataract surgery, but there have been dramatic increases for chronic eye conditions such as glaucoma, diabetic eye disease and age-related muscular degeneration. Easy, cheap operations such as cataract procedures are what the treatment centres want to focus on.' However, free market critics argue that the reforms have not gone far enough. Professor Nick Bosanquet of Imperial College has argued in a paper for the Reform think tank (Bosanquet 2004) that even if the government achieves its target of reducing the maximum wait to four and a half months, 'the NHS after a decade of effort will only be on the borderline of standards considered internationally acceptable.' He maintains that Spain and Denmark have achieved significant improvements in waiting times through reform of their procedures, notably the introduction of new financial incentives, rather than through extra funding.

A big qualification needs to be added. Most of the focus has been on hospital treatments, and then on GPs. But the nation's health is also crucially dependent on other factors such as diet, smoking, drinking and exercise. Labour has had a public health minister since 1997 and various initiatives have been launched, but the government has been reluctant to be seen to be intervening too much, and nannying. Life expectancy has improved over the last twenty years, to a large extent as a result of a decline in smoking. The number of adults who smoke has declined from 45 to 26 per cent over the last thirty years. But obesity among women has risen from 8 to 24 per cent since 1980. These problems are not shared equally. Working-class women are twice as likely to be as obese as upper-class women. One result is that male life expectancy between the classes has widened, not narrowed, over the past thirty years. It is very hard to shift these trends. Even a ban on smoking in public places may make a difference of only a couple of percentage points to the rate of smoking by 2010. Changing diets is even harder. Moreover, people on average walk more than a fifth less per year than in 1990.

In education, the picture is patchy. Much more money has been spent. Schools are being rebuilt. There are more teachers, particularly in secondary schools, while teacher recruitment has also risen, even slowly in subjects like science and mathematics. The record on class sizes, one of the original five pledges, has been mixed. The number of primary school pupils in classes of more than thirty has halved, from 33 per cent in 1997 to 15 per cent in 2004. But the average size of primary school classes has only fallen from 27.5 in 1997 to 26.2 in 2004. In secondary schools, the number of pupils in classes of more than thirty has risen since 1997, from 8.7 per cent to 12 per cent, though the average has remained virtually unchanged at 21.8. The number of pupils per teacher has fallen since 1997 from 22.8 to 21.9 in primary schools, but has increased fractionally from 16.2 to 16.4 in secondary schools.

Performance has generally improved. The percentage of pupils achieving level 4 at Key Stage 2, for eleven-year-olds, rose from 63 to 77 per cent in English between 1997 and 2004, and in mathematics from 62 to 74 per cent. But after a sharp initial improvement in the late 1990s, performance was on a plateau from 2000 onwards. In English, for example, results are still way below the 85 per cent target. The same is true of the 80 per cent in mathematics. The independent Statistics Commission argues that the official figures for test scores between 1995 and 2000 substantially overstated the underlying improvement. But there was, nonetheless, some rise in standards. The number of low-performing secondary schools – those with less than a quarter of pupils achieving five A to C grades at GCSE/GNVQ levels – has fallen by over two-thirds from 600 in 1997. But that still leaves an intractable remainder. Overall, performance at GCSE has continued to improve steadily, with the percentage gaining five or more grades A to C rising from 46.3 per cent in 1997–98 to 53.4 per cent in 2003–04. But there has been no obvious change in trend since 1997. However, the results of the growing number of specialist schools have improved faster than the average. But truancy has remained a serious problem, with no signs of any real reduction. There has been no real improvement in the percentage of sixteen- to nineteen-year-olds in education and training, stuck at about 75 per cent.

Overall, the real test will come in a few years' time when children who were five in 1997 sit their GCSEs. David Miliband, a former Minister for School Standards, has argued that these children are going through a much changed educational world – with rebuilt schools (most with a specialist status) and with more motivated teachers, a mixture of academic subjects according to aptitude, and better results. Perhaps, but the record so far is mixed.

Law and order has been a bitterly contested area. The government has poured out legislation and initiatives to combat crime and anti-social behaviour. The police have been reorganised, given more resources and powers; the Crown Prosecution Service has been shaken up; a Youth Justice Board has been established in the hope of discouraging reoffending; criminal procedure has been overhauled; and a whole range of new offences have been established, with tougher powers to deal with drug traffickers, football hooligans, sex offenders and those using or carrying guns. Police numbers have risen substantially, and over 5,000 community support officers (who assist the police without possessing their full powers) are now in place. After an alarming rise in street crime in 2001–02, Tony Blair personally intervened, and a high-profile Street Crime Initiative helped secure a 17 per cent fall in robberies across the targeted police forces. More was invested in police squads, video ID parades and action in and around schools.

This is a massive subject in its own right, but the broad evidence from the British Crime Survey is that overall crime fell by 30 per cent between 1997 and 2004. Violent crime was down by a quarter. However, within the overall decline, the mix of violent crime has shifted towards violence by strangers, with street crime not down much nationally. Violence against the person has risen sharply since the end of the 1990s, though this may partly reflect changes in reporting and recording procedures. It is arguable how much this overall decline is due to the Blair government's various initiatives, as opposed to actions taken earlier and broader social trends since the crime figures peaked in 1995, two years before Labour came to power. The mix of crime matters, since violent crime is regarded by the victims as more damaging than property crimes. Moreover, the public remains very concerned about anti-social behaviour, and less than a quarter believe there has been an improvement over the past two years. Drug and alcohol abuse are associated with a high percentage of crimes, and there has been little improvement in the trends there.

Immigration and asylum have been major political – and electoral – problems for the government since 1997. The number of asylum seekers shot up from 1999 onwards – from around 30,000 in 1997 to a peak of 84,000 in 2002 – and the Home Office appeared to have lost control of the problem, especially as there was a low rate of exclusion of failed applicants. But procedures were tightened with tougher controls on welfare benefits and more immigration officers appointed, including many checking passengers before they enter the UK. Border controls were being strengthened with fingerprinting of all visa applicants. So by the time of the 2005 election Labour was able to claim that asylum applications were well down on the 2002 peak, with faster procedures for considering appeals and a more than doubling of removals. Moreover, Britain did not rank very high, and was near the EU average, for the number of persons applying for asylum per thousand inhabitants. The government sought to balance its toughness over asylum with making the case for more skilled workers coming into the country, subject to English language tests for everyone who wants to stay permanently.

The underlying political question was how far the British public would accept that such flows were an inevitable part of a more integrated world. Total migrant inflows into Britain have risen over the past ten years by more than 30 per cent, of which increase over half are students. This is linked to attitudes toward minority ethnic groups, who made up 8 per cent of the UK population in 2001, up from 5.2 per cent in 1991. However, the public believes ethnic minorities constitute 23 per cent of the population, and race and immigration are the third highest public concern according to various opinion polls. Muslim communities have been most worried about discrimination, particularly after the 9/11 attacks and the Iraq war, with the media focus on a few extreme clerics fomenting violence. This issue has become particularly acute after the terrorist attacks in London on 7 July 2005 and the discovery that the suicide bombers were British-born Muslims.

Of all the main public services, few even in 10 Downing Street and the ever-optimistic Delivery Unit would pretend that there has been much progress so far in transport. This reflected a combination of a lack of interest from Blair and Brown as well as a succession of short-lived, often poor, ministers. In addition, a succession of rail crashes (two outside Paddington, at Hatfield and at Potters Bar) raised fundamental questions about rail privatisation. The fragmentation, particularly in maintenance and repairs, raised questions over safety procedures and standards. After the Hatfield crash in October 2000 an emergency repairs programme was introduced, which caused enormous disruption. And while performance, in terms of trains arriving on time, subsequently recovered, it had not yet returned to pre-Hatfield levels by mid-2004 – even though use of trains was rising sharply, with an increase of a quarter in the number of passenger miles since 1997. There was also a bitter controversy over the collapse of Railtrack, which was brought under Whitehall control, leading to lengthy recriminations and a legal challenge. At the same time, the Treasury had a lengthy argument over how to finance the rebuilding of the London Underground, which delayed work.

The most innovative transport ideas came, ironically, from Ken Livingstone, whom Blair had prevented from being Labour's candidate for mayor of London before he was elected to that office in 2000. As part of a series of changes to transport in the capital, Livingstone introduced a congestion charge in the central area, initially £5 per day but increased to £8 from summer 2005. Despite protests from small businesses and retailers, the charge succeeded in producing a sharp reduction in congestion. Central government was encouraged by the success of the London charge to press forward with ideas for road-pricing in order to cut congestion, especially after ministers had to concede that their target for stabilising congestion at 2000 levels by 2010 would not be met. Road congestion in Britain is far worse than in the rest of Europe. A pilot scheme will belatedly be introduced within five years, and any charges would vary depending on the type of roads used and at what time of day.

Overall, the picture in the public services is uneven. Clear progress in health; some advances in education; a fall in crime but continued fear of robbery and anti-social behaviour; and all still to do in transport, despite some recent improvement in rail punctuality. For the Government, the main challenge is moving from central direction and a multiplicity of targets to a self-sustaining framework where change and higher standards are driven by consumers of services choosing between a range of providers. The key, though, is whether the public believes that services are improving, and therefore willing to pay the necessary taxes, and even accept increases in tax rates. Here the evidence is mixed. The public is satisfied with local services where people have direct experience, but remains sceptical about the national picture. According to a MORI survey in December 2004, while over two-thirds think their local hospital is providing a good service (and even more were satisfied with their last visit), more than half do not think that, in the long term, the government's policies will improve the state of Britain's public services. That epitomises Blair's dilemma after more than eight years in office, and his position as the unfulfilled prime minister.

6

A Bridge Too Far

'The tragedy for British politics – for Britain – has been that politicians of both parties have consistently failed, not just in the 1950s but on up to the present day, to appreciate the emerging reality of European integration. And in doing so, they have failed Britain's interests ... The history of our engagement with Europe is one of opportunities missed in the name of illusions – and Britain suffering as a result.'

Tony Blair, speech at the European Research Institute, Birmingham, 23 November 2001.

'Tony Blair is arguably the most pro-European prime minister in modern times, certainly since Edward Heath. It is an irony of history, and a personal tragedy for him, that his commitment to support President Bush in war on Iraq should have torpedoed his strategic objective of restoring Britain as a respected major player in Europe, and, as an integral part of that project, taking Britain into the euro.'

Robin Cook, *The Point of Departure*, 2003.

Tony Blair has been a traditional British prime minister in trying to act as a bridge between the United States and Europe. This has involved trying to reconcile contrasting, and often conflicting, attitudes and interests. But the differences have proved to be too great even for so skilled and resilient a conciliator as Blair. The bridge has been severely damaged by the Iraq war, and his efforts to repair it have been largely unsuccessful. Europe and Iraq are closely interlinked. Blair has been left in a precarious position between the two sides of the Atlantic, neither at the heart of Europe nor with a decisive influence in Washington. While pressures for further European integration have stalled, Blair's repeated talk of Europe being 'our destiny' sounds hollow.

Foreign policy is at the same time both the most ephemeral and the most lasting aspect of government. Prime ministers build a reputation and even an influence as a result of some foreign policy success. But this is often temporary and has little lasting effect when circumstances change and they leave office. As I have written elsewhere about Margaret Thatcher (in Pugliese 2003, pp. 11–12): 'Paradoxically, many of those features of her premiership that were most striking at the time were also the most transitory, particularly in foreign affairs: the Falklands, her crucial interventions with Ronald Reagan over arms control and the nuclear balance, in spotting the early significance of Mikhail Gorbachev, in standing up against terrorism. These were all notable achievements at the time. However, to the extent that her influence with Reagan and Gorbachev reflected their personal rapport, it did not, and could not, last. Even by the end of her own premiership these personal aspects had faded and her distinctive legacy and influence had dimmed, as seen in the arguments over German unification.' I concluded: 'Her premiership did not produce a lasting change in Britain's place in the world. In 1990, as in 1979, Britain was still a medium-sized European power with an uncertain role.'

Exactly the same can be said about Blair. He achieved an international reputation, for good and ill, only just behind Thatcher and Winston Churchill among British prime ministers of the past century, particularly in the United States. But this did not, could not, resolve the dilemmas of what Alan Milward has called 'national strategy' in his absorbing study of postwar British policy towards Europe (2002). This is more than just the conventional wisdom of the time, but refers to a set of assumptions about Britain's place in the world, shared by policy-makers in and out of Whitehall and by most of the leading politicians of all parties. This strategy can change, and has done so, but the shifts are little to do with the results of general elections: they reflect deeper currents of opinion and the impact of external events.

The critical such event in postwar British history was the Suez debacle of 1956, which forced the British government to come to terms with a reduced role in the world and its inability any longer to act without American support. As often, it was not a clear dividing line and the adjustment was not immediate, nor was it clearcut. But the shock waves set in train several reviews of Britain's role in the world. The conclusions were ambiguous and inconsistent: both a belief that Britain should never again come into open conflict with the United States and the hesitant start of the closer involvement in Europe. That was the origin of the transatlantic bridge that Blair still championed more than forty years later.

The policy was inherently and deliberately contradictory. It was the avoidance of a choice elevated into a new national strategy. Now, there is nothing inherently wrong in this. Much of politics, especially foreign policy, involves avoiding choices, or making the best of a number of options. The problem is when the balancing act is no longer sustainable. The bridge strategy has meant that Britain should be both a European and an Atlantic power, an active member of what became the European Union and the USA's closest ally in Europe. It was this conflict that led de Gaulle to exercise his first veto over Britain's application to join the then Common Market in January 1963.

However, every prime minister from Harold Macmillan onwards sought to maintain this balancing act, with the exception of Sir Edward Heath for a brief period in the early 1970s. For Heath, putting Europe first and not seeking a special or insider relationship with Washington was essential not only to overcome President Pompidou's doubts about agreeing to British entry, but also to make a success of membership. Yet his successors were much more comfortable with the balancing act: trying, not always success-fully, to get close to the American president of the day whenever a big crisis developed and, at the same time, to develop closer relations with the rest of Europe. The balance between the USA and Europe varied, depending both on the personalities and on circumstances.

Of course, the United States pursued its own national interests, as any history of the postwar world amply demonstrates. But successive adminis-trations had to take account of European views. The ambiguities and tensions in the transatlantic relationship were containable because America and Europe had sufficient interests in common in the face of the military and security challenge of the Soviet Union during the Cold War. American presidents both encouraged Europe to work more closely together – always favouring British membership of the European Community – and operated on a multilateral basis. Of course, there were often strains and disagreements. But the idea of a transatlantic bridge was just about sustainable, even if never liked by German and French leaders who resented British claims to privileged access in Washington. Moreover, the instinctive desire of prime ministers to be close to American presidents, and a wariness about new European developments, left Britain as the perpetual awkward partner.

Tony Blair adopted this foreign policy approach when he became prime minister in May 1997. His prime motivation, as in so many other areas, was backward looking, to distance himself from Labour's extremist image in the 1980s, when the party managed to be both anti-American and anti-European. Blair embraced Europe since he was determined to be seen as forward looking and progressive. By the late 1980s, Europe appeared to offer a social democratic alternative to Thatcherism at home. And the United States became more attractive, especially to Blair and his friends, after the arrival of Bill Clinton in the White House. Above all, Blair was determined to show that New Labour could be competent in foreign and defence affairs, traditionally strong areas for the Conservatives.

In opposition, Blair was more concerned to show he could be trusted than to say anything distinctive on foreign affairs. There was no sense of a new Blair approach, let alone a doctrine. During a visit to the USA in April 1996 he reiterated the traditional British policy in what became a familiar mantra: 'It is absurd to imagine that, for Britain, there is a choice between the relationship with Europe and that with America. On the contrary, the real value to the US of the British role in Europe lies in the influence we can and will exert to keep Europe firmly linked to the US in defence, outward looking, open to trade and investment.' His main comments as leader of the opposition were to emphasise how, in contrast to the divided Conservatives, Labour would end Britain's isolation in Europe. Each of his party conference speeches in opposition had contained positive references about Europe. He argued that Britain's global influence was dependent on its influence in the EU and he promised that Britain should not remain at the edge of Europe. This approach always had a double meaning: first, to give Britain more influence over developments in the EU; and second, to end the ambivalence in Britain's relationship by persuading the public to embrace a closer involvement with the EU.

Under the overall commitment to 'give Britain leadership in Europe', the Labour manifesto in 1997 promised both to hold a referendum on participation in the single currency, 'based on a hard-headed assessment of Britain's economic interests', and to lead reform in the EU. There were references to rapid completion of the single market, a high priority for enlargement, urgent reform of the Common Agricultural Policy, greater openness and democracy in the EU, signing the social chapter (from which Britain had an opt-out under the Maastricht treaty) and retention of the national veto 'over key matters of national interest, such as taxation, defence and security, immigration, decisions over the budget and treaty changes, while considering the extension of Qualified Majority Voting in limited areas where that is in Britain's interests'. But the foreign policy section did not refer to the USA, let alone to Iraq. There was a commitment to 'strong defence within NATO'; tougher and more transparent controls on exports of arms, including a ban on sales to regimes who might use them for internal repression or international aggression; appointing a Cabinet minister to run a new Department for International Development and starting to reverse the decline in UK aid spending; making the protection and promotion of human rights a central part of our foreign policy and working for a permanent international criminal court.

The seeds of his later reluctance to make a full-hearted commitment to Europe were clear from the start. The very growth of sceptic opinion which he attacked in the Conservative Party also led him and Gordon Brown in November 1996 to promise a referendum on membership of the euro. This attempted isolation of the euro issue was to avoid being outflanked by the Tories and to retain the support of sceptic newspapers. At its most nauseating and cynical, this involved the appearance of an article under his name in the *Sun* in April 1997 proclaiming 'my love for the pound'. Throughout his premiership, Blair has been ambivalent. He has made speeches every six to twelve months, or least did before the Iraq war, arguing for an end to the previous doubts about Britain's role in the EU. In Aachen in summer 1999, Blair talked about his 'bold aim ... that over the next few years Britain resolves once and for all its ambivalence towards Europe. I want to end the uncertainty, the lack of confidence, the Europhobia.' Three years later, in Cardiff, he returned to the same dilemma: 'For Britain, there is a simple choice to be made. Are we fully partners in Europe, at the centre of its decision-making, influencing and shaping its direction; or are we at the back of the file, following warily a path beaten by others? For fifty years, that has been our choice. For fifty years we have chosen to follow, first in joining; then in each new departure Europe has made. Now we have an historic opportunity to put our relations with the rest of Europe on a more serious footing and choose not to hang back but to participate fully and wholeheartedly.' These excellent analyses, and statements of good intentions, did not change anything. There was usually little follow-up.

Immediately after the 1997 election, there was a short-lived honeymoon period in Europe. Blair quickly signalled that he wanted to make a fresh start and develop a more positive relationship with the EU than the negative and minimalist approach of the late Major years. The Foreign Office also saw a chance to revive their long-cherished but often fruitless hope of breaking into the Franco-German duopoly at the centre of Europe by building strong bilateral relationships with Jacques Chirac and Helmut Kohl (and then Gerhard Schroeder after his election in September 1998). The election of Blair was widely welcomed, particularly on the centre-left, even though there was some irritation at his triumphalist tone, particularly from the French after the election of Lionel Jospin and a socialist government a few weeks later. The French socialists were no fans of the Third Way espoused by Blair and Clinton with all its transatlantic, Anglo-Saxon overtones. Moreover, Blair's attempt to form a common ideological bond with Schroeder was also short-lived. Their joint paper, *Europe: The Third Way/Die Neue Mitte* (Blair and Schroeder 1999), sought to set out a new way forward for social democrats, based on economic reform, a competitive market framework, sound public finance and active labour market policy to get people back into work via changes to the tax and benefits system. These proposals, already in process of introduction in Britain, were more controversial in the rest of Europe. After attacks by the left of the SPD, Schroeder quickly distanced himself from the paper, and his inconsistent pursuit of reform led to disillusionment with him in the Blair inner circle. Over time, Blair's closest relationships were more with centre-right leaders like José María Aznar of Spain and Silvio Berlusconi of Italy, rather than with centre-left leaders like Jospin. Blair's most longstanding ally on the centre left was Goran Pederssen of Sweden.

Within a few weeks of the May 1997 election, Britain had ended its opt-out from the social chapter of the Maastricht treaty and had signed up to what became the Amsterdam treaty. Britain also actively pushed enlargement of the EU and backed what became the Lisbon agenda of economic reform to make labour, capital and product markets more flexible and innovative. This was intended to raise growth rates and employment, in the hope that the EU's performance would match that of the United States. Blair followed this up with a series of bilateral initiatives with various countries to push forward reform – with, amongst others, the leaders of Germany, Spain, the Netherlands, Sweden and, most controversially, at a later stage with Berlusconi, who was widely disliked on the left.

Blair also took the lead in December 1998 at a summit at St Malo with President Chirac in launching a joint Anglo-French initiative on European defence. The declaration included the phrase that the EU 'must have the capacity for autonomous action, backed by credible, military forces, the means to decide to use them, and a readiness to do so, in order to respond to international crises ... acting in conformity with our respective obligations to NATO'. The reaction from the Clinton administration was a mixture of anger at what was seen as a lack of adequate prior consultation by the British government and suspicion that the primacy of NATO might be undermined by the French suborning the British. The British sought to reassure the Americans about the primacy of NATO: that Europe would only want to run its own operations when the USA did not want to be involved. Meanwhile, the French questioned the sincerity of the British commitment to European defence after the UK participated in the controversial American-led raids on Iraq in December 1998, only a few days after the St Malo agreement.

This episode – the bold initiative in a pro-European direction followed by a classic instance of following the American lead on a joint military operation – epitomised the ambiguities in the British position. Blair did not, however, accept there were any contradictions. On the eve of a visit to Washington in February 1998, he talked to American journalists about his belief in a bridge between Europe and the US. During his first term, he pursued the familiar policy of getting close to the American president, first

Bill Clinton and then George W. Bush. Indeed, as I explain in *Hug Them Close* (2003, pp. 118–20), it was during his three and a half years of working with Clinton that he developed his conviction that Britain should always work closely with the USA. The key event was the Kosovo conflict of spring 1999 when Blair clashed with Clinton over the conduct of the campaign. Blair drew four overlapping conclusions: the priority of being on the inside with whoever was American president, trying to influence decisions in private while being publicly supportive; second, America's overwhelming military superiority as the sole superpower, linked to the dangers of the US acting alone or not intervening; third, the serious political and military weaknesses of Europe reinforcing the case for closer foreign and defence cooperation; and fourth, a special role for Britain, and particularly himself, as a bridge to help Europe understand where America is coming from, and to explain European concerns to America. So his conclusions were both Atlanticist and European; again the belief that to talk of a choice between the two was wrong and, indeed, damaging.

At the end of Blair's first term in 2001, many European leaders were disillusioned with his government, believing that the early promise had not been fulfilled. Britain seemed further from, rather than closer to, fulfilling Labour's 1997 election pledge to hold a referendum on taking Britain into the euro. Within only five months of his triumphant entry into 10 Downing Street, Blair had surrendered control over the decision to Gordon Brown and the Treasury. An alternative option was seriously considered within the Blair camp at this stage, and urged by amongst others Lord Jenkins of Hillhead, then at the peak of his influence on Blair. This was to hold a referendum on the principle of euro entry in 1997–98, leaving the decision on timing to a vote by Parliament depending on whether the economic conditions were right. However, Blair decided against because he was not sure he could win a referendum until New Labour had demonstrated its competence in government. He saw a referendum as too much of a diversion from this priority in the first term.

Brown, initially the more enthusiastic of the two about euro entry, became more cautious, partly because of the favourable reception to his decision to make the Bank of England responsible for setting interest rates and controlling inflation, which was seen in the Treasury as a viable monetary alternative to euro entry. So after a period of confusion in

October 1997, Brown announced five tests which must be met before the government would recommend entry in a referendum. These five economic tests were and are:

1. Are business cycles and economic structures compatible so that we and others could live comfortably with euro interest rates on a permanent basis?
2. If problems emerged, is there sufficient flexibility to deal with them?
3. Would joining EMU create better conditions for firms making long-term decisions to invest in Britain?
4. What impact would entry into EMU have on the competitive position of the UK's financial services industry, particularly the City's wholesale markets?
5. In summary, will joining EMU promote higher growth, stability and a lasting increase in jobs?

Forests of trees have been cut down in pursuit of the meaning and assessment of these tests. They have been seen either as largely subjective, or some sub-Wagnerian set of forbidden questions. Whatever their meaning for economists, the tests have been a shield for the government to hide behind. At the insistence of Blair during the tortured negotiations of October 1997, Brown did not rule out the possibility of entry in that parliament, and made clear that the government did not see any constitutional objections to participation. For New Labour, it was a matter of economics. But in saying that, and by announcing the five tests, Blair had given Brown a permanent veto over British policy on the euro. It was quickly clear that there was no chance of entry during the first term. An argument between Blair and Brown about the wording of a statement on euro preparations in spring 1999 underlined the Treasury's hostility to entry.

In retrospect, October 1997 was the last – and perhaps the only – time that there was a serious prospect of British entry. Brown, Ed Balls and the Treasury took an increasingly sceptical line over European issues, from the proposed EU constitution to new policies. This partly reflected long-established institutional suspicion of Brussels, and partly a desire to preserve Britain's competitive position against new regulations. Brown had a long battle over plans to harmonise taxes on savings. He feared that harmonisation would both push up tax rates and threaten financial markets in London. So, using his threat of a veto, Brown forced changes in the proposals away from harmonisation to exchanges of information to prevent tax evasion.

The chances of entry receded as the British economy did well on its own outside the euro, while the performance of the eurozone economies, particularly Germany, remained sluggish. It was no surprise when the promised assessment in June 2003 about the five tests was negative. This was the largest single piece of work ever undertaken by the Treasury, involving eighteen separate studies of various aspects of the impact of EMU, as well as a 246-page long White Paper of conclusions. The intention was to show that the exercise was driven by economics, not politics, though the two cannot be separated. The Treasury argued that had the UK joined EMU at its start in 1999, 'the UK economy could potentially have experienced greater economic instability than has actually been the case.' The conclusion (2003) was unequivocal:

> Overall the Treasury assessment is that since 1997 the UK has made real progress towards meeting the five economic tests. But, on balance, though the potential benefits of increased investment, trade, a boost to financial services, growth and jobs are clear, we cannot at this point in time conclude that there is sustainable and durable convergence or sufficient flexibility to cope with any potential difficulties within the euro area. So, despite the risks and costs from delaying the benefits of joining, a clear and unambiguous case for UK membership of EMU has not at the present time been made and a decision to join now would not be in the national economic interest.

To appease the dwindling band of supporters of euro entry, Blair talked in June 2003 about launching a roadshow to make the case for entry – still presented as a when rather than an if – as well as promising a further review the following year to see whether another assessment was justified. But both promises were quickly exposed as empty. The government did not pursue a consistent programme of advocating entry and no further assessment occurred. By early 2004, Blair accepted the Treasury view that euro entry was off the agenda for the foreseeable future, certainly in his own premiership, not least because of the problems of the European economies. Many of Blair's domestic advisers were relieved that Britain had not entered. So instead of the strongly pro-euro language of his early years in Downing Street, Blair talked more in take-it-or-leave-it terms. In his ever adaptable way of changing his argument to meet the circumstances, he emphasised that he had always seen entry more as an economic question.

In contrast to his caution on Europe, Blair also adopted an increasingly moralistic strain in his foreign policy statements. This was a departure from traditional foreign policy outlined above. The doctrine of humanitarian intervention reflected the change in the nature of conflict in the post-Cold War era, from confrontations between nations to civil wars and the slaughter or expulsion of minority groups – what became known as ethnic cleansing. These views were first expressed during the Kosovo conflict in spring 1999. In his speech in Chicago in April 1999 on the 'Doctrine of the International Community', Blair argued that 'the most pressing foreign policy problem we face is to identify the circumstances in which we should get actively involved in other people's conflict.' This was a radical departure from the 350-year-old doctrine of non-interference in the affairs of other countries which had restrained western European countries from intervening militarily in the Bosnian civil war in the first half of the 1990s. But Blair said this longstanding approach must be 'qualified in important respects. Acts of genocide can never be a purely internal matter. When oppression produces massive flows of refugees which unsettle neighbouring countries, then they can properly be described as "threats to international peace and security".' He then set out various tests before force should be used: exhaustion of diplomatic options; practicality of any military operations; preparation for a long-term commitment; and the involvement of national interests.

As Blair readily acknowledged, there were not absolute tests. Why Kosovo, Afghanistan, Iraq and Sierra Leone? But why not Rwanda or Darfur, let alone Chechnya? The lines were blurred, and there were big questions about who should authorise such operations. The United Nations Security Council did not specifically approve of the action to force the Serbs out of Kosovo because of Russian opposition. Yet the operation was widely backed and involved NATO in a military action for the first time. But the conditions were very different in the case of Iraq. In practice, national interest has been crucial. Blair's moralistic language could soar well ahead of any practical realities, notably in his speech to the Labour conference in the aftermath of the 9/11 attacks, when in messianic language he talked of a fight for freedom and justice 'to bring those same values of democracy and freedom to people around the world ... the starving, the wretched, the dispossessed, the ignorant, those living in wanton squalor, from the deserts of North Africa to the slums of Gaza, to the mountain ranges of Afghanistan: they are our cause.' Where would it end? This appeared to be a justification for intervention everywhere.

Humanitarian intervention could be seen as part of the commitment to human rights in the Labour manifesto, and the 'ethical dimension' in a socialist foreign policy, which Robin Cook announced in his mission statement as Foreign Secretary in 1997. But the two were distinct in inspiration and in their implications, as was seen over Iraq. In his desire to remake the world, Blair also overlapped with the outlook of some of the neo-conservatives in the Bush administration who wanted to export/encourage/impose democracy throughout the world. At the other end of the spectrum, Blair's outlook led to his concern over Africa, his sponsorship of the Africa Commission and the push with Gordon Brown for increased debt relief and assistance for poorer countries. For Blair, Iraq and Africa reflected a similar view of the world.

During his four years as Foreign Secretary, Cook sought to put human rights at the heart of foreign policy: condemning and, if necessary, imposing sanctions on regimes violating human rights; refusing to supply weapons and equipment to such governments; a commitment to ensuring that trade objectives did not undermine rights, by the use, for example, of child labour; and backing the establishment of an international criminal court. The process commitments, like setting up the ICC and incorporating the European Convention into British law, proved to be relatively straightforward, despite continuing tensions with the USA over the court. But the record on the other pledges has been mixed. In some cases, there has been a conflict of objectives, notably over arms sales and the protection of jobs in defence industries in Britain (up to 90,000 of which are dependent on exports). In most cases, the interests of defence exports came first. The ambiguities were highlighted by sales of arms to both Indonesia and Sierra Leone, which produced the 'arms to Africa' mini-scandal in 1998.

In other human rights issues, the British government could condemn, but it could not bring about change on its own, or even as part of the EU. That was highlighted by the failure to stop the barbarity of Mugabe's murderous regime in Zimbabwe, largely because the South African government would not back tougher action. Britain and most other Western governments also skirted around human rights abuses in Russia and China.

The biggest strains in Blair's foreign policy came increasingly from Europe's relations with Washington. Following outgoing president Bill Clinton's advice (Riddell in *Hug The Close* 2003, p. 2) to get as close to George W. Bush as he had been to him, Blair soon developed close relations with the new Republican president. As in his relations with European leaders, ideological or party affiliation mattered far less than working with whoever happened to be in power at the time. The new Bush administration quickly created transatlantic tensions over missile defence and the US intention to withdraw from the 1972 Anti-Ballistic Missile Treaty, and, particularly, over its denunciation of the Kyoto agreement on climate change and its opposition to the proposed international criminal court. The dismissive manner in which these decisions were announced without consultation fed European suspicions. Blair sought to minimise differences and act as the interlocutor – the bridge, to use his favourite metaphor. But France and Germany disliked such talk of a bridge. Chancellor Schroeder was reported as saying that the traffic across Blair's bridge always seemed to be in one direction.

The 9/11 attacks on New York and Washington instantly, temporarily and misleadingly produced transatlantic unity. European leaders rushed to offer both their sympathy and practical support. In France, *Le Monde* proclaimed with a Gallic flourish that '*nous sommes tous Américains*', while Schroeder expressed 'unlimited solidarity'. But it was Blair who instinctively understood the significance of the attacks for the United States, and particularly for the Bush administration. It was then that he decided that the USA must not be left on its own, and that Britain should remain closely alongside. This reflected fears that the US might react, or rather overreact, unilaterally. This view dominated his thinking and behaviour over the following eighteen months up to the start of the Iraq war in March 2003. At each stage, he was more concerned with what the Bush administration was thinking and planning than with the opinions of his fellow European leaders.

The strains appeared quickly in the autumn of 2001. Europe discovered that the emotions and solidarity of mid-September did not mark a change in the Bush administration's approach. International support had to be on American terms and, apart from British military involvement in the Afghanistan campaign, European help was mainly secondary. Blair in effect became Bush's ambassador-at-large, covering more than 40,000 miles in the eight weeks after the 9/11 attacks while having 54 meetings with other leaders. Blair's independent actions, or at first with Chirac and Schroeder, did not go down well in the EU. A meeting by the three leaders during the Ghent EU summit in mid-October 2001 was criticised by Romano Prodi, the President of the European Commission, as a 'shame' and as 'solo diplomacy'. These tensions descended into farce when Blair arranged a Sunday evening dinner in 10 Downing Street on 4 November 2001, on the eve of a short visit to Washington. The guest list, originally just the French president and German chancellor, expanded over the succeeding days as other leaders were invited, or invited themselves. The list included the leaders of Italy, Spain, Belgium (which held the EU presidency) and the Netherlands (which arrived late during the meal). Blair was trying to be both a messenger between Europe and America and a missionary around the world on the part of President Bush. In neither role did he appear to be acting in the EU's collective interests.

But these difficulties were nothing compared with the open divisions of the following eighteen months. The twists and turns of the build-up to the Iraq war have been fully covered elsewhere (including Riddell 2003, Kampfner 2003, Daalder and Lindsay 2003, Gordon and Shapiro 2004) and highlight the growing strains and tensions in Blair's foreign policy. In late January 2002, in his annual State of the Union address to Congress, President Bush described states like North Korea, Iran and Iraq as 'an axis of evil, arming to threaten the peace of the world'. These remarks were widely criticised in Europe as crude, naïve and dangerous. The pressing issue was increasingly Iraq, where, as discussed below, Blair privately accepted by summer 2002 that the US would probably take military action and that Britain would almost certainly participate, provided the right diplomatic conditions were met. This meant a new United Nations Security Council resolution and the return of weapons inspectors to Iraq. All the time Blair was saying that no decision on military action had been taken and attempted to maintain a joint US/EU position. But even the facade of unity was undermined during the summer of 2002 as Gerhard Schroeder took a strongly anti-war line in his party's campaign for re-election that September. This infuriated Bush, who saw Schroeder's attacks as a personal betrayal, and their relationship was permanently damaged. A common transatlantic position was reached during October and November over what became UN Resolution 1441. But this only masked differences between the American belief that another vote was not needed before military action and the French and Russian view that 1441 did not provide an automatic trigger for war. The unanimous Security Council vote on 8 November 2002 was the deceptive high point of transatlantic unity, with the British deluding themselves that their successful diplomacy might avoid war.

Blair's attempt to reconcile – at times, almost to deny – these differences was publicly destroyed in the first three months of 2003. The transatlantic bridge collapsed, exposing the contradictions in his foreign policy. The British government failed to recognise the signs of a revival in the Franco-German alliance, which the Foreign Office had been trying to break open by bilateral initiatives with Berlin and Paris. At an EU summit in Brussels in late October 2002, Britain, and particularly Blair, was outmanoeuvred by a surprise joint French and German initiative on the future financing of the Common Agricultural Policy. Chirac and Blair clashed openly on these proposals. Chirac complained that he had never been spoken to in this way before. This may have been absurd but it led to the postponement of the planned Anglo-French summit until the New Year. The closer Franco-German cooperation was highlighted in January 2003 when members of the Bundestag and the National Assembly met to celebrate the fortieth anniversary of the Elysée treaty signed by President de Gaulle and Chancellor Adenaeur.

The gulf became wider over the following weeks as the US determination to take military action became more apparent, and as French and German opposition became more vocal. Blair was increasingly seen as on the US side. Two events symbolised the breach. First, on 22 January 2003, Donald Rumsfeld, the US Defense Secretary, sought to divide Europe when asked about European opposition to military action. 'You're thinking of Europe as Germany and France. I don't. That's old Europe. If you look to the east, Germany has been a problem, and France has been a problem. But you look at the vast numbers of other countries in Europe. They're not with France and Germany on this, they're with the United States.' Rumsfeld touched on a sensitive spot. His remarks were partly correct since many of the central and eastern European countries had instinctive sympathy for the US position, but that did not make them anti-EU, which they had been trying so hard to enter for the previous decade. There have also been deep divisions over economic and social policy. But the split was much more complicated than just old versus new Europe. There were differences between the views of heads of government, like José María Aznar of Spain, who backed President Bush, and his electorate, who were strongly opposed to military action. Rumsfeld's remarks were extremely provocative and indicated a change of policy at least by some in the Bush administration. For most of the post-1945 era, the US policy had been to encourage a united Europe; now, there seemed to be a deliberate attempt by powerful forces in the administration to divide the EU and work with *ad hoc* coalitions of the willing, rather than with formal alliances. That put the Blair government on the spot as a supporter of transatlantic cooperation through bodies such as the EU, and was crucial in undermining Blair's bridge strategy.

The second symbolic event came at the end of January 2003 when eight heads of European governments – of Britain, Denmark, Italy, Portugal and Spain among existing EU members, and of the Czech Republic, Hungary and Poland among new entrants – signed a widely publicised article supporting the enforcement of Resolution 1441. This was backed up a few days later when the leaders of ten other central and eastern European countries signed a similar pro-US letter. These letters appeared to confirm Rumsfeld's claim and infuriated French and German leaders.

Blair was left looking increasingly isolated over the following weeks. He faced growing domestic opposition – notably the massive public demonstration of more than one million people in London on 15 February 2002 – and was spurned by the French, German and some other EU leaders. At the same time, he was unable to secure a majority for the further UN resolution to authorise the use of force, which the Bush administration anyway regarded as unnecessary. The final, open breach in Europe occurred in mid-March when President Jacques Chirac appeared on French television to say: 'My position is that, regardless of the circumstances, France will vote no because it considers this evening there are no grounds for waging war in order to achieve the goal we have set ourselves – to disarm Iraq.' There has been much dispute about whether Chirac was referring just to the resolution proposed by Britain, or whether, as Blair claimed, to any resolution setting a timed ultimatum requiring Saddam to comply or face the automatic use of force. But Chirac's use of the phrase 'regardless of the circumstances' gave Blair an opening to argue that a further resolution had been unreasonably blocked. There was then a spate of French-bashing, led by Jack Straw and enthusiastically joined by the jingoistic tabloids. This helped ease the short-term pressures on Blair, but at considerable long-term cost.

When faced with a fundamental strategic choice, Blair had opted for the United States rather than for Europe. More crudely, he was widely attacked for being merely Bush's poodle. However, his instincts were the same as virtually all his predecessors apart from Sir Edward Heath, even though few would necessarily have been as bold as Blair.

So, could the diplomatic train wreck of March 2003 have been avoided? There are three interlinked questions. First, could Britain have opposed the war like Germany and France? Second, could Britain have broadly backed the US action but not participated in the invasion – perhaps providing troops later for the occupation like Italy and Spain? And third, could Britain have maintained European unity?

On the first point, it is too easily forgotten that Blair genuinely believed that Saddam was a threat and that he was developing weapons of mass destruction. That had been his view well before the 9/11 attacks. For all the subsequent arguments about 'sexed up' dossiers, Blair, his key advisers and the intelligence agencies in France, Israel, the USA and Britain all took this view. There was a big element of wishful thinking, an overreliance on dubious sources and an unwillingness to revise long-established assessments (as discussed in the Butler report, 2004). Blair did not deliberately distort the genuine worries of the intelligence world, even if the nature of the threat was exaggerated in published statements (such as the endlessly discussed 45-minute claim). The real criticism is of his judgement. Nothing new had been found, or suspected, to change the largely successful policy of containment adopted since the first Gulf War in 1991. What had changed, as Blair admitted, was the US attitude. The 9/11 attacks had led to a new approach in Washington, and Blair was determined to ensure that the United States, as the sole superpower and Britain's closest military ally, was not left alone. This was a plausible objective, as well as one with a long pedigree. Blair was over-optimistic about the degree of his real influence in the White House, as opposed to access, obtained for being such a staunch ally, but this was a more credible and mainstream foreign policy than his critics have acknowledged. It would have represented a radical reversal of the post-Suez policy for Blair to oppose the military action, potentially jeopardising American cooperation on intelligence and nuclear matters.

Second, should Blair have committed himself so early to the military route, as he effectively did from the spring and summer of 2002? By then, he and his advisers may have hoped that a firm stand, backed by the return of UN inspectors, might force Saddam to back down, but they all recognised that military action was probable – as is shown by the memorandum written on 23 July 2002 by Matthew Rycroft, one of the 10 Downing Street private secretaries, and published in the *Sunday Times* on 1 May 2005, four days before the general election. This was a note of a meeting held by Blair with senior ministers, intelligence and defence advisers Jack Straw is reported as saying that 'it seemed clear that Bush had made up his mind to take military action, even if the timing was not yet decided,' while in the conclusions, the prime minister said: 'We should work on the assumption that the UK would take part in any military action.' This contradicted the public comments of Blair and other ministers over the following seven months that all options were still open. They may have been legally, but not in practice, or in the understanding of the key figures in London and Washington. The Bush administration had good reason to believe that Blair was with them from then onwards, despite caveats about going to the UN. They were right, but it weakened any limited bargaining position that Blair might have had. That is why the search for a further UN resolution in February and March 2003 was always a face-saving device, necessary to protect Blair's increasingly vulnerable domestic political flank but never really believed in, or actively pushed, by Bush and his advisers.

But even then, just before the start of fighting, was there an alternative course? Many ministers and even close Blair advisers think there was. Blair could have followed Heath's approach during the Yom Kippur War and adopted a policy of detached neutrality, declining to provide military help or the use of British bases for any attack on Iraq. Another possibility might have been Harold Wilson's policy in the late 1960s during the Vietnam War when he broadly backed the American strategy, albeit with qualifications, but resisted Lyndon Johnson's pleas to send even a token force of British troops. This possibility arose in early March 2003, shortly before the war started, when the political arithmetic looked uncertain for Blair in the Commons ahead of the key vote, and Donald Rumsfeld tactlessly said that the US might have to manage without British troops. The immediate angry reaction from London, forcing a rare Rumsfeld clarification, showed how this option was never acceptable to Blair, though it might have been to some others in Whitehall. For him, Britain had to go the whole way. If the government believed that the operation was right, then troops should be committed. That was also the view of British military commanders, not least because a very large number of troops were in Kuwait, alongside the Americans, waiting for the order to invade Iraq. Staying where they were at that stage would have been regarded by them as a humiliation. However, some of Blair's closest Cabinet colleagues believe that the government could, and should, have gone no further then, especially given the uncertainties over the legal position. On this view, the government should have said that in the absence of wide international support and a further UN resolution, Britain would not join in the military action. That might have made Blair's own position very vulnerable, but it was a serious option.

But could Blair have avoided the divisions with much of the rest of Europe?

The prime minister himself suggested one possibility in his speech on 18 March 2003 in the Commons debate about whether to go to war:

> I tell you what Europe should have said last September to the US. With one voice it should have said: 'We understand your strategic anxiety over terrorism and WMD and we will help you meet it. We will mean what we say in any UN resolution we pass and will back it with action if Saddam fails to disarm voluntarily; but in return we ask two things of you, that the US should choose the UN path and you should recognise the fundamental importance of restarting the Middle East peace process, which we will hold you to.

Blair may have been correct in his aspiration, but his view rests on several possibly over-optimistic assumptions about both US and European behaviour. Would the US have accepted such a bargain and really gone down the UN path and been willing to confront the Sharon government over the peace process? And would France and Germany have backed military action against Saddam? It is possible that a split was unavoidable in view of the belligerent approach of many in the Bush administration and their desire to divide Europe. Moreover, the weakness of Schroeder before and after the German elections of September 2002 led to a revival of the Franco-German alliance on Chirac's terms, making it much harder for Blair to bridge transatlantic differences. Sir Stephen Wall, Blair's European adviser at the time, has argued (2004) that the failure to reach agreement was not just about a different world view:

> It had a lot to do with neo-Gaullist posturing by President Chirac, with opportunistic posturing by Chancellor Schroeder, and with the incautious courting of President Putin on the part of both. Added to that, the United Kingdom's inability to define its identity and role prevents us from filling a void in European leadership as France and Germany, under their present leaders, talk the European talk but walk a walk that is increasingly about national self interest.

These months represented a major failure in British foreign policy, both of intelligence and execution. The government, or at least 10 Downing Street, had failed to appreciate either the renewed closeness of Chirac and Schroeder or the firmness of the French determination to oppose military action. Blair failed to devote nearly enough time to talking to Chirac, Schroeder and other European leaders as he did to his relations with the Bush White House. A more even-handed diplomacy might not have prevented differences over the war given Blair's overriding priority of not deserting the United States, but more skilful personal diplomacy by him could have mitigated the consequences. So the careful balancing act of British diplomacy of avoiding a choice between the USA and Europe failed.

Transatlantic divisions remained in the aftermath. The Bush administration did not really trust the Europeans, especially after most countries failed to supply significant forces to help rebuild Iraq, and some like Spain withdrew after a period. The bloody shambles in Iraq after the fall of Baghdad in April 2003, and the incompetence of the US authorities in failing to prepare properly, did little to provide reassurance that the operation had been worthwhile. Admittedly, after the January 2005 elections, there was a democratically elected Iraqi government of a sort, but the violence continued on a large scale, especially around Baghdad. Of course Iraq was better off without Saddam, but that did not excuse all the errors of US policy and the many horrors. The follow-up which Blair sought in the revival of the Middle East peace process did not really occur. The only positive development was the election of Mahmoud Abbas as leader of the Palestinian Authority after the death of Yasser Arafat in autumn 2004. But he had an uphill task to establish a proper democratic government in face of a lack of resources, corruption, the strength of the Hamas terrorist group and lack of sufficient help from the Israeli government. Moreover, the Sharon government decided to introduce a number of unilateral steps, starting with a planned withdrawal from Gaza, rather than pursuing negotiations for a comprehensive deal. Indeed, settlements were expanded in the West Bank, notably around Jerusalem, isolating the predominantly Palestinian areas in the east of the city. This was intended to pre-empt any later negotiations about the West Bank.

The Iraq war was not only the overarching event of Blair's second term and possibly of his whole premiership, but it also undermined his attempt to present a pro-European case. Talk of old and new Europe and the demonisation of France were hardly the best way of combating Euroscepticism, let alone of winning a referendum on entry to the euro. Opinion polls showed, for example, a slight increase in opposition to joining the euro after the Iraq war compared with before.

That was reflected in the debate in the 2003–05 period over a constitutional treaty for the EU, which followed the report of a Constitutional Convention, chaired by former French president Valéry Giscard d'Estaing and consisting of representatives of member governments, national parliaments, the Commission and the European Parliament. The Blair government accepted that the EU had to change to accommodate 25 member states. There were two stages of negotiation: first in the convention; and second, by member governments in an intergovernmental conference, which concluded in June 2004. The convention produced a package that was intended to meet the concerns of big countries, and particularly Britain and France by emphasising co-operation by member states. This included proposals for a permanent President of the European Council, serving for a period of two and a half years, in place of the rotating six-month presidencies. In addition, there would be a European foreign minister, combining the roles of the High Representative and the Commissioner for External Affairs. There would also be an EU external action service to provide diplomatic support. Most controversial for Britain was the very idea of a constitution, even though it was strictly a treaty like earlier treaties such as Maastricht, Amsterdam and Nice. But the draft highlighted the supremacy of EU law, which had always been true in areas of community competence, and gave the EU a single legal personality. This provoked sceptic fears about a European superstate. Moreover, the Charter of Fundamental Rights was seen as providing a loophole for the introduction of new EU laws and regulations affecting British business. This was despite British amendments to ensure that new rights were not introduced into British law. Qualified majority voting was also extended in some areas, notably in extending community competence in justice and home affairs, though in none of the British 'red lines', like taxation.

Blair was able to claim, fairly, that the EU constitution was a good deal for Britain, certainly by comparison with any likely alternative. But such was the mood of Euroscepticism in Britain that he was on the defensive from the start. A treaty that was criticised in much of the rest of Europe, particularly on the left, as too pro-British and too pro-market was attacked in Britain by sceptics for selling out national interests by supporting a federal United States of Europe. Opinion polls consistently showed a majority of the public against the constitution. Blair and some of his senior colleagues – especially Jack Straw – were worried that demands for a referendum by the Conservative Party and the vocal Eurosceptic press would dominate any future election campaign and damage Labour's chances. Consequently in April 2004, ahead of final agreement on the constitution, Blair was persuaded to announce that a referendum would be held to ratify any treaty. He did this without consulting the Cabinet as a whole, and the announcement was seen as a sign of political weakness. Contrary to his talk of being 'best when boldest',

Blair had opted for a minimalist, risk-averse position on Europe, putting off awkward positions when possible.

The paradox was that the British position in Europe had advanced in many ways since 1997. In particular, enlargement of the EU to 25, formally completed in May 2004, not only fulfilled a longstanding British foreign policy goal of incorporating the former communist states of eastern and central Europe within the EU, but it also promised a Europe more to Britain's liking: more Atlanticist on security issues, and more free-market on economic matters. Britain was more comfortable with enlargement than, say, France, with its worries about losing its previously dominant position within the EU. French newspapers and politicians complained about excessive British influence in Brussels, and a tilt in a 'liberal, pro-market'/Anglo-Saxon direction after the appointment of José Manuel Barroso, a former prime minister of Portugal, as President of the Commission from autumn 2004. On foreign and security policy, also, work towards a more effective joint EU voice and capability continued despite, and to some extent because of, the divisions over Iraq. Shortly after the fall of Baghdad in April 2003, Jack Straw launched a joint initiative with the French and German foreign ministers to negotiate with the Tehran regime over Iran's nuclear programme. This was intended to pre-empt a more aggressive approach by the Bush administration. Despite criticism from hawks in Washington, the State Department offered guarded support, partly because it did not have a better alternative in the short term.

These efforts were in parallel with the development of a European defence policy, building on the St Malo declaration of December 1998 and the Helsinki communiqué of a year later. Britain has backed both the creation of the European Defence Agency, involving ministers and officials from EU countries to improve common procurement, and an EU battle-groups initiative. Apart from perennial problems of the balance with NATO, the real problem has been capability, with the EU as a whole falling well behind the Helsinki goal of having up to 50,000 to 60,000 troops deployable within sixty days and sustainable for at least a year in peace-keeping and related tasks. The US has remained worried about EU defence activities separate from NATO, but the EU's short-term ambitions and capabilities have remained modest, though in 2004 it was able to take over NATO's peacekeeping mission in Bosnia.

The government also shifted its position on justice and home affairs. Initially, Labour followed the Conservative policy of maintaining national border controls, unlike the countries within the area covered by the Schengen agreement. However, under the influence of Jack Straw, first as Home Secretary, Britain has participated in more of these arrangements, such as police and justice cooperation, and then, from 2002 onwards, in immigration and asylum. As concern mounted within Britain about rising numbers of asylum seekers, the Blair government argued that a common European approach was needed to control inflows.

Britain also remained active in pushing economic reform, despite its exclusion from the eurozone. The government has pressed for completion of the single market in energy, telecommunications and financial services (the latter a particularly fraught area), as well as for reductions in regulations and more flexible labour, capital and product markets. Progress has been mixed. A scorecard on the Lisbon agenda drawn up in early 2005 by Alasdair Murray and Aurore Wanlin of the Centre for Economic Reform think tank argues: 'The EU's Lisbon process has reached the half-way stage with few obvious signs of improvement in the performance of the European economy. The EU has already admitted that it will miss a number of key targets.' The new Barroso Commission made the revival of the Lisbon agenda, growth and employment a top priority, but it immediately ran into problems over the proposed services directive, to allow a legally authorised provider from any member country to operate in any other state.

The sluggish performance of the eurozone economies compared with Britain has undermined support for the pro-European position. Business enthusiasm for the EU has been noticeably on the decline, while the European argument in Britain has often been put by ministers in minimalist terms of red lines, of national interests being defended, rather than highlighting the advantages of membership. Hardly surprisingly, given the negative way that Europe has been discussed by politicians and a sceptical media, public opinion has remained hostile to the EU and to initiatives like the euro and the constitution. A Eurobarometer poll in October and November 2004 showed that the number saying that EU membership was a good thing was lowest in the UK of all 25 member states. For the first time in twenty years, more people think that membership of the EU is a bad rather than a good thing. In 1998, at the high point of Blair's pro-Europeanism, the balance was two to one in favour.

The rejection of the European constitution by the French and Dutch electorates on 29 May and 1 June 2005 raised questions about the broader direction of Europe.

These votes were initially seen as offering a way out for Blair since the constitution was, in effect, dead and he would not have to hold a highly risky referendum some time in 2006 – especially as a 'No' vote might have ended his premiership. But this was a short-sighted view. The European constitution offered the best hope of the type of primarily intergovernmental arrangements that Blair preferred, in contrast to the closer integration favoured by many in France, Germany and Spain. The constitutional treaty was formally put on ice at an acrimonious EU summit in Brussels in mid-June 2005, but this merely highlighted deeper divisions over the funding of the EU (with bitter arguments between Britain and France over the UK rebate and reform of the Common Agricultural Policy) and over the future direction of the EU. Europe was divided over social and economic strategy.

Blair had also failed to make the case for Europe to the British people. He repeatedly said in private – first about the euro and then about the constitution – that he could ratchet up opinion in favour of Europe whenever a referendum was called. Even in May 2005, he was said by advisers to be relishing the prospect of the battle over Britain's position in Europe, which he had mentioned so often in his speeches. But that is an illusion. It has always been a case of tomorrow. There has been an occasional big speech, but then nothing.

Moreover, as Roger Liddle, former European adviser to Tony Blair and since November 2004 a member of Peter Mandelson's cabinet in Brussels, has argued (Liddle 2005), the old coalition of pro-European Tories, big business, the Liberals (now Liberal Democrats) and much of Labour has fractured. The old pro-European arguments of the 1960s and 1970s based on Britain's weakness compared with the rest of Europe no longer apply. 'As Britain's relative economic performance has strengthened, the power of the old "declinist" argument for Europe has weakened. In parallel, the attraction of the European model has itself declined.' Liddle argues that the centre-left has to change the terms of the European political debate away from the 'no alternative' view of the past to making a more positive political argument that only the EU acting together can deal with the new global challenges. Despite being instinctively more pro-European than most previous prime ministers apart from Heath, Blair has been hesitant about going on the offensive over Europe in face of public scepticism and domestic political pressures.

Blair cannot be faulted on his intentions. Better relations with Europe were one of his top priorities on becoming prime minister. He ended the frostiness and isolation of the late Major years by his energy and charm, developing good relations with a number of key European leaders and launching joint reform initiatives. His personal imprint on these changes was considerable. But his efforts were not sustained. He became frustrated with the way that decisions were taken at EU summits, often returning home as soon as possible. The achievements of his government on Europe – pushing forward, or backing, new proposals on economic reform, enlargement, increased cooperation on defence and home affairs – should not be dismissed. They matter and are markedly different from the record of the previous few years. Despite Iraq, Britain has been an active player in the EU; and both the economic reform programme of the Barroso Commission and the now defunct constitution have been in line with British aspirations. But this has failed to move British public opinion in a pro-European direction. The whole is much less than the sum of the parts.

With the constitution on one side, Blair was able to take the initiative at the start of the British presidency in July 2005. In a skilful and widely applauded speech to the European Parliament on 23 June, he argued that the choice was not between a 'free market' Europe and a social Europe – demolishing the caricature that 'Britain is in the grip of some extreme Anglo-Saxon market philosophy that tramples on the poor and the disadvantaged.' Moreover, 'there is not some division between the Europe necessary to succeed economically and social Europe.' Instead, he made the case for reform, for a new approach across the board. He said Britain was prepared to compromise on the budget rebate provided the Common Agricultural Policy was renegotiated. He said the real objection was to leaving existing arrangements in place until 2013. His main emphasis was on the need to modernise the social model, not to abandon it. 'Business as usual' would not work. Noting the 20 million unemployed in Europe and productivity rates falling behind the USA, he argued that the social model should be changed to enhance Europe's ability to compete. In effect, he was urging the adoption of the British model, the combination of economic growth and social protection. It is a strong case and one shared by many other European leaders. But there is a big difference between having an opportunity to exercise leadership, as Blair had at the start of the British presidency, and changes being agreed. All the applause will not change minds in the short term, especially given the political uncertainties in France and Germany. Talking sensibly is not enough. Blair is suffering from the legacy of his eight years of ambiguity.

Above all, he has avoided the necessary strategic rethink required by both the end of the Cold War and a very different approach by the Bush administration. His transatlantic bridge policy – in effect the national strategy of the previous fifty years – failed not just because of Iraq, but because of a growing diversity of interests between Europe and the United States. This should not mean building up Europe as a superpower in rivalry to the US, the multi-polar view put forward by Jacques Chirac: that would increase, rather than reduce, tensions and weaken the EU's influence. As Blair rightly argued in his speech to the Joint Session of Congress on 17 July 2003, the night that David Kelly killed himself: 'There is no more dangerous theory in international politics today than that we need to balance the power of America with other competitor powers, different poles around which nations gather ... It is dangerous because it is not rivalry but partnership we need: a common will and a shared purpose in the face of a common threat. An alliance must start with America and Europe.' But such an alliance is more likely to wither rather than grow if Europe is divided, as many in Washington would like.

There was, and is, an alternative to Blair's approach as it developed after the Iraq war. Britain should not seek to define itself against Washington in the French fashion, but should work with European allies to develop a common position, if possible, in order to cooperate across the Atlantic. This would involve changes in the mindset in Whitehall compared with what happened during the run-up to the Iraq war. The danger is of a continuing ambiguous role in Europe and, at best, intermittent influence in Washington. Chris Patten pointed out in early 2004 that 'as the disproportion between America's and Britain's might increases, the only role for us is that of a very junior partner, partly of value simply because we are there.' As the example of the talks with Iran has shown, if Britain works with European allies then it can have more influence in discussions with Washington. As Patten argues, most of the things that Europeans want 'are more likely to be achieved if we can work with America. That is manifestly true, for example, about global issues like better environmental management and regional issues like the Balkans. It is almost equally the case that most of the things that America wants are easier to accomplish if Europe is a partner. Witness the present search by the US administration for a wider Middle East policy that will really encourage free trade and participative democracy.' The alternative strategy put forward by some on the Eurosceptic right of throwing our lot in completely with Washington is nonsense. There are common interests – in fighting terrorism, and on some, though far from all, global economic issues. The 51st-state path would result in the certainty of Britain being patronised by the US and ignored by much of Europe. The dilemma has been expressed succinctly by Andrew Gamble in his perceptive book on the subject (2003, p. 231):

> Many of the tensions in British politics, and the travails of its political parties, are because Britain has been drawing ever closer to Europe, but this has been resisted by a significant part of the political class which prefers America, and also by a large part of the electorate, which is hostile to both Europe and America and would prefer to remain detached from both.

Blair's legacy in foreign affairs is distinctly patchy, largely but not solely because of the Iraq war. He has understood the new challenges facing the world: over terrorism and ethnic conflict (brutally brought home by the bomb attacks in London on 7 July 2005), in the Middle East, the problems of Africa and the economic competition from China and India. His government's record in many of these areas has been strong, even if the performance has not always matched the good intentions. But he has offered a lead: for instance over climate change and Africa. Despite US resistance, Britain has both backed the Kyoto protocol and taken action to achieve its targets by reducing carbon dioxide emissions. The British aid budget has been doubled and Britain, particularly Gordon Brown, has taken the lead in cancelling the debt of the poorest countries and in trying to gain international support for wider debt relief, with only limited success in face of US reservations.

It is intriguing to speculate how a Brown foreign policy might have been different from the Blair performance. A greater emphasis on international development, less on defence. Definitely no euro, and generally probably more sceptical rhetoric, with no references to Europe as our destiny, though the outcome might have made little difference in practice. The biggest uncertainty is about relations with the United States. In one sense, Brown is more of an instinctive Atlanticist than Blair – all those holidays on Cape Cod, discussions with American economists, liking for their pro-enterprise and liberal market model. Yet he has also been a sceptic about the introduction of market solutions into the running of public services. It is hard to see him developing the close personal relationship which Blair has had with Bush and his advisers, and any Brown premiership may not begin until towards the end of Bush's time in the White House. Brown publicly backed the various military actions taken by Blair, largely it seemed at times for domestic political reasons. It is fascinating, but ultimately fruitless, to speculate about whether he would have adopted the same approach to the Iraq war as Blair: possibly not. But now, he would face the same dilemma of whether and how to modify the longstanding national strategy of the transatlantic bridge. And Brown would have the same problem that it is no good telling the rest of Europe that the British way on economic reform is right. That is not the same as persuading them.

The greatest setbacks since 1997 have been in European policy. Despite some of the advances set out above, the whole has been much less than the parts. Even without the war, Britain would still probably not have been in the euro, and there would still have been the divisions over the direction of Europe, between the liberalising free-market vision and the more familiar social/protectionist model. Even before the war, Blair was never willing to devote himself fully to his European goals. Perhaps without the war, he might in his second and third terms have been willing to take greater risks. But he failed in his repeated aim of ending the decades of British distance, reservation and hesitation about Europe. Britain remains the perpetual awkward partner. This was not all his personal fault. Circumstances were against him. It is possible that changes of government in Germany and France may provide a new coalition of support for the type of outward-looking, economically liberal Europe which Blair favours. Possible, but not certain. But it would be very late in his premiership and a long way from his early hopes. At present, Europe has been one of the central failures of his premiership. The limits of his achievements were shown in May and June 2005 when he was seen, wrongly, as having shifted in a sceptic direction. He had not, but his stressing the virtues of the British approach in face of the failures of the European model was seen in this light.

The weaknesses in the post-Suez national strategy of trying to be the bridge between America and Europe have been exposed. Instead of transforming Britain's foreign policy, Blair has become a victim of its contradictions.

7

How We Are Governed

'Before the election in May 1997, we identified a range of problems: a government that was over-centralised, inefficient and bureaucratic; local government in need of reform; something approaching a national crisis of confidence in our political system; excessive secrecy that both encouraged and reflected the arrogance of power and lack of accountability; and a want of principled protection for human rights.'

Lord Irvine of Lairg, Lord Chancellor, speech delivered on 16 July 1999 and published in *Human Rights, Constitutional Law and the Development of the English Legal System*, 2003.

'Governing parties are more than just tenants of the constitutional structure; they have a right, even a duty, to modify it where they judge that the people will thus be better served (though any such modification ought to be made openly, with proper discussion and accountability). But they remain less than owners; they are more like trustees, with an obligation to maintain the structure and hand it on to eventual successors in good working order. The Hutton and Butler scrutinies in effect called into question whether the obligation was being fully secured.'

Sir Michael Quinlan, former Permanent Secretary at the Ministry of Defence, in W. G. Runciman (ed.), *Hutton and Butler: Lifting the Lid on the Workings of Power*, 2004.

The most lasting legacy of the Blair premiership is likely to be the one area in which Tony Blair himself has shown least interest – the constitution. His government has introduced big changes to the way Britain is governed, with far-reaching implications for the Westminster parliament, for the courts and judges, for individual liberty and for central–local government relations, yet the involvement of the prime minister himself has been marginal, with the significant, and special, exception of Northern Ireland. While his lack of interest in the constitutional programme did not matter in the first term since so much had been planned beforehand, his detachment has contributed to an increasing incoherence and confusion since 2001.

One of the main paradoxes of the Blair premiership is the contrast between these largely pluralist changes to the constitution and his often centralist style of leadership. There have been numerous examples of legislation giving power to other institutions at the same time as the centre had sought to retain continuing control over what happens. A Welsh Assembly was set up, yet the prime minister tried to influence who ran it. A new mayor was created in London, yet the national Labour leadership tried to determine who stood as the party candidate. In both cases, the result was failure, humiliation and further damage to Blair's standing. The effect has been that he, and his government, have got less credit and more criticism than they deserve for the constitutional changes they have introduced.

Consequently Blair has been accused by a mixture of the right, the old and the bold (the retired establishment), and libertarians of abusing and undermining the constitution, and especially Parliament. There is something in these charges, but they are exaggerated. The critics often ignored the changes during the course of Blair's premiership, notably in Parliament after the 2001 election.

Blair is himself partly to blame, for the explanation lies both in his character and in the creation of New Labour. He has made virtually no speeches about the constitution since 1997, and during conversations with him I have never had a sustained discussion about the subject. This is not only because other issues, like the economy, public services and Europe, are of more interest to him and, he rightly believes, for most voters. His attitude was revealed in a Commons debate in July 2000 on the decline in the power of Parliament to hold the executive to account. Blair dismissed proposals for pre-legislative scrutiny and fine-tuning the Ministerial Code. 'These are good issues for academics and constitutional experts, but they are not the big issues that Parliament should debate when we consider our role in modern society and our relationship with the executive today.' You can say that the constitution is a low electoral priority, but it is curious not to show much interest when constitutional legislation is such a major feature of your programme.

His lack of interest is more fundamental. For a lawyer, Blair has had surprisingly little instinctive feel for constitutional issues. Questions about the mechanisms of power are much less important for him than how power is used. He simply does not understand, or have any interest in, debates about the proper boundaries between ministers, special advisers and civil servants. That is why a Civil Service Bill has always fallen off the legislative agenda in the Queen's Speech. Similarly, he has had practically no interest in what happens in Parliament, though he and his ministers have increasingly been forced to pay attention to the views, and the votes, of MPs and peers. Blair has not only been distant from what happens in the House of Commons, but he has caused his own government repeated problems by his lack of understanding of the politics of the House of Lords. Revealingly, when he has referred in passing to these issues, he has talked about 'modernising' democracy. But as the debate over reform in the Commons has shown, modernisation is not the same as shifting the balance of power.

More significantly, Blair has always been ambivalent about the exercise of power, and hence what constitutional change means. The Liberal Democrat peer and strategist Richard Holme (Lord Holme of Cheltenham), who was closely involved in the then LibDem leader Paddy Ashdown's negotiations with Blair from 1994 until 1998, spotted the dilemma early on in the Blair premiership. In a speech at the LibDem conference in September 1997 (Riddell 1997), he said the challenge for Mr Blair and his colleagues is whether they 'sincerely believe in pluralism, or do you want to create a New Labour hegemony?' Is it a sharing of power or a takeover? Did Mr Blair, in short, want to work in partnership with the Liberal Democrats or to swallow them up? This question had a crucial bearing on the debates over electoral reform and the report of the commission under Lord Jenkins of Hillhead in 1998. Under the influence of

Jenkins, Blair had frequently regretted the division of the progressive left for much of the twentieth century between Labour and Liberals (now the Liberal Democrats), which had so benefited the Conservatives. He wanted to end that schism. There were two routes: to bring the forces of the centre-left within New Labour's big tent, or to move to a new, more pluralist politics of co-operation, and probably of coalition involving electoral reform. Events showed that Blair wanted to dominate rather than to share power. It was not just that much of the Labour Party disliked the Liberal Democrats and rejected pluralist politics, with notable exceptions such as Robin Cook. Blair himself has famously 'not been persuaded' by the argument for proportional representation, and has been cautious on other aspects of constitutional reform. He has believed in strong leadership to achieve change rather than negotiation. This wariness about pluralism has also been shown in his caution over introducing an elected element into the House of Lords.

Not only has he been detached from much of the constitutional agenda, but it was not his creation. Unlike most other New Labour policies, the constitutional proposals were largely inherited from John Smith. The demands for Scottish, and more ambiguously Welsh, devolution; for a London mayor; for a Human Rights Act; for freedom of information legislation; and for House of Lords reform had a long history. Most were responses to the long period of one-party rule by the Conservatives from 1979 to 1997. This was particularly true in Scotland, where the fall in the number of Scottish Conservative MPs from the mid-1980s and the fierce battles over the introduction of the poll tax led to widespread complaints about laws being imposed from Westminster. This led to the formation of the Scottish Constitutional Convention involving the Labour and Liberal Democrat parties, as well as representatives of business, the trade unions, the churches and other bodies. Its carefully worked-out proposals provided a blueprint for the later devolution legislation. The Human Rights Act emerged from the arguments of lawyers and civil liberties groups.

After taking over as Labour leader in July 1994, Blair's impact on these proposals was mainly cautious. He did not want his whole first term to be dominated by constitutional reform, the tail wagging the dog, as he once put it. Despite Labour's big lead in the opinion polls in the 1994–97 period, Blair was never sure right up to election day that the party would have a big majority. He was worried that the legislative programme might be obstructed or undermined by the Tory-dominated House of Lords. That led him controversially to propose referendums in both Scotland and Wales over devolution. This announcement infuriated the Scottish Labour Party, who saw the proposal for a referendum (with separate questions on the principle and on tax-varying powers) as a threat to their long-cherished plans. In the event, Blair's worries about the size of his Commons majority were groundless. The referendum in Scotland in September 1997 proved to be a way of entrenching the change, as well as ensuring a smooth passage through Parliament. The margin in the Welsh referendum was wafer thin, reflecting the greater divisions and doubts in the principality, and leading to a continuing debate about the way Wales was governed. But again, the mere fact of holding a referendum ensured that the changes could not be easily repealed by a later government. Without such popular consent, the Thatcher administration pushed through legislation in the mid-1980s abolishing the Greater London Council and the metropolitan counties.

Labour developed an ambitious programme for constitutional change. During the mid-1990s there was a widespread sense that the way that Britain had been governed was unsatisfactory, being too centralised and giving the government too much power. The quotation from Lord Irvine at the beginning of this chapter (2003, p. 88) sums up the general feeling, as well as providing a yardstick by which to judge the later record. His analysis was widely accepted:

> The United Kingdom has suffered from a long drift towards ever greater centralisation of political power. This has caused many to feel that they have little or no opportunity to influence the important decisions that affect their daily lives. The accountability of government to the people has been damaged by a culture of secrecy. And human rights cases in Britain have had to be taken to the European Court of Human Rights in Strasbourg, instead of being pursued in our domestic courts.

A new constitutional settlement was seen as a central part of national renewal. The extent of the consensus on the progressive left was highlighted by a joint document prepared by Labour and the Liberal Democrats shortly before the 1997 election. This was known as the Cook/Maclennan agreement after its two authors, Robin Cook for Labour and Robert Maclennan for the Liberal Democrats. As Peter Facey of the New Politics Network (2005) pointed out in a pamphlet looking back on the agreement, it did not come out of a vacuum, but 'identified and codified what had become the consensus position of progressive reformers at the time'. Implementation of a large part of it – 80 per cent in Cook's view – 'fundamentally changed the way Britain is now governed'.

The Labour manifesto for the May 1997 election made a long list of specific commitments:

- Removal of the right of hereditary peers to sit and vote in the House of Lords and a greater party political balance amongst life peers.
- Modernisation of the House of Commons.
- Controls on party funding.
- A referendum on the voting system for the House of Commons.
- A Freedom of Information Act.
- A Scottish Parliament with tax-varying powers.
- A Welsh Assembly.
- A more accountable and democratic local government.
- A strategic authority for London.
- Regional chambers leading to directly elected regional assemblies in England.
- Incorporation of the European Convention on Human Rights into UK law.
- Support for the peace process and devolution in Northern Ireland.

This was an ambitious list by any standards.

On coming to power in May 1997 the new government acted quickly to implement these pledges. Several Cabinet committees were set up to plan and take forward the programme, with four chaired by Lord Irvine of Lairg, the Lord Chancellor. As Robert Hazell of University College London, the auditor *par excellence* of this programme, has written (2001): 'Six cabinet committees devoted to constitutional reform (out of thirty cabinet committees in total) is a measure of the collective ministerial effort devoted to the programme.' And unlike some other Cabinet committees, these ones met. White Papers were quickly produced and legislation introduced, taking advantage of the government's majority of 179, the support of the bigger Liberal Democrat group of 46 MPs and the low morale of the defeated Tories. So what the Callaghan government of the late 1970s had spent months and years agonising over and failing to achieve in the 1979 referendums, the Blair administration succeeded in doing relatively smoothly.

In the first, long session of parliament, nine separate constitutional acts were passed: allowing referendums to be held for devolution in Scotland and Wales and on creating a mayor and assembly in London; then setting up the devolved bodies in Edinburgh and Cardiff; two measures on Northern Ireland following the Good Friday agreement; registering political parties; establishing regional development agencies; and, perhaps most important of all, the Human Rights Act to incorporate the European Convention. Later in the 1997–2001 parliament, legislation was passed in 1999 to remove all but 92 hereditary peers from the House of Lords; to change the method of electing the European Parliament to a regional list system of proportional representation; to create a mayor and assembly for London, following the earlier referendum; to alter the way local government is run to strengthen the executive, including elected mayors; to establish a limited right to official information; and to set up an electoral commission to regulate elections and party funding.

The Blair government devoted much attention to Northern Ireland, building on the work of the Major administration. Both Tony Blair and, a few years earlier, John Major admitted to me in similar language that one of the most unexpected aspects of being prime minister was the amount of time they had to give to dealing with Northern Ireland. The leaders of the various groups expect to deal directly with the prime minister. Since 1997, Blair has probably spent as much time with Gerry Adams and Ian Paisley as he has with some of his Cabinet colleagues, and much more time than with junior ministers, let alone backbench MPs. The affairs of Northern Ireland are separate from all the other constitutional matters dealt with in this chapter, and are not given the space they deserve. Blair himself, unusually, took a lot of interest in them.

He decided early on that any attempt to achieve a lasting solution must involve direct contact between him and Sinn Fein, the political arm of the IRA. There had already been meetings during the Major years between

Northern Ireland ministers and leading members of Sinn Fein/IRA, but Blair himself met Adams and his senior colleagues. After lengthy negotiations, in 1998 all the main parties signed the Good Friday agreement. This involved setting up a Northern Ireland Assembly to allow locally elected representatives to exercise real responsibility over domestic policies, with special provisions to ensure cross-community support; a new North–South ministerial council, to help deepen cross-border relationships; and a new British–Irish Council, bringing together the two governments and the devolved institutions in Northern Ireland, Scotland and Wales, as well as the Channel Islands and the Isle of Man.

This is not the place to set out the full details of the subsequent on/off – and mainly off – history of devolution, the frustrated hopes over decommissioning and the polarisation of Northern Ireland at a series of elections between Paisley's Democratic Unionists and Sinn Fein, at the expense of previously dominant constitutional parties, the Ulster Unionists and the SDLP. Critics argue that Blair has legitimised Sinn Fein. But the significant point is the view of most, if not all, the paramilitaries that the 'war' is over. The level of killing, and of terrorist incidents, has been reduced, even if gangsterism and protection rackets remain rife in many areas. However unstable the position, there looks unlikely to be a return to the scale of killing and disorder seen in the 1970s and early 1980s. This was underlined by the IRA's announcement in late July 2005 that it was calling off the armed struggle – opening the way for a revival of the political process.

By any standards the record of legislation after 1997 is impressive, testament both to careful planning before the 1997 election and to energetic implementation afterwards. Labour could claim – though Blair seldom did – to have fulfilled most of his election promises and to have gone some way towards revitalising British democracy. The devolution arrangements worked pretty well: despite fears that it would bring closer the break-up of the United Kingdom, the reverse has happened. After some early successes in the first elections in 1999, the nationalist parties have not won converts and have been on the defensive. Admittedly, there have been grumbles about the spiralling cost of the new Scottish Parliament building at Holyrood, but the new parliament itself quickly developed a distinctive character and some innovative procedures in its handling of legislation and petitions by voters. The Labour/Liberal Democrat coalition worked well and survived, with the main teething problems coming from the perennial internal battles in the Scottish Labour Party and the incestuous political/media relationships of the Scottish elite. The same is broadly true in Wales after the fiasco of the self-destruction of Ron Davies, the imposition of the hapless Alun Michael and, after his failure, the successful leadership of Rhodri Morgan. In London, the complicated attempts by the Labour leadership to prevent Ken Livingstone becoming the party candidate for mayor of London were counterproductive, as he won easily as an independent.

Over time, the Labour-dominated or Labour-controlled Scottish and Welsh executives developed policies which were different from those being pursued by their party colleagues in London. A study by Michael Keating of Aberdeen University *et al.* noted:

> The Labour Party may be the dominant political force in London, Edinburgh and Cardiff. But Scotland and Wales have stuck more to the traditional social democratic model of public service delivery. This has led them to stress non-selectivity, professionalism and uniformity, while rejecting foundation hospitals, star-rated hospitals, school league tables, beacon councils, elite universities and selective schools. Scotland also scrapped up-front university tuition fees and rejected top-up fees. At the same time, free care for the elderly has been introduced north of the border. (Keating *et al* 2005)

The differences in policies partly reflects contrasting electoral circumstances since, in both Scotland and Wales, Labour faces competition from the left, while in England the party, and Blair in particular, are concerned about appealing to the middle classes. The results have also been different: for instance, the Welsh record on hospital waiting lists was inferior to the English experience, where big changes in the structure of provision had been introduced, as Blair dryly noted during the 2005 election campaign. Yet in this way devolution has challenged one of the basic principles of the post-1945 settlement, that entitlements to services from the state, particularly in welfare and social services, should be the same throughout the country. Concern that relatively poor parts of the country would suffer from devolution was one of the main arguments against the Labour government's proposals in the late 1970s from younger, left-wing MPs like Robin Cook and Neil Kinnock, who later became converts. In practice, however, high levels of public spending have ensured that Scotland and Wales have retained more collectivist/social democratic policies.

Moreover, Ken Livingstone in London had been much bolder than the central government in introducing a congestion charge. Blair acknowledged the success of the charge, and his government moved warily to endorse road-pricing as a way of managing traffic flow. Livingstone was also readmitted to the Labour party ahead of the 2004 mayoral election, when he comfortably won a second term.

These changes amount to a clear movement towards a quasi-federal structure, albeit with different arrangements for different parts of the UK, and a culture of rights presided over by the judiciary. This did not mean that Britain was going in the direction of the United States or Germany with their written constitutions, elaborate balance of central and state/Länder powers, and powerful supreme or constitutional courts. Devolution is not the same as federalism. The Scotland Act of 1998 was explicit that 'The UK Parliament is and will remain sovereign in all matters'; adding that the provision for the Scottish Parliament to make laws 'does not affect the power of the Parliament of the UK to make laws for Scotland'. The powers of the Scottish Parliament and Welsh Assembly derive from Westminster, not from the Scottish or Welsh people. This contrasts with the grand declaration in the Claim of Right, the foundation document in 1988 of the Scottish Constitutional Convention, that 'we do hereby acknowledge the sovereign right of the Scottish people to determine the form of government suited to their needs.' In practice, the supremacy of Westminster over the domestic affairs of both Scotland and Wales has been limited, as is recognised in the behaviour of ministers since 1999. As Professor Vernon Bogdanor has argued (2005): 'Westminster is in practice no longer sovereign over the domestic affairs of Scotland and Wales ... At the very least, the sovereignty of parliament means something very different in Scotland, and to some extent Wales, from what it means in England ... Westminster is no longer a parliament for the domestic and non-domestic affairs of the whole of the United Kingdom. It has been transformed into a parliament for England, a federal parliament for Scotland and Northern Ireland, and a parliament for primary legislation for Wales.'

The Human Rights Act of 1998 created similar ambiguities. The Law Lords could not strike down or annul legislation passed by Parliament, preserving the latter's sovereignty. However, as part of the ingenious compromise, the Act did have a significant impact on how sovereignty is exercised in practice. A declaration by a court that a law is incompatible with the European Convention has created political pressure to amend the offending legislation. This happened after the Law Lords ruled in December 2004 that the provisions in the 2001 anti-terrorism legislation detaining foreign nationals without trial, mainly in Belmarsh prison in south-east London, were incompatible with the convention because they were discriminatory and disproportionate. This forced the government into an urgent review and the introduction of a highly controversial replacement law, which permitted orders to restrict the movement of both UK citizens and foreign nationals suspected of terrorism who could not be brought before the courts. This case highlighted the impact of the Act. There is also a fast-track procedure for remedying problems. Under the legislation, when introducing new Bills ministers have to state whether they are compatible with the European Convention. Moreover, a Joint Committee on Human Rights has been set up to scrutinise new Bills, which has already had a significant impact in forcing amendments, though the suggested Human Rights Commission with a monitoring role has not been set up. This is, in addition, to the main benefit of allowing British citizens to bring cases before British courts rather than go through the considerable delay and cost of going to the European Court of Human Rights in Strasbourg.

The freedom of information legislation, though enacted in 2000, only came into full operation at the beginning of 2005 after both a long preparatory period and lengthy arguments. An early, more liberal draft prepared by David Clark when he was in charge of the Cabinet Office was dropped after he was sacked in the July 1998 reshuffle. A much tighter version was introduced after lengthy bargaining between Jack Straw, who as Home Secretary took over responsibility for the Bill, and Lord Irvine. While many areas such as Civil Service advice to ministers and sensitive economic, intelligence, defence and foreign policy matters are still excluded, the act has had an impact in producing the disclosure of more background information to decisions, as well as more ephemeral, though more publicised matters like the Blair family's official guests at Chequers.

One of the least discussed but most important measures was the Political Parties, Elections and Referendums Act of 2000. This established an independent, non-partisan Electoral Commission to supervise the conduct of elections, and particularly party funding. For the first time, limits were laid down regarding what parties could spend during election campaigns, as well as requiring disclosure of their contributors. This followed various allegations about big, secret donors seeking influence. The commission has also conducted research, particularly after the sharp fall in turnout at the 2001 general election from 72 to 59 per cent, only recovering a couple of points in 2005. More controversially, the commission has sponsored pilot schemes and experiments to boost turnout. However, its advice to be cautious about all-postal ballots until the law on registration has been tightened up was brushed aside by the government with embarrassing results in the June 2004 elections. There were allegations about fraud and abuse in postal voting. The most serious proven case, in Birmingham, had nothing to do with all-postal voting and was the result of an earlier relaxation in the law. But the incident highlighted the tension between the government and an independent regulator in a sensitive area. This was another illustration of how decision-making had become more diffuse and complicated.

Yet substantial though these changes were, there has been little sense of an overall picture. In 10 Downing Street, and in Blair's attitude, there was almost a sense of ticking a box when a new measure was enacted. Lord Irvine was right to claim that the changes were internally consistent, one of the achievements of his coordinating role. But that did not make for a coherent whole, a charge Lord Irvine disputed (2003, p. 96): 'We made decisions, based on empirical evidence, about precisely which aspects of our constitution needed earliest attention, and on what basis. We are conscious of the way different elements of any constitutional settlement can impact on each other. Of course, many parts of the package are not interdependent. They address particular problems, which are the product of lengthy and complex pre-histories of their own.' But while only passionate constitutional reformers favour a Big Bang approach of wholesale change, the Blair government's piecemeal changes have lacked a sense of direction or strategy.

Much of the problem in the second term was uncertainty about what type of constitution the government wanted. Frequent talk of modernisation just muddled the debate. How far did the government want to move away from a centralised state dominated by the winner-takes-all politics of the first-past-the-post system towards a more pluralist politics in which power was shared? The evidence was mixed. In time, the Blair team was prepared to recognise the implications of devolution for the devolved bodies, not least because they were largely controlled or dominated by Labour itself. But the Blair government was far less willing to share power at the centre. That was partly a matter of style: the powerful centre (in practice a duopoly between 10 Downing Street and the Treasury) wanted to retain control of the levers of power to drive forward change.

There was a more basic ambivalence, which was shown in the debates over electoral reform; over the future of the House of Lords; over the 'modernisation' of the House of Commons; and over central–local government relations. Changing the electoral system to secure a closer relationship between votes cast and seats won has been a longstanding demand of the Liberal Democrats in their current and previous incarnations. There is no perfect electoral system. It all depends on circumstance and on the nature of the body being elected. What is right, say, for the European Parliament, which does not form a government, may not be appropriate for the Commons, which does. There is a variety of conflicting factors.

Any move away towards a more proportional outcome involves changing the single-member constituency system. Some Labour ministers and MPs favour the alternative vote, under which people state a list of preferences (1, 2, 3 on the ballot paper), and votes are reallocated until one candidate gets over 50 per cent. While this prevents the election of a candidate with, say, 35 per cent of the vote, this system is not proportional and can produce an even more exaggerated majority for the leading party, and would probably have done so in 1983, 1987 and 1997. The beneficiary is the third party and the loser the second party. To achieve a proportional outcome between votes and seats involves either a number of additional seats being allocated on top of the single-member constituency ones to ensure a fairer balance, or distributing seats regionally in relation to the share of votes. The first, additional member system, combining constituency and top-up seats, is used for elections to the German

Bundestag and for the elections to the Scottish Parliament, Welsh Assembly and London Assembly. The second, regional list system has been used since 1999 for elections to the European Parliament. There are many other variants, notably the single transferable vote, the favourite of most PR enthusiasts, which involves multi-member constituencies. This is used in the Irish Republic for elections to the Dail and in Northern Ireland for some elections, but in June 2005 was rejected by the government for use in elections to the Welsh Assembly. Whatever the system, the exclusive link between the constituency and his or her representative is broken, for there is another tier of representative. This seems to work reasonably well where used, but members of the Commons are very protective about their constituencies. In many respects, this is desirable since they regard looking after their interests and grievances as a central part of their job. But it can lead to the illusion that they somehow own their seats, a belief that can be quickly destroyed when they lose. But any threat to the single-member system quickly mobilises a majority of Conservative and Labour MPs.

Any proportional system is unlikely to give a single party an overall majority. The chances depend on the precise design of the system. A higher ratio of top-up seats to constituency ones, as in Scotland, makes the absence of a single winner more likely. A lower ratio gives the dominant party a better chance of forming an executive on its own, as in Wales. Indeed, the existence of such a system is likely to encourage a wider range of parties standing and being represented, as has happened in Scotland since 1999. Multi-party politics, without a single party having a majority, means co-operation and coalitions. Parties have to talk, negotiate and share power. That is the reverse of the tribal, adversarial tradition in Britain.

As part of his elaborate courtship dance with Paddy Ashdown, Blair dangled the prospect of PR, or rather its examination. Blair and Ashdown talked often about how closely the two parties should cooperate, even discussing coalition at least twice. As a mark of goodwill, though little more, a Joint Cabinet Consultative Committee was set up, involving leading members of both parties, to discuss areas of cooperation, notably on the constitutional agenda. This was a continuation of the Cook–Maclennan talks and offered the hope of a more pluralist, co-operative style, though the joint committee was hated by Labour traditionalists like John Prescott. Blair sought to fulfil his manifesto promise by setting up an independent commission under Lord Jenkins of Hillhead to recommend an alternative to the first-past-the-post system.

The Jenkins commission, which reported in October 1998, was aimed at reconciling the conflicting aims discussed above. Its solution was a system called 'AV Plus', that is the alternative vote for single-member constituencies with a relatively small top-up to provide an element of proportionality. This ingenious, and elegantly expressed, solution would have left most MPs in single-member constituencies and still produced single-party governments on many occasions. Yet even this compromise was rapidly disowned by Jack Straw, as Home Secretary responsible for electoral matters but an opponent of PR with a strong dislike of the Liberal Democrats. So faced with the hostility of most of his Cabinet for either PR or the Liberal Democrats, an anyway lukewarm Tony Blair did nothing with the report, which was quickly forgotten. Blair's cool reception of the Jenkins report marked the end of attempts to forge links with the Liberal Democrats. Shortly afterwards, in early 1999, Paddy Ashdown announced his intention to stand down as party leader after eleven years. Charles Kennedy, his successor, deliberately distanced his party from Labour, particularly after the 2001 election and ahead of the Iraq war, which he strongly opposed. The Joint Cabinet Committee was allowed to wither away, before being formally abolished after the 2005 election.

The other part of the 1997 manifesto promise, to hold a referendum on the voting system for the House of Commons, did not happen. Nor did the review of the working of PR systems promised in the 2001 manifesto occur, though an Independent Commission on Proportional Representation was set up to look at the experience since 1997: it reported in 2004. Every single new body created or proposed since 1997 used a variant of PR rather than first-past-the-post: the Scottish Parliament, the Welsh Assembly, the Northern Ireland Assembly, the London Assembly, the proposed regional assemblies in England and, more tentatively, an elected element in the House of Lords, while the method of electing members of the European Parliament was changed to PR. Yet the Blair government drew a line between these largely successful innovations and the Commons. Sharing power was all right elsewhere, but not at Westminster. This was underlined after the 2005 general election when Labour won a comfortable working majority with less than 36 per cent of the overall vote, and the support of under 22 per cent of the overall electorate. These were by far the lowest shares in electoral history for any single-party government in Britain. Yet Blair and Lord Falconer, whose Department of Constitutional Affairs was now responsible for electoral matters, claimed that the public was not really interested in these matters and arguments over electoral reform.

Parallel ambiguities bedevilled debates over the future of the House of Lords. Labour came to office promising to end the 86-year-old stalemate over the future of the second chamber, the unresolved business left over from the 1911 Parliament Act. The Blair government adopted a two-stage approach: first, introducing legislation in the 1998–99 session to remove the hereditary peers; and second, setting up a Royal Commission to look at the future of the House ahead of further legislation. Despite a great deal of harrumphing and nostalgic guff about the irreplaceable contribution of hereditary peers, their removal went reasonably smoothly after the threat of obstruction to the rest of the legislative programme by opposition peers was removed by a compromise deal. This deal was formulated under the auspices of Lord Weatherill, the former Commons Speaker who was convenor of the crossbench peers, but was negotiated by the Lord Chancellor Lord Irvine and Lord Cranborne, the leader of the Conservative peers and the latest and possibly the last in the long Cecil line to play a major role in the affairs of the Lords. Cranborne negotiated behind the back of William Hague, his party leader, and was forced to resign, only to be succeeded by Lord Strathclyde, his close ally.

Under the deal, 92 hereditary peers were allowed to remain. This ensured that most of the active and most committed hereditary peers had a role in the new House. They were elected, a strange contradiciton for hereditary peers, and their numbers were fixed in proportion to their party affiliations in the House. This was intended to be merely a transitional expedient before the adoption of longer-term reform, but as this further stage was delayed again and again, there was the bizarre experience of by-elections being held to fill vacancies after hereditary peers died. In retrospect, it is questionable whether this deal was strictly necessary, or whether continuity could have been established by offering life peerages to a similar number of the most active hereditary peers.

In parallel, the Royal Commission under the chairmanship of Lord Wakeham, a Conservative former leader of both Houses, had consulted on the longer-term future of the Lords. Its report came out in January 2000, shortly after the bulk of the hereditary peers had left the Lords. The Wakeham Commission largely endorsed the existing role and powers of the Lords, with the exception of secondary legislation. Its main proposal was to recommend a partly elected and a partly appointed chamber, with various options for the elected element of 12, 16 or 35 per cent of the whole chamber. The elected element would represent the nations and regions of the UK, and the others would be selected by an independent Appointments Commission. Nothing happened before the 2001 election, apart from the establishment of a non-statutory Appointments Commission, with a limited remit of vetting new peers and recommending crossbenchers.

After the 2001 election, when Labour promised a 'more representative and democratic' House, the government produced its own plan suggesting that around a fifth of the second chamber would be directly elected, its proposals differing in a number of detailed ways from the Wakeham report. Most of the criticism of the government's White Paper was for not going far enough towards an elected House. A joint committee of both Houses was set up under the chairmanship of Jack Cunningham, a former Labour cabinet minister. This had the task of recommending various options to be voted on by both Houses. But behind the scenes there were serious tensions between Robin Cook, Leader of the Commons from June 2001 until his resignation over the Iraq war, and Lord Irvine, the Lord Chancellor. Cook favoured a large elected element, while Irvine backed a largely appointed second chamber. Irvine had the ear of Blair, his former pupil as a barrister. Labour MPs were divided between pluralists, who accepted the desirability of checks on the power of the Commons and hence the government, and the supremacists, who did not want any challenge to the Commons and to the ability of the ruling party to implement its programme. Blair was instinctively in the second camp, which included most Labour whips, along with many left-wing MPs who were not his allies on other issues and many from the old Labour right who were hostile to constitutional reform.

In January 2003 Irvine had infuriated Cook and supporters of a large elected element by saying that a part-elected, part-appointed House was a hybrid solution which would prove unworkable. Just before the issue came to a vote in February 2003, Blair made a similar statement at Prime

Minister's Questions. This may have helped the balance and, on 4 February 2003 all seven of the options from a wholly elected to a wholly appointed second chamber, as well as total abolition of the Lords, were rejected by the Commons in a confused series of votes. The narrowest vote was on an 80 per cent elected House, defeated by just three votes. On the same day, the by then largely appointed House proclaimed its desire for personal self-preservation, rejecting all the elected options and voting by three to one to remain an appointed House. The government then promised to bring forward a Bill to abolish the remaining hereditary peers and make the Appointments Commission statutory. But this produced charges of breach of faith by both the Conservatives and the Liberal Democrats, who between them could easily outvote Labour in the Lords. Their case was that Lord Irvine had given an explicit pledge that the removal of the remaining hereditary peers would be accompanied by proposals for the long-term composition of the House. So there was a stalemate, and in March 2004 the government announced that it would not be introducing further legislation on the Lords before the next election. This was also partly because Lord Falconer of Thoroton, Lord Irvine's successor, faced considerable difficulties in the Lords over the proposals to abolish the post of Lord Chancellor, as discussed below. This Bill might have been jeopardised by a further contentious argument over reform of the Lords.

In the 2005 general election, Labour proposed to codify and formalise the conventions of the Lords and their relations with the Commons in the handling of legislation, including the operation of the Parliament Act, as well as reviving the old proposals on removing the remaining hereditary peers. Both Houses would again be given a free vote on composition of the Lords, though with Blair repeating his doubts about a hybrid House. There was no prospect of early action, with another joint committee being set up to look at the conventions over the powers of the House and legislation unlikely until the 2006–07 session.

The prospect was for a further unstable stalemate: unstable because the half-reformed House regarded itself as more 'legitimate' in the words of Baroness Jay, Labour leader of the Lords, when most of the hereditaries were removed, and therefore more willing to challenge the will of the Commons, in effect the Blair government. The largely appointed Lords proved much more troublesome than the chamber dominated by hereditaries, defeating the government twice as often in the 2001–05 period than during the previous four years, and four times as much as the Thatcher and Major governments were defeated. The challenges were mainly over Home Office and similar Bills raising issues of human rights and civil liberties, and the government had particular problems over various criminal justice and anti-terrorism measures, as discussed later. Tony Wright, chairman of the Public Administration Committee for much of this period, remarked on the irony that supporters of constitutional reform and an elected second chamber looked to the Lords to put right what had passed the Commons.

This stalemate has arisen because the government, and therefore the Commons, has not had a clearcut view about what type of Lords it wants. Does it want a genuinely bicameral system, as in the United States or Germany? The second chamber can challenge the main elected House and, in the case of the US Senate, has particular powers of its own over the confirmation of senior public appointees. Or alternatively, do we want to continue with an essentially unicameral system? Under this option, a second chamber lacking democratic legitimacy has a subsidiary role tidying up the defects of legislation sent from the Commons and acting as an occasional trip-wire to force the Commons to look again. Blair and most of his Cabinet still favour the latter. In practice, this enshrines the largely unchecked power of a government with a clear working majority in the Commons, subject, of course, to maintaining discipline amongst its own MPs.

The debate over the future of the Lords became interlinked with the long drawn-out saga of the abolition of the post of Lord Chancellor, and the whole affair was made worse by characteristic mismanagement by 10 Downing Street in the reshuffle of July 2003. Blair had wanted to change the role of Lord Chancellor from his tripartite role of Cabinet minister, head of the judiciary who appointed top judges, and presiding officer of the House of Lords. He wanted a full-time Cabinet minister in charge of the courts and probation system in what would become the Department of Constitutional Affairs. At the same time, he wanted to set up a statutory Judicial Appointments Commission and to turn the Law Lords, technically a committee of the Lords, into a free-standing Supreme Court, with its own building and greater resources, though with no change in powers. Many of these propositions were opposed by Lord Irvine, who had anyway become more distant from Blair and had a fractious relationship with David Blunkett – then Home Secretary – as with Jack Straw before him. Removing Irvine – Blair's mentor during his early legal career – proved to be a personally fraught business for the prime minister.

As part of the reshuffle when Falconer was promoted to take over from Irvine, these constitutional changes were announced in a press notice, even though they had far-reaching implications for the House of Lords itself. The Lords, let alone the senior judiciary, are very touchy about their rights and standing, so there were many protests, both about the shambolic handling of the proposals and about the content. No one in 10 Downing Street seems to have thought through the implications, least of all that the Lord Chancellor's role as presiding officer of the Lords could not just be abolished overnight. This descended into farce as the disorganised Falconer quickly had to put on the Lord Chancellor's robes. More seriously, he had to spend twenty months negotiating, consulting and reassuring before the proposals became law shortly before the 2005 general election. Blair initially could not understand what all the fuss was about, as he told me shortly afterwards. He had been told that the Law Lords wanted a Supreme Court (some of them did) and he wanted a full-time constitutional affairs secretary in charge of the courts. That showed both his and his office's lack of understanding about the Lords and his own insensitivity about handling fellow politicians.

The whole episode was bizarre since what was being proposed was less political involvement in the running of the judiciary, not more. Yet the judges were in a prickly mood after the criticism by Blunkett and others. Falconer had to put up with being patronised by Lord Woolf, the Lord Chief Justice, who made a silly speech about his being a 'cheerful chappy'. The Law Lords seemed to want to have it both ways, both being in the House of Lords as a legislative chamber and having increased resources. Yet the whole notion of the senior judges sitting, speaking and voting in a chamber of the legislature would be unconstitutional in virtually any other country, as would the idea of the head of the judiciary being a member of the Cabinet. The judges attracted a great deal of sympathy and support from fellow peers for their desire to have one of their own, or at least a senior lawyer, in the Cabinet, to resist the blandishments of more political and partisan ministers. Why not a soldier at the Ministry of Defence or a doctor at the Department of Health?

At the other end of the Palace of Westminster, Labour came to office promising reform of the Commons, though it was vague about what this meant. Immediately after the election, a Modernisation Select Committee was set up under Ann Taylor, Leader of the Commons. The title exposed the ambiguity about the committee's role. What did modernisation mean? The word was part of the New Labourspeak of the time, trying to convey an impression of being forward looking. But in the parliamentary context, the meaning was ambiguous. Who would benefit? MPs, with fewer late night sittings? The government, through greater control of its legislative timetable? Or Parliament as an institution, in gaining greater powers to hold ministers accountable and scrutinise the executive? The lack of clear objectives is highlighted in a Hansard Society report (2005) on changes in Parliament since 1997, which distinguishes between modernisation as efficiency and modernisation as scrutiny. The former has had more success than the latter.

These ambiguities became clearer as the parliament continued. There was a hint in the government's first action, even before the Queen's Speech, when it announced that the two previous quarter-of-an-hour sessions of Prime Minister's Questions on Tuesdays and Thursdays would be consolidated into one half-hour session on Wednesday. This move was done without any consultation with either the other party leaders or MPs. While this *fait accompli* triggered protests, the idea had been considered, though rejected, during the Major premiership and this was probably the only time it could be pushed through. It cut the number of chances to question the prime minister, while not altering the total time, and further concentrated the parliamentary week. (For more details, see Riddell 2004.)

The Modernisation Committee quickly produced a report in July 1997, building on innovations introduced by Tony Newton, the former Conservative Leader of the Commons. The report proposed the timetabling of government bills; publication in draft to allow pre-legislative scrutiny; the greater use of special standing committees to hear witnesses before Bills are considered in detail; and the carry-over of some Bills from one session until the next. This was intended to permit scrutiny of all parts of a Bill, while allowing the opposition parties to raise issues of concern to them, but assuring the government that it can get its legislation through. The Labour whips disliked this package. The proposals were not put into the standing orders of the Commons and little changed. Instead of agreed timetabling of bills, imposed guillotines were used more and more.

Following the arrival of a record number of women MPs in the 1997 election, much attention was given to changes in working hours to make the Commons more 'family friendly'. Much of this was good sense, though it proved controversial with many older, male MPs whose family homes were a long way from London – and the changes were partially reversed in 2005, producing a patchwork of sitting hours during the week. But the focus on this aspect of 'modernisation' both discredited the concept and distracted attention from the basic questions of scrutiny and accountability.

Some of the innovations, such as the parallel debating chamber in Westminster Hall (also fully reported in Hansard), have been welcome and worthwhile. But as Philip Cowley and Mark Stuart have argued (in Seldon and Kavanagh 2005): 'Few of the proposals had the potential to enhance the scrutinising role of the Commons. Of the fifteen substantive reports published by the House of Commons Modernisation Committee between 1997 and 2001, only two contained proposals to help enhance the power of the Commons in relation to the executive. The others were designed for cosmetic or tidying up purposes, or for the convenience of members.'

The government's reluctance to surrender power was shown after Margaret Beckett took over from Ann Taylor as Leader of the Commons in July 1998. Mrs Beckett is a highly competent minister, the ultimate safe pair of hands, but her instincts are partisan, not pluralist. Her view on the centrality of party cannot be dismissed out of hand. Many critics of Parliament glibly demonise the power of the party whips and call for MPs to be more independent. Much of this is nonsense, as well as ignoring the rising trend of rebellions by MPs of the governing party, particularly marked on the Labour side after 2001. Party is the cement of any parliamentary system, vital for both coherence and effectiveness. Most MPs are loyal most of the time to their parties without any pressure from the whips. A truly independent House would produce chaos and incoherence which would further appal the critics. Any governing party with a majority is entitled to get its business through. The question, rather, is one of balance, of allowing the opposition parties and MPs, whether individually or on committees, to scrutinise the executive. But a variety of suggestions for strengthening select committees were dismissed by Mrs Beckett, producing an angry stand-off at the end of the 1997–2001 parliament over proposals produced by the Liaison Committee, consisting of the chairmen of all select committees. At the same time, both the Conservatives and the Liberal Democrats produced their own reform plans, and a Hansard Society Commission chaired by Lord Newton of Braintree (as Tony Newton had become) prepared a wide-ranging series of proposals to strengthen select committees. There was a clear cross-party mood in favour of change, of 'Shifting the Balance', in the words of the title of the Liaison Committee report. The obstacle was the government.

However, a new opportunity arose after the 2001 general election when Robin Cook unexpectedly became Leader of the Commons. He was not only a pluralist and long-term supporter of constitutional reform, but he saw a fresh opportunity to rebuild his political career and extend his range of support. Cook picked up the ideas for reform and pushed through proposals in May and October 2002 to strengthen the select committee system, by providing the committees with more resources, including more researchers, as well giving them a list of core tasks, including scrutiny of expenditure, public appointments, regulators and quangos in its area. There were also proposals to allow a greater carry-over of Bills from one session to the next, to prevent or at any rate reduce the logjam at the end of each parliamentary year in November; to have a formal parliamentary calendar for the year announced well in advance; to publish more Bills in draft form; and to bring forward Prime Minister's Questions from 3 p.m. to noon on Wednesday as a result of starting the sitting at 11.30 a.m. (one change which was not later reversed). The biggest row was, predictably, over patronage. After a bruising defeat for the government in summer 2001 over an attempt by the whips to block two senior Labour MPs from continuing to serve as committee chairmen, Cook's proposal to establish semi-independent procedures for the selection of members of committees to reduce the power of the whips was narrowly defeated – though party procedures, especially in Labour, have been more democratic. However, a plan to pay most select committee chairmen an extra £12,500 a year on top of their backbench salary was eventually implemented. This raised questions of patronage, of who would pick the MPs to hold these better-paid posts. However, an attempt after the 2005 election by the Labour whips to put a number of ex-ministers in as chairmen – including some who had only just left office – was defeated by Labour MPs.

In a significant change, Blair reversed his previous stance and agreed to appear twice a year before the main select committee chairmen on the Liaison Committee. Starting in July 2002, he was questioned for two and a half hours over the whole range of the government's responsibilities in a televised session. The committee concentrated on three or four topics, and while the sessions were often illuminating about Blair's thinking, they were seldom challenging for him. His five hours before this committee a year compared with the twelve hours plus with the press at his monthly Downing Street news conferences.

After Cook resigned in March 2003 the pace of reform flagged. There was no real government interest or commitment, apart from a few moves to improve access and removing the archaic term 'strangers' when referring to visitors to the Commons. The net balance was favourable, notably for select committees. However, Cowley and Stuart (in Seldon and Kavanagh 2005) argue that 'the impact of several of the reforms has turned out to be peripheral at best.' They note that the carry-over provisions have only applied to a small number of Bills; the much sought-after innovation of pre-legislative scrutiny has not prevented problems later on in the passage of Bills, as with the Gambling Act of 2005; and the automatic timetabling of Bills became seen simply as helping the government. However, the other side of this picture in explaining the mixed progress is the executive-mindedness of many MPs. Their aim is to serve on their parties' front benches, whether in government or opposition. For them, work on a select committee is merely a stepping stone, or a consolation after loss of office. So the government is not entirely to blame. But a lead from the prime minister might have turned modernisation into something more than a fashionable slogan.

The ambiguities in the government's position were also apparent in central–local relations. There were two main changes: first in the organisation of local government; and second, steps towards regional government. The two were in part competing as Blair was a champion of elected mayors, while John Prescott, in charge of the department covering local government for all but a year of the period, favoured regional government. Prescott was seen by many of Blair's advisers as obstructing innovation. The 2000 Local Government Act created the split between the executive and representative functions on local councils. It was left to councils themselves which of various options they took: a directly elected executive mayor with a cabinet appointed from among councillors; cabinet with leader elected by the council; directly elected mayor with full-time council manager. This was linked with changes in finance to simplify the allocation of grants; the replacement of compulsory competitive tendering by a 'best value' inspection regime; and greater freedom for beacon or strongly performing councils. There were only a dozen directly elected mayors by 2005, and they were resisted by many Labour traditionalists and local government stalwarts, in whose eyes the system was discredited by the election of a number of independents, including controversial figures such as Ray Mallon, the tough former policeman, in Middlesbrough, and Stuart Drummond, the former 'monkey' mascot of the local football club in Hartlepool. The 'monkey man' tag was widely used to discredit the whole idea. But Drummond proved to be a popular mayor and was easily re-elected in May 2005, as were a number of other mayors.

Proposals for regional government in England have been a flop. Eight regional development agencies were set up in 1998 as a step towards elected regional assemblies. But they were appointed by ministers, accountable to Parliament rather than their regions, and their budgets were fixed in Whitehall. These were complemented by voluntary, non-statutory chambers. In Blair's second term, more detailed proposals for regional government were produced, but the lack of enthusiasm of 10 Downing Street ensured they would be weak bodies with little money – 'almost designed to fail', in the words of one close Blair adviser. The idea was for a rolling programme, starting in the areas where there was expected to be greatest support. Originally, three regions were designated – the north-east, the north-west, and Yorkshire and Humberside. But following setbacks in the June 2004 elections, the government opted just for the north-east, the area with the longest history of demanding devolution and thought to have the strongest regional identity outside London. But even with an all-postal ballot, the proposal there was rejected by around three-quarters of those voting. So regional government was abandoned, and there followed a renewed interest in mayors and city regions to give a clearer local identity.

The reasons for the rejection are complicated: partly a protest at the Blair government, but more significant probably was dislike of adding a new tier of elected politicians to a body which did not have much to do. It was the weakness, rather than the strength, of the proposed regional assembly that was significant. This goes to the heart of the New Labour dilemma over local government. For all the talk of the 'new localism', as trumpeted by the Treasury in the second term, there has been a reluctance to allow local authorities real freedom where it mattered: over money. This was typified by the cloying phrase 'earned autonomy', used to describe the greater flexibility allowed to good performing councils: 'good', that is, as judged by Whitehall. The inspection regime was simplified for councils seen as doing well. But the basic balance between central and local funding remained. The money came from the centre, producing a heavy gearing effect, so that on average, if a council wants to raise spending by one pound beyond what is allowed for in the central grant, it will have to raise council tax by four pounds. The resulting problems led to very high council tax increases in 2003–04, hitting pensioners in particular. The Treasury chipped in to limit rises ahead of the 2005 election, but a review of local government finance did not reach a definite conclusion and a further review was carefully timed to come after polling day. But the underlying dilemma remains of how to make council tax fairer and how to broaden the financial base of local authorities. That has been a failure of every government since the early 1970s – the combination of ingrained centralism, especially in the Treasury, and fears of the political and electoral consequences of allowing, or forcing, local councils to raise more of their funds themselves.

Charles Clarke, then education secretary, explained in a speech in October 2004 why the centre was reluctant to give all power back to local authorities, which he described as an 'unrealistic and even naïve' demand. He believed the public expected education and child protection 'to be provided as national services which means that local government's role is in effect (and I use this word advisedly) as active agents for central government in relation to these key services'.

The government's constitutional credentials came under increasing fire over its criminal justice and anti-terrorism measures. Successive Home Secretaries – Jack Straw, David Blunkett and Charles Clarke – have been seen as leaning to the authoritarian rather than libertarian side. On many points they were correct. Fear of crime or anti-social behaviour – of mugging or louts in your neighbourhood – is real, particularly in working-class and poorer neighbourhoods. There is nothing 'right-wing' about recognising these concerns, nor in believing that the criminal justice system has been so inefficient as to benefit criminals rather than assisting their victims. It is no longer good enough to rely on a sense of local community solidarity or neighbourliness. Those living on drug-ridden estates and suffering from obnoxious neighbours now have no one but the state to help them. In this context, anti-social behaviour orders seem less a threat to civil liberties than a protection of the poor and disadvantaged.

The problem, in part, has been that by adopting tough language on law and order, partly to protect their flank against the Conservatives, successive Home Secretaries appeared less concerned with civil liberties. They faced frequent conflict with the judiciary in their desire to set out mandatory minimum sentences and to limit judicial discretion. There was conflict, for example, over proposals to limit trial by jury, though only in a tiny minority of very complicated, mainly fraud cases. The greatest friction was over anti-terrorism legislation, as discussed above in relation to the Belmarsh judgement of December 2004. The dispute was about a balance between potential and actual threats to the public against the rights of suspects.

At root, much of the criticism of the government's position was because some judges and lawyers did not really believe that the terrorist threat was so serious and immediate as to require exceptional measures which would restrict the liberty of some individuals. That was partly because of the discrediting of intelligence claims after no weapons of mass destruction were found in Iraq. The intelligence authorities, and ministers, were seen as trying to scare the public. But their warnings were shown to be correct by the terrorist attacks in London on 7 July 2005. The government then proposed a wide range of new measures against potential terrorists and their supporters which risked further conflict with the judiciary. Earlier in the year Lord Steyn, a senior Law Lord, had argued in a public speech that while nobody doubts the 'very real risk of international terrorism', the Belmarsh decision 'came against the public fears whipped up by the governments of the United States and the United Kingdom since September 11, 2001 and their determination to bend established international law to their will and to undermine its essential structures'. But there is, and was, an enormous difference between the torture and abuse of rights in the Guantanamo Bay camp and detention in the Belmarsh prison.

Another problem has been that the instinctive reaction of the Home Office and the security authorities has been restrictive. The post-9/11 law allowing the detention without trial of foreign nationals who could not be deported to their home country was crude. After the Law Lords' ruling that the original 2001 law was incompatible with the European Convention, the government came up with a graduated, though still controversial, series of alternatives, falling short of full imprisonment.

Ministers were seen, not just by the judges but more widely, as centralist and determined to control everything. This mood was reinforced by criticisms of Blair's style of government, as discussed elsewhere in this book, as well as by alleged cronyism in public appointments. There were clashes between the government, notably Sir Andrew Turnbull, the Cabinet Secretary up to summer 2005, and the Committee on Standards in Public Life over ministerial involvement in appointments to public bodies, as well as on other issues such as the handling of complaints against ministers and boundaries between ministers and civil servants.

The Blair government was generally seen as having a blind spot for the type of ethical issues being considered by the committee. This informality also landed the government in trouble. Blair never really understood the need for proper procedures where there might be a conflict of interest. Just five months into his premiership, he became involved in a row over the apparently dubious combination of a £1 million donation to Labour funds from Bernie Ecclestone, who ran Formula One racing, and a government decision to exempt motor racing from its ban on sports sponsorship by tobacco companies. Blair insisted, not entirely persuasively, that the two were separate and he had done nothing wrong. His defence in a television interview was that he was sure voters realised that he would never do 'anything improper. I never have. I think most people who have dealt with me think I am a pretty straight sort of guy'. Blair got away with it then, but his reputation was damaged over time by a succession of alleged scandals, some absurdly exaggerated, some in which he was not involved at all. He could appear sanctimonious, believing that merely saying he had behaved properly was enough.

Despite the weight of constitutional legislation, Blair and his government alienated not only civil libertarians, but also much of the traditional establishment over their style of government – too much a court and too presidential. The presidential charge was always an oversimplification since power has been shared between Blair and Brown. But there was a sense of a personal court uninterested in constraints on power, or in formal procedures. Both the Hutton and Butler reports (in January and July 2004) contained damning evidence about the informality of the government's operations, as well as over the wide-ranging influence of Alastair Campbell as the then head of communications. Lord Hutton seemed undisturbed by the revelations of informality, though Lord Butler, the former Cabinet Secretary, was concerned in his report on the intelligence background to the war. His report was misleadingly seen by some as a whitewash. Its carefully judged language disguised the impact of its criticisms, both on the lax procedures in the Secret Intelligence Service in passing on what turned out to be unreliable information and about the way the government operated.

In a key concluding passage, the Butler report noted the informal style of the Blair premiership – what has become known as 'sofa government' – and notably the frequent absence of formal papers circulated in advance. While being careful not to suggest there should be 'an ideal or unchangeable system of collective government', the report declared (2004, p. 148): 'We are concerned that the informality and circumscribed character of the government's procedures ... risks reducing the scope for informed collective political judgement.' These remarks proved a rallying point for other critics of the government, as in the quotation from Sir Michael Quinlan at the beginning of this chapter.

Dislike of the Iraq war has been a motive for many of the critics, who have claimed that the government acted illegally since ministers knew there were no weapons of mass destruction and invading Iraq to remove the Saddam regime was against international law. Whatever happened later, Tony Blair himself still believed in the existence of Iraq's WMD. There has been a long-running controversy over the legality of the military action, and whether the advice of Lord Goldsmith, the Attorney General, was changed and modified to meet the political needs of the government just before the Iraq war. Lord Goldsmith firmly denies doing this, and the eventual publication during the 2005 election campaign of his previously unpublished advice of 7 March 2003 on the legality of military action against Iraq was not conclusive. This memorandum showed that, while a further UN resolution to authorise the use of force was the 'safest legal course', Lord Goldsmith did not say that the failure to secure a resolution – as happened later that month – made military action illegal. Rather, any such action must be subject to strict conditions, notably proportionality, and related to securing compliance with Iraq's disarmament obligations. Regime change cannot, he said, 'be the objective of military action'. This is a massive topic all on its own, but the key point in this context is that many lawyers and critics of the government believe that Blair acted illegally, and this is one the main charges against him on the broader constitutional front.

The critics tend to bring together the Iraq war, informality in decision-making, Blair's alleged neglect of Parliament; excessive spin and centralism. Sir Christopher Foster, a distinguished former government adviser, put the case for the prosecution succinctly in the introduction to his book *British Government in Crisis*:

> We are badly governed. Some reasons for this are now widely acknowledged: Cabinet being replaced by prime ministerial government; the dominance of a political culture of spin; the rise of unelected special advisers and political cronies to positions of great power; the marginalising of Parliament and the substitution of the media as a 24-hour-a-day forum for political debate; but most important our inability to restrain a perilous and deeply flawed foreign policy in Iraq or to bring about a lasting improvement in our public services despite more billions spent on them. (Foster 2005, p. 1)

This charge sheet – echoed in the late Anthony Sampson's *Who Runs This Place?* (2004) – brings together, even confuses, questions of style and constitutional principle or precedent. The two are very different. You may believe that Blair's neglect of formal procedures or circulating Cabinet papers is unwise, as the Butler report did, but that is a matter of how government works rather than of constitutional rights or rules. On Iraq, Blair permitted regular weekly discussions from September 2002 until the start of the fighting in March 2003, while there were several debates in the

Commons, plus two key votes on motions of substance. The agreement to hold the votes was regarded by both Jack Straw and Robin Cook as a significant constitutional innovation, a precedent which it would be hard for any future prime minister not to follow ahead of major military action. But what the critics really dislike is not the procedures that Blair followed, but his decision to go to war.

The other main flaws of the Foster and Sampson critiques are 'golden ageism' and exaggeration. Foster offers an interesting and in part persuasive account of changes in the way we are governed. But the implicit assumption is that things were done better in the past. After all, if we go back to when Foster first became an adviser to transport ministers in the Wilson governments of the 1960s, procedures may have been followed, meetings duly noted, but the results were hardly wonderful. That was when there was the debate about whether Britain was governable at all. Moreover, unelected special advisers, political cronies and spin were not invented by Blair. They were also hallmarks of the Wilson era. Even Alastair Campbell was not unique in his combativeness. Joe Haines and Bernard Ingham engaged in spin as much as Campbell. This is not to defend the excesses of the Blair style: only to point out they are neither unprecedented nor great constitutional scandals, as the critics imply.

Both Foster and Sampson fail to take account of changes in the Blair style and important innovations since the late 1990s, or of how his attitude has changed, and has had to change, over the last two or three years. They barely mention the Cook reforms to strengthen select committees, Blair's agreement to appear in front of the Liaison Committee twice a year or the Commons votes ahead of the Iraq war. These are important constitutional changes, some involving Blair directly. The common view that Labour MPs are 'lobby fodder' and subservient to the government whips is nonsense. As Cowley and Stuart (in Seldon and Kavanagh 2005) have pointed out, the number of rebellions between 2001 and 2005 was, at nearly 22 per cent, the highest in the postwar period when measured as a percentage of all votes. These revolts were also much larger in scale, not just the 139 voting against the Iraq war in March 2003, but also the large rebellions which nearly defeated the tuition fees Bill in January 2004, against foundation hospitals, and against anti-terrorism legislation. These reflected a combination of the specific issues, the resentments of former ministers and those passed over for promotion, and recidivism, as once an MP has rebelled the more likely he or she is to revolt again. One of the ironies of the eventual approval of the legislation banning hunting with dogs in November 2004 is that this was a victory for Labour MPs against the wishes of Tony Blair and several senior ministers who would have preferred a compromise. Moreover, the Lords has become more assertive. So while Blair is not a House of Commons man in the traditional sense, he has not been able to ignore Parliament.

After more than eight years in power, what is striking is not just how much has changed on the constitutional front, but how many unanswered questions there are. As noted, there have been several far-reaching changes in the balance between the centre and the nations; in introducing proportional systems of election for a wide range of bodies; in the removal of most of the hereditary peers from the House of Lords; in the Human Rights Act, etc. All these laws have changed the balance between the government and the governed. Yet there has been something half-hearted about it, as if Tony Blair and many of his inner circle did not really believe in, or even understand, the changes.

The questions still on the agenda include the central/local government balance, both of powers and funding; the structure of local/city government in England; the future composition and powers of the House of Lords; and whether to change the electoral system for the House of Commons – leaving aside such perennial questions as the government of Northern Ireland and Britain's relations with the European Union. There are also big unresolved questions about the disengagement of the public, particularly young people, with mainstream politics, especially after the fall in turnout at the 2001 general election. How to involve the public more – to bridge the gap between voters and politicians – has scarcely been addressed so far.

Tony Blair will leave a large constitutional legacy, but it is one that he remains both half unwilling to acknowledge and even more reluctant to discuss. Gordon Brown has a greater interest in constitutional matters and has hinted (Peston 2005, p. 320) at his interest in completing the process of turning the House of Lords into a more democratic chamber as well as reinvigorating local government (though this has traditionally clashed with the Treasury's centralist instincts) and giving Parliament a formal role in decisions on the use of armed force. Brown has also given lectures (notably to the British Council, 2004) on Britishness, which he has defined less in constitutional terms than in values – liberty, decency, a sense of duty and fair play – shared across the boundaries of England, Scotland, Wales and Northern Ireland. This steps around the dilemma of the role of a Scottish MP in United Kingdom politics after devolution.

But the constitutional reforms since 1997 cannot just be seen as a task completed. Lord Wilson of Dinton, Cabinet Secretary from early 1998 until summer 2002, has noted (2005) how 'the British tend to ignore big constitutional change. They behave like a patient who submits to surgery under anaesthetic, but only considers whether he wants the operation some time later when he begins to feel the consequences.' Lord Wilson has a point. We – the political and media worlds, let alone most voters – have not woken up to the significance of the reforms. Of course, it will take years to judge their full impact. At present we are in a transitional phase, with a quasi-federal structure in the United Kingdom and a culture of rights testable in the courts – all qualifying, though not replacing, the sovereignty of the Westminster Parliament. Changes in political circumstances – say, the plausible scenarios of a series of hung parliaments where no single party has an overall majority – would force electoral reform back onto the agenda. The questions about pluralism or hegemony, sharing or monopolising power, which Blair has left unresolved will have to be answered by his successors.

8

The Legacy

'I have said this is my last election. At the election following there will be a different leader. What this manifesto shows is that, when at that election this party is under new leadership, it will continue to be the modern progressive New Labour Party of the past ten years that the British people can support with confidence.'

Tony Blair, speaking at the launch of the Labour manifesto, Mermaid Theatre, London, 13 April 2005.

Anyone who is prime minister for more than eight years has an opportunity to change the political landscape which few leaders enjoy. Asquith, Franklin Roosevelt, Attlee and Thatcher and their administrations unquestionably made a substantial, and lasting, difference. But it is impossible at present to deliver such a verdict on Tony Blair. The 'settlement' he talked about so much during the 2005 election campaign remains elusive.

Blair has certainly been one of the most remarkable prime ministers of the past century. He has an intuitive feel for the mood of the moment, great personal charm and persuasive power. The nearest British comparison is perhaps Lloyd George, whose wizard-like qualities at the 1919 Paris peace conference were brilliantly caught by Keynes. As he wrote later (1933) in terms that equally apply to Blair: 'Who shall paint the chameleon? Who can tether a broomstick?'

At times of intense pressure and national drama, Blair has a sure touch and can outshine all his rivals and opponents. He showed these talents after the death of Diana, Princess of Wales, after the 9/11 attacks and again – at the time of the completion of this book – during the rollercoaster first week of July 2005 when he combined the roles of national salesman, in helping win the 2012 Olympics for London; mourner and national leader after the terrorist attacks on London on what instantly became known as 7/7; and, at the same time, chairman of an extraordinary gathering of world leaders in Gleneagles on climate change and the future of Africa. All but his most severe critics admired his verve, courage and skill during that period. That is a crucial part of leadership. But performance is not the same as achievement.

The assessments of Blair vary enormously. For many, Iraq is all, and his decision to take Britain to war condemns him utterly, not least because he allegedly lied over Iraq's weapons of mass destruction. And, partly as a result, his hopes of reconciling Britain to Europe have been fatally undermined. The disillusion was greatest amongst those whose hopes were highest. Sir David Hare, the playwright, who received his knighthood under the Blair government, thought 'Blair was much the best prime minister of the past fifty years' (2003). But Iraq changed that. 'Big figures make big mistakes, and Blair has made the greatest mistake in British foreign policy since Suez. I don't understand how Blair can have concentrated on driving through an illegal invasion against the wishes of the UN. It's a mystifying position for any British prime minister to be in, let alone a Labour prime minister.'

But even for many of those for whom Iraq is not the whole story, Blair's premiership has been a failure. Ross McKibbin, an Oxford political historian, has attacked his leadership since the 2001 election as 'feckless and irresponsible' (2005). This is not just over the 'moral disaster' of Iraq, but also because 'he has had opportunities unavailable to any other Labour leader, and has thrown nearly all of them away.' McKibbin argues that 'the greatest of these opportunities would have been the democratic reform of the constitution.' Many others, such as David Marquand (2004), have criticised New Labour's public service reform programme for undermining professionals. From the opposite side, a common argument on the right is that under Blair the state has encroached ever more on the lives of ordinary people and businessmen, while much of the money spent on public services in recent years has been wasted, with no real improvement in health and education.

Another line of criticism is to acknowledge, at least in part, the achievements of the Blair government, but to claim that other people were responsible. Several supporters of Gordon Brown argue that he can take credit for most of the real achievements of the government, such as a stable economy and the reduction in poverty, while Blair is depicted as largely a front man with few ideas of his own. Anthony Seldon takes a more nuanced approach but argues (2005, p. 714): 'The assault on poverty aside, which was Brown's agenda, almost everything Blair has done personally – in education, health, law and order and Northern Ireland – has also been an extension of Conservative policy between 1979 and 1997. Blair, the Pollyanna prime minister, believes that the glory will come in the years ahead and his place in history amongst the pantheon of great national leaders will be secured.'

Blair's supporters have come from two sharply contrasting groups. First, there are backers of the Iraq war, both in Britain and particularly the United States, who regard Blair's courage in backing President Bush as trumping whatever doubts they may have about his domestic policies. That was broadly the view taken by Rupert Murdoch at the 2005 election. Many Conservatives admire and support Blair over Iraq but not generally because of their disagreements over his domestic approach. Second, and in complete contrast, Blair is praised for his domestic record by some who strongly opposed the Iraq war. Chief among these supporters are those who stress fairness and the reduction of poverty. Polly Toynbee and David Walker (2005, pp. 327–8) wrote: 'By 2005 Britain was a richer and fairer society than in 1997. It was healthier, safer and in many respects better governed ... Blair's era was a better era to be British than for many decades.' Their main criticism of Blair is 'for joining Bush's war' and for 'failing to offer an inspiring progressive legend'. So their overall verdict is 'good, but not good enough, with still time on the clock to do better in a third term'. And Toynbee has given much of the credit on fighting poverty to Brown rather than Blair. That leaves a very small number who support Blair both on Iraq and on his domestic agenda, of whom the most consistent in the press has been John Rentoul of the *Independent* group.

My own conclusion, as is clear from the previous chapters, is that Blair has not been a failure as prime minister. But nor has he been as successful as he should have been. Opinion polls consistently show a clear majority of voters is dissatisfied with the record of both Blair personally and of his government. There has been a sense of disappointment, in marked contrast to the almost euphoric mood in May 1997. There was a paradox then. The leadership was cautious in its specific promises – as epitomised by the five pledges discussed in Chapters 2 and 5 – but the 1997 campaign also fuelled excessive expectations that everything would change if only the Tories were thrown out and Labour was elected. Talk of 'saving' the NHS was absurd and bound to lead to disillusion as performance failed to match the earlier hopes. But the disappointment has run deeper: that the Blair government has wasted a rare opportunity to change Britain.

So why have not Blair and his government done better? The reasons reflect a mixture of inexperience in the ways of government and uncertainty both about what they wanted to do and how to do it. First, the electoral strategy needed to win in 1997, and to win two more terms, was at odds with a coherent governing strategy. The aim was to occupy the centre ground and to erect a big tent to attract as wide a range of supporters as possible. Blair was also obsessed with avoiding the mistakes of Labour during the previous two decades. This led to the triangulation approach, defining New Labour as distinct from both the Conservatives and Old Labour. But that tactically effective device had adverse results. Triangulation alienated party supporters, many of whom were only fair-weather backers of Blair as long as he was a winner, rather than identifying with him or liking him. That created a climate of suspicion, which was aggravated but not created by the Iraq war. Too often, there was a sense of policies being pursued despite the opposition of many MPs and local activists, rather than because of their enthusiastic support. This applied to tuition fees and much of the choice and diversity agenda in health and education. That is a fragile base on which to construct a long-term settlement.

Moreover, as Geoff Mulgan, the former head of the Downing Street Strategy Unit, has argued, the rebranding of New Labour 'was not an ideology or a strategy of transformation. It was mainly a way of winning elections. Unfortunately, the very factors that made it a success as an electoral project inevitably weakened it as a transformative governing project. Despite substantial progress in reducing poverty and opening up opportunities, the big tent approach made it hard to take on the most powerful interests – the London media, the super-rich, big business and the City – that often stood in the way of progressive reform. Policies in areas as varied as curriculum reform, environmental regulation and the taxation of pensions for the rich were unnecessarily constrained.'

Yet the absolute priority of winning and the big tent approach produced not only caution in policy-making but also confusion. All the focus had been on reassurance – over tax rates and continuing Tory spending plans – and there was too little thinking about what needed to be done. Instead, there were either promises to reverse Conservative policies (on, for example, the internal market in the NHS or grant-maintained schools) or a largely content-free blizzard of low-cost initiatives. These were a substitute for proper policy analysis. It is often claimed that Labour came to power in 1997 full of plans they were eager and impatient to implement. That is true in some areas, such as Bank of England independence, constitutional reform, and the five pledges, but not more generally, where many of the policies were vague and soon proved to be inadequate – as in transport, health and secondary schools. Many of the initial anti-Tory measures were reversed in the second term as a quasi-market was, for example, created in health, and secondary schools were given more independence. The 'initiativitis' phase only bred cynicism about the government promising more than it could deliver, fuelling the reaction against 'spin' that so damaged Blair and Labour.

The turning point came nearly three years into the first term when the flu/NHS crisis of early 2000 brought to a head worries at the top of the government about whether current policies were working. Both Blair and Brown, and their advisers, concluded that changes needed to be made. This was the key formative period for the Blair premiership in domestic policy when the pledge sharply to increase both spending on the NHS and total public expenditure was made. Moreover, it was during 2000 that Blair started to abandon the original mantra of 'standards not structures'. The NHS plan of July 2000 signalled the first steps towards the choice and diversity agenda in public services. This developed over the following two years with the proposals for diagnostic and treatment centres, foundation hospitals, city academies and more specialist schools.

However, it is not just that it took several years for ministers to devise a coherent strategy for reforming public services. There has also been a confusion about the role of central government. Blair in particular took time to understand how to use the levers of power, and he had no time for the traditional ways of Whitehall – at first, and for a long time, not wanting the full Cabinet to consider big decisions, or even have a formal agenda. Blair and his close allies preferred a more informal style, relying on loose meetings with affected ministers and advisers and e-mails rather than minutes. That also reflected his disdain for many of his fellow Cabinet ministers and his own party, and, increasingly, the strains with Gordon Brown and the Treasury, which wanted to keep all the economic decisions to themselves. The result was an often *ad hoc* style of decision-making which reduced the chances of proper deliberation and consideration of the options. Only much later, after the Iraq war and particularly after the 2005 general election, was a more collective method of decision-making revived with a shake-up of the Cabinet committee system.

When he became prime minister, Blair was also wholly ignorant about big organisations. He had never managed anything in his life and it showed. The 'scars on the back' remark in 1999 revealed not just Blair's frustration with the pace of change, but also his uncertainty about how to achieve reform. 'Tony wants' does not make much difference to a harassed doctor or nurse in an accident and emergency department, or to a teacher trying to control an unruly classroom, or to a police constable trying to deal with drunken and unruly teenagers in a city centre at the weekend. One of the most damaging charges against the Blair government has been that it has intervened too much and imposed too many regulations on local professionals and businesses alike. An excess of directives and new initiatives from Whitehall has been a frequent complaint from local managers and professionals. Throughout, there has been a tension between centrally imposed targets and talk of devolution of management to a local level. If we have national standards of performance, then the national politicians whose careers stand or fall by meeting these targets will demand a say in how these services are run. This is not an argument against league tables and the publication of more information: far from it. The public provision of such information is vital to push forward change and secure higher standards. But the centrally driven structure could not work over the long term. Hence the shift to increasing consumer choice, by parents and patients where possible, and extending local accountability of, for example, police commanders, where choice is not possible – in order to make reform self-sustaining.

But even the much reduced list of targets that can be read on the Treasury's website shows a central government with ambitions way beyond its reach. Action by the state may influence people's behaviour in various ways, but there is a danger of creating unrealistic expectations, and hence later blame, by setting targets on lifestyles which are way beyond its control. Setting a target for cutting the under-eighteen conception rate by a half by 2010 is highly desirable, but no one in Whitehall or any town hall can do much directly or indirectly to affect the outcome.

Similarly, fighting anti-social behaviour is a desirable objective. But how far can central or local government really alter the attitudes or conduct of young people – particularly their drinking and drug habits? Smoking, binge drinking and obesity are undoubtedly serious public health problems. But what is the balance between official discouragement and prescription? It has been worse when there have been contradictions between policies: for instance, between the liberalisation of licensing hours and rowdy behaviour by young drunks. One reason for disillusionment with the Blair record is that the rhetoric has exceeded what can possibly be achieved by the government – reinforcing the impression of the nanny state.

New Labour has therefore suffered both from the primacy of its electoral objectives over a governing strategy and from not having a coherent view of what the state can do. That has delayed the creation of successful policies and made the public sceptical about its record. That is why, in retrospect, Blair regarded much of his first term as wasted and believes that he only got into his stride with public service reform in the second term. This is also why he has become impatient now, aware of time partly wasted in the past, and only a finite time left to make his mark. But he has paid the price for the earlier mistakes and the overselling of minor changes in public scepticism about later achievements. Even when there was clearcut evidence of improvements in health and primary schools, many voters believed the government was all spin and no substance. While in the first term New Labour overpromised, and under-achieved, in the second term it was given insufficient credit for its much more firmly based achievements.

There have been obvious pluses – the stability of the economy, low inflation and interest rates; the rate of job creation; the reduction in child and pensioner poverty; definite evidence of improvement in the NHS and, more ambiguously, in schools; the big expansion of pre-school and nursery provision; the beginnings of a credible long-term funding structure for universities; and a partial, though uneven, shift to a more pluralist and less centralist structure of government. And, despite the terrorist attacks of July 2005 and worries over street crime and disorderly behaviour, Britain is generally a safer place in which to live.

In many of these areas there are as many qualifications as unequivocal verdicts. Perhaps that is the nature of all politics. But it would be premature to say, for instance, that secondary education policy is yet a success, even though there are many positive signs in school results and in the recruitment of teachers. No one can say that transport policy is yet more than ambivalent work-in-progress, since it has taken nearly eight years to create a viable long-term strategy. There are many uncertainties: House of Lords reform; the central/local government balance; the sustainability of public spending plans; pensions and the growing retired population; the green agenda and civil nuclear power; combating anti-social behaviour.

The foreign policy record is more ambiguous than either Blair's critics or supporters recognise. He has followed not only a very traditional approach of trying to balance Europe and the United States but also one which worked for a long time during the post-1945 era. The trouble is that the circumstances which sustained the 'bridge' strategy have changed. The end of the Cold War and the appearance in Washington of an administration wanting to pick and mix allies and cool to a common European voice has left Blair stranded in the middle. Many of his instincts, notably in handling the Bush administration post-9/11, were shrewd. His underlying argument for backing the US in the run-up to the Iraq war – that the United States should not be left to act alone – was a plausible strategy. But because he could never publicly admit that this was his main motive, he was left over-emphasising the threat from Saddam's WMD, and was then left looking shifty, and to many a liar, when no WMD were found. I do not believe that Blair deliberately lied since, like most of his intelligence advisers and agencies abroad, he genuinely believed in the existence of Iraq's WMD programme, not least because Saddam had used chemical weapons against both Iran and his own people. At the key period in the first half of 2002, Blair was acutely aware of fears of proliferation of nuclear, biological and chemical weapons involving Al-Qaeda and the activities of A. Q. Khan as a supplier, potentially to Saddam. The increasing sham of the oil-for-food programme threatened the whole policy of sanctions and containment. Only subsequently did outsiders know that Saddam's defiant stance and language was largely bluster to hide the weakness of his military position.

But Blair possibly deluded himself and certainly deluded the public in the emphasis he placed on the threat, and in refusing to revise his view when the UN inspection teams under Hans Blix did not find any evidence of such weapons in early 2003. By then, the die had been cast, and Blair was committed to going to war on highly controversial legal grounds, though not necessarily illegal ones. (In this respect, the highly publicised row over the Attorney General's legal advice in the first three months of 2003 looks overblown. Lord Goldsmith was arguably right both to commend the legal desirability of a further United Nations resolution to authorise military action against Saddam and then, in mid-March when it was clear that no such resolution was obtainable, to argue that there were still legal grounds for going to war. This was a second-best position, but not necessarily a wrong one.) The key point over Iraq has been the outcome: a continued high level of bloodshed and insurgency despite democratic elections and painfully slow attempts to create a broadly based government. The question for Blair, and for Bush, is whether the removal of Saddam and the hopes of creating a democratic Iraq justify the war and all the subsequent suffering and increased insecurity. That will continue to divide the British public and, in the eyes of a substantial minority, to be a permanent stain on his premiership. Whatever Blair's motives and intentions – and I am more sympathetic on this count than many of his critics – prime ministers have to be assessed on their judgement and, above all, on the results.

Moreover, Blair's rejection of President Chirac's attempt to build up Europe as a competing superpower rather than a partner of the USA was correct. But he failed to recognise sufficiently the dangers of being seen as Washington's cheerleader in Europe, rather than as part of a joint EU voice in Washington. That was partly unfair, since Blair was said to be robust in his private talks with the Bush administration. But there was little real evidence of much benefit to British foreign policy interests. At a stretch, Blair may have helped push Bush to a closer engagement with the Middle East peace process and to the debt relief and increased aid package for Africa agreed at the Gleneagles summit in July 2005. But when US corporate – and especially oil – interests were involved, as over climate change and targets to reduce global warming, Blair's influence was very limited.

Blair also talked much sense about the reform of the EU to make it more competitive, and adapting the traditional European model of social protection to create more jobs. This approach, adopted after the French and Dutch rejection of the EU constitution in May 2005, may have helped secure his domestic political base but it did not secure agreement within the European Union. The whole question of Britain's role in the EU remained unresolved after more than eight years in office, and the British public was, if anything, more sceptical than it had been in 1997.

Another way of looking at Blair's record is to focus on the main challenges facing Britain. The prime minister's Strategy Unit in February 2005 updated an audit of where Britain stands in relation to the main problems facing the country, and by comparison with its main competitors. Due allowance has to be given for the source of the report, and self-audit has obvious limitations, encouraging euphemisms and overgenerosity in assessments. But even so the audit provides a fascinating commentary on what has been achieved and what has not. Many of the key influences are long term. The positives are mainly the ones listed above and in earlier chapters: economic stability, closing the productivity gap, improving educational attainment, tackling child and pensioner poverty, reducing crime and improving health outcomes and the capacity of the NHS. As interesting are the 'challenges', such as 'meeting the growing demands on transport infrastructure, ensuring enough houses are built, getting the hardest-to-reach groups back into work, and further improving the life chances of those born into the poorest households'. Moreover, key influences on longer-term prosperity – low adult skills, innovation and investment – still lag behind international standards. The report also highlights structural problems as varied as lack of sufficient business innovation, low entrepreneurial activity, drugs, maintaining progress on sustainable development and achieving further reductions in greenhouse emissions. A particularly vivid illustration in the report is from Charles Booth's poverty maps of London in the 1890s, which highlighted deprived areas by colouring them black. An area of Bethnal Green is shown which still faces serious problems of poverty today, as the second most deprived ward in London, though with a wholly different ethnic make-up.

If you take a longer-term perspective, the Blair record looks better. As Howard Glennerster of the London School of Economics argues (2005): 'Every other Labour government has begun with ambitious social goals and then either retrenched or sometimes abandoned them. This is the first to have begun with modest ambitions and steadily enlarged them, building on economic success.' He notes that after the 1980s welfare states appeared doomed, and on the left there has been complacency with the postwar legacy of public service institutions. Despite the ducking and weaving and the headline-chasing, 2005 feels very different. The income peaks and troughs have stopped growing. Tax and benefit policy has left the rich worse off than they would have been and the poor significantly better off. The odd fact is that much of the attack on inequality has been undertaken in an almost clandestine way.

Merely not to have made a mess of the economy is an achievement when you look back at the records of previous Labour governments. True, the Attlee, Wilson and Callaghan administrations inherited much more serious economic difficulties. And Blair and Brown had a largely benign inheritance. But Brown built on the shifts in economic policy begun by the Major government, notably by making the Bank of England responsible for setting interest rates. It is fair to point to continuities with the previous Conservative government in this and the post-2000 policies on public services. But in most cases the Blair government has taken its policies much further. Similarly, to highlight Brown's contribution as opposed to Blair's is only partly right. The Chancellor deserves most of the credit on the economy and the anti-poverty strategy, but Brown would not have been able to achieve what he has done without Blair's political support and, above all, without Blair's electoral and campaigning skills which have given Labour three terms in office. Blair's ability to communicate with and reassure Middle England has permitted Brown's attack on inequality. Blair and Brown are complementary, as was seen during the 2005 election campaign. The one would not be nearly as successful without the other, despite recurrent, and worsening, tensions and rows between them and their advisers. That is why it will be so fascinating to see how Brown does on his own, without Blair. It is likely to be much harder than Brown and his advisers currently think.

But does all this add up to a settlement, comparable to the post-1945 and post-1979 ones? The circumstances were very different in 1997. As Mulgan has argued (2005), New Labour 'came to power not, as in 1945, with a strong consensus behind reform, but in the aftermath of a period in which the self-confident (and self-deluding) ideologues of Thatcherism had roundly defeated their opponents on the left'. Similarly, Glennerster has argued (2005) that Attlee was 'building on a long groundswell of support, deep study by major commissions of inquiry in the Second World War and a readiness for far-reaching change. Nearly full employment had brought more equality and prosperity. Blair inherited the opposite set of circumstances – a powerful hostile ideology that had seemed to sweep all before it, deep and new economic divisions and inexperience in government.'

I would go further. Unlike either 1945 or 1979, New Labour has consciously and deliberately not been trying to construct a settlement wholly different from its predecessors. It has not sought to nationalise or privatise, or to change the balance in industrial relations, or in the management of the economy. In many key areas, Blair and Brown accepted the Thatcherite settlement: in the importance of monetary and fiscal discipline, in not seeking to reverse the industrial relations legislation of the 1980s and in not promising to reverse the privatisations and pro-business measures of the previous decade and a half. Moreover, the big electoral swing that carried New Labour into office in May 1997 was more to do with a rejection of the style and divisions of the Tories than a desire to reverse or abandon their main policies. Rather, a key part of Brown's strategy was to make sure that the Tory economic approach work better, through a more rigorous monetary framework and more pro-enterprise and pro-competition policies. Prudence came before purpose in Brown's lexicon. As argued throughout this book, the New Labour strategy only emerged in the course of its period in office. There is nothing wrong or unusual in that. The same was true of the Liberals after the 1906 election and Roosevelt after 1933 or, for that matter, Thatcher after 1979. It took several years before what we now regard as their distinctive legacies became clearly defined.

A Blairite settlement would now involve a combination of financial stability and low inflation; an active state; taxpayer-funded core public services such as health and schooling, but tailored to personal needs and choice of provision; a quasi-federal structure of government; and an internationalist, broadly European foreign policy. If the definition of a settlement is that it is broadly accepted by your political opponents, then New Labour is only halfway there. The Conservatives have accepted key measures such as making the Bank of England responsible for setting interest rates and devolution to Scotland and Wales. Much though the Tories might hanker for the golden days of the hereditary peers, they are not going to restore them to the Lords and, officially at least, the party is committed to an elected element. But big divisions still exist over Europe.

The central question remains public services. In the 2005 general election the Tories went part of the way towards accepting the Labour approach. They promised to match Labour spending plans on education and health. This meant that, even after some pretty ambitious promises on efficiency savings and squeezing other budgets, the Tories would have ended up by 2009–10 with a public spending share of national income only two percentage points smaller than Labour's projected share. This is not the stuff of big ideological shifts, despite Labour's exaggerated talk about £35 billion of cuts. In essence, the Conservatives accepted much of the spending landscape as defined by Labour. Where they differed was in proposing that patients would be subsidised to opt out of the state sector and allowed to top up with their own money in buying private treatment. This was a real dividing line.

Looking ahead, one of Blair's main former advisers on public services reckons that we will only know if there is truly a settlement on New Labour terms in four or five years' time. This will be determined by whether there is widespread support for primarily taxpayer-funded core services, even if there is more private financing of university education and child and elderly care. If the Conservatives accept that most schools and health care are financed by the taxpayer, with what this means for levels of public spending and taxation, then there will be a new settlement. This is quite separate from whether health care and schooling are provided by voluntary and private groups, as in much of the Continent, notably Sweden and the Netherlands, but still financed by the state. The big debate in the

Conservative Party over the next few years will be how far to challenge state funding of health and education and how far to allow topping up by individuals from their own money. That would, in turn, undermine the central principles of equity in the NHS and the state school system.

Another measure may be the number of people, particularly the better-off middle classes, who choose to remain within the state-funded sector. As a middle-class parent in London, one of Blair's ambitions has been to increase the number of his fellow middle-class professionals who send their children to state-funded schools in the capital. That point has not remotely yet been reached in inner London, though it is true in many other areas of the country. It is already apparent, however, that the speedier treatment for many non-urgent medical conditions has put pressure on the private health insurance sector. Indeed, the private health sector increasingly sees its role as providing treatments for the NHS.

There has been a fierce debate about where the New Labour approach stands in broader ideological and historical terms. (I have nearly twenty books on my shelves by political scientists debating the significance and place of New Labour. Few are light reading.) This discussion has been confused by the tactic of triangulation and the deliberate attempt to project an image of freshness and modernisation as if history began when Blair was elected Labour leader in July 1994, or when he became prime minister in 1997. That is obviously nonsense. No government is completely new. It operates within a framework of policies and expectations set by its predecessors. But the confusion has been fuelled by the search for an ideological justification, notably the ever-elastic term The Third Way – now reformulated, but equally elusive, as progressive governance or consensus.

New Labour's repudiation of its recent past, and its acceptance of the broadly Thatcherite economic framework, has led many critics on the left to depict the Blair government as part of the neo-liberal orthodoxy established in the 1980s. On this view, as set out in a more subtle way by Richard Heffernan (2001, p. xiv), Thatcherism's greatest success was in transforming the Labour Party, and New Labour has been 'the climax of a gradual and incremental accommodation' with the Conservatives' neo-liberal approach. 'Labour's governing agenda begins with the *status quo* bequeathed by Thatcherism because its policy and programme is cast within a pre-existing political, and economic paradigm, one fashioned as a result of the worldwide resurgence of market liberalism into which Thatcherism tapped. More often than not governing practice exemplifies continuity rather than discontinuity.' There is something in this view, though it is also true of other successful social democratic governments since the early 1990s, such as the Labour Party in Australia in the days of Paul Keating or in New Zealand under Helen Clark, as well as the centrist New Democrats in Bill Clinton's heyday. In Europe, the Swedish Social Democrats provide the prime example, though less so the German SPD, whose internal divisions have reflected its only partial acceptance of these global changes.

A counter-view is that new Labour remains recognisably in the social democratic tradition. Indeed, many of its policies – for example, on reducing child and pensioner poverty, on introducing the national minimum wage and on allocating substantial resources to run-down inner city areas – would never have been introduced by a Conservative government. David Miliband, one of the formative influences on Labour thinking in opposition, in 10 Downing Street in the first term and now in government, has talked (2002) of New Labour standing for 'steadfast social democratic values', though innovative means, to achieve their delivery. This has involved reaching back 'into the history of progressive thought in Britain to develop a "liberal socialism" – social democratic commitment to social justice through collective action enriched by commitment to individual freedom in the market economy'. Steven Fielding has argued (2003, p. 3) that Blair 'deliberately made the party's break with its past appear more apparent than it actually was' for electoral reasons. The contrasts which the prime minister and his allies have sought to make with Old Labour have mainly been with the failures of its lurch to the left in the early 1980s. If you go back earlier, then the Blair government has similarities with previous Labour administrations in seeking to encourage private-enterprise capitalism, while supporting an active state and increasing public spending on health, education and other public services. In terms of public services, the Blair government can be viewed as more successfully social democratic than the Wilson and Callaghan administrations, which were forced to squeeze spending in face of recurrent financial and foreign exchange crises. The main contrast is in the much reduced role of the trade unions since 1997, both in the economy and in the Labour Party, compared with their dominance in earlier decades.

Patrick Diamond, a young adviser in Downing Street during the second term and pupil of Anthony Giddens, has sought to portray New Labour as not really new but as recognisably part of the long tradition of Labour revisionism and of ethical socialism. In particular, by rewriting Clause Four in 1994–95, New Labour has fulfilled the task that an earlier generation of revisionists sought and failed to achieve. New Labour has neither discarded the key tenets of social democracy nor created an entirely new ideology. Diamond sees New Labour as the 'unfinished revolution in British politics' – with the potential to 'complete the revisionist project instigated by Gaitskell, Crosland and Jay in the 1950s'. This sees the establishment of a successful and lasting social democracy as being coterminous with the modernisation of the British economy and state. However, Diamond is cautious in his view of what New Labour has so far achieved (2004, p. 247): 'New Labour has yet to match the successive structural transformations instigated by the Thatcher administrations in the 1980s. Yet governments are defined by their institutional legacies. New Labour needs to invent new social and economic institutions, and reallocate resources and assets, on a scale that matches the privatised industries, the National Lottery, council house ownership, and the savings schemes introduced under the Conservatives.'

It is possible to view New Labour as both post-Thatcherite and social democratic: post-Thatcherite in accepting the new framework of economic policy created in the 1980s, and social democratic in the sense of trying to improve public services for all and broaden social opportunities. As Blair argued in his speech to the European Parliament in June 2005, the old socialist model of intervention and job protection nowadays works against both reducing unemployment and creating new opportunities for the excluded. The key is the link between pro-competitiveness policies and social justice. That argument is more persuasive than the critics' claims that New Labour is sacrificing the poor and destroying an ethos of public service. The more pertinent question is how far these economic and social objectives can be reconciled without pushing up taxes and intervening on a scale that undermines incentives.

Blair's problem is less now in devising and putting forward a coherent view of how the economy and public services should be run than in the long task of implementation and, above all, in winning over his own party.

Yes, Labour is a very different party from the early 1980s, but it is not really Blairite in its heart and instincts. Blair is respected by many, but he is still seen as a distant, remote, un-Labour figure. These feelings are correct. Blair does not feel comfortable with the Labour Party. As Philip Stephens has argued (2005): 'The central fact of his premiership – its strength and weakness – has been his distance from his own party. The most successful leader in Labour's history has always been detached from it.' There is a striking contrast with Brown. Blair has 'never felt the emotional attachment, the sense of belonging, that perfectly describes Brown's progress through Labour's ranks'. Brown respects Labour's traditions, ideals and instincts. Blair is not really at home with them.

The prime minister's repeated protestations that he was not born into the party, but chose it, reveal the deeper ambiguities of his relationship to Labour. That was evident at the celebration in February 2000 of the party's centenary. Blair dutifully paid tribute to the party's great figures. But, as noted in Chapter 1, he believes the creation of the Labour Representation Committee separate from the Liberals in February 1900 was a historic mistake. By splitting Labour from 'other progressive forces', the decision ensured that the party was in office for a mere 23 years in the twentieth century, opening the way for Conservative domination. So Blair has sought to mould Labour to fit his strategy of achieving an equal dominance in the twenty-first century from the centre – to give a role for a centre-left party after the victory of capitalism in the long ideological battle of the twentieth century. The tactical shifts needed to achieve this position – triangulation, the big tent approach, and 'talking right but acting left' – have, however, partly estranged him from his own party.

So when we look at whether Blair has achieved a new settlement – and at the nature of his legacy – the question is as much to do with his own party as with the Conservatives. When he has talked about entrenchment, and wanting another three years or so in office, Blair – and certainly his more zealous advisers – have meant entrenching the changes from a Labour/Brownite reaction, as much as from the more remote possibility of a Conservative or Liberal Democrat reaction. The quotation at the beginning of this chapter from the long opening statement delivered by Labour leaders at the launch of their manifesto in April 2005 seems based on hope as much as certainty. Much would depend on the attitudes of the man standing alongside him on the platform then, Gordon Brown. Of course, Brown has accepted most of the policies proposed and implemented since 1997, not least since he had been responsible for a large number of them. There have been differences over the extent of the introduction of market forces and competition in public services. But otherwise it has been as much a matter of style and positioning, and personal rivalry. A Brown premiership will certainly disappoint those on the left looking for a big change of direction, a fresh start after the hated Blair years. But positioning matters and the fear of the Blairites is that Brown may abandon the centre ground in his language and campaigning style – if not in most of his policies. Rather, Brown may look more to the left to try and regain the support of many traditional Labour supporters who have either stayed at home in the last two general elections or switched to the Liberal Democrats in 2005. Brown faces the danger that, while he may enthuse and regain the support of such traditional Labour supporters, boosting majorities in safe seats, he may put at risk the support of Blair's people in Middle England in all those seats which Labour won in 1997. These fears explain the impatience in the Blair camp to press on with the reform programme, to ensure that the choice and diversity agenda is so firmly established by 2007 and 2008 as not to be reversible.

Any assessment of the Blair premiership now is obviously tentative. Political fortunes and fashions change frequently. Blair's standing fell sharply in the aftermath of the May 2005 election, as his political and media critics claimed that he would find it hard to manage Parliament and urged him to set an early date for his retirement. He was reported to be depressed by all this carping even though he had won an unprecedented third election victory for his party. But within six weeks his stock had recovered sharply, and by the end of July 2005 he was seen as a commanding figure, a leader both at home and in Europe. The turning point was the end of May when the defeat of the European constitution in the French and Dutch referendums ended his need to hold such a ballot in Britain some time in 2006. Such a referendum would have dominated the intervening period, with speculation about whether he would have to resign if the 'Yes' side lost. The answer is that had 'Yes' lost the referendum, Blair would certainly have had to resign, and he had been reconciling himself to going down fighting.

But that danger was suddenly lifted, and he could plan for a period of at least two, and possibly three, years in 10 Downing Street. The bruising EU summit at Brussels and his confrontation with President Jacques Chirac energised him further, as was reflected in his successful speech to the European Parliament a week later. Cabinet colleagues reported a fresh buoyancy and determination. The triumphant and tragic events of the first week of July reinforced this shift, showing Blair at his formidable best. Yet such fluctuations in a prime minister's standing are misleading. Just as his position was not nearly as weak as his critics would have liked in May, so it was not as strong as his supporters claimed two months later. The terrorist threat could rebound on Blair, not least by reminding voters of the Iraq war. Blair remains a leader in the final, possibly long, phase of his premiership. It may be an Indian summer, but that never lasts for ever.

Calling Tony Blair the 'unfulfilled prime minister' is seen by some as implying that I think he is a failure. That is wrong. Unfulfilled is a relative term, not an absolute verdict. It is a comment on his achievements relative to the potential and opportunity he had in 1997. By those measures, he is unfulfilled. That is acknowledged by his own impatience. But Blair has already been a more historically significant prime minister, for both good and ill, than all but a handful of his predecessors in Downing Street over the last century. The achievements of his government – some due to him, and some to others – are real and substantial. He has achieved much more than, say, Bill Clinton did in his eight years in the White House. But he has not yet transformed the political landscape. Any Blairite settlement is still in doubt. His legacy remains bitterly contested.

Bibliography

NOTE: For writings and speeches by Tony Blair, entries marked with an asterisk are to be found – in their entirety or in edited form – in Paul Richards (ed.), *Tony Blair In His Own Words* (London, Politico's, 2004).

Adonis, Andrew, 'Let Blair Be His Own Education Secretary', *Observer*, 15 December 1996.

Balls, Ed, and O'Donnell, Gus (eds.), *Reforming Britain's Economic and Financial Policy: Towards Greater Economic Stability*, HM Treasury: Basingstoke, Palgrave Macmillan, 2002.

Balls, Ed, Grice, Joe, and O'Donnell, Gus (eds.), *Microeconomic Reform in Britain: Delivering Opportunities for All*, HM Treasury: Basingstoke, Palgrave Macmillan, 2004.

Balls, Ed, *Trust and Economic Policy*, The Lubbock Lecture, Said Business School, University of Oxford, 20 June 2005.

Barber, Sir Michael [Head of Prime Minister's Delivery Unit], *Delivery Update*, report to the Cabinet, July 2004.

Blair, Tony, 'What Labour Needs to Do', *Guardian*, 30 June 1992.

*Blair, Tony, speech to the Labour Party conference, Blackpool, 4 October 1994.

Blair, Tony, speech at special Labour Party conference on Clause Four, Central Hall, Westminster, 29 April 1995.

Blair, Tony, speech to News Corporation Leadership Conference, Hayman Island, Australia, 17 July 1995.

*Blair, Tony speech to the Labour Party conference, Brighton, 3 October 1995.

Blair, Tony, statement at the launch of Labour's New Year campaign document, Millbank Tower, London, 8 January 1996.

Blair, Tony, speech to British-American Chamber of Commerce, New York, 12 April 1996.

Blair, Tony, 'Doctrine of the International Community', speech in Chicago, 22 April 1999.

Blair, Tony, and Schroeder, Gerhard, *Europe: The Third Way/Die Neue Mitte*, London, Labour Party, 1999.

Blair, Tony, 'New Challenges for Europe', Aachen, 20 May 1999.

Blair, Tony, speech to the Venture Capital Association, London, 6 July 1999.

Blair, Tony, interview with Andrew Rawnsley, *Observer*, 5 September 1999.

Blair, Tony, interview on *Breakfast with Frost*, BBC1 television, 16 January 2000.

Blair, Tony, speech at the Centenary Anniversary of the Labour Party, The Old Vic, London, 27 February 2000.

*Blair, Tony, 'Touchstones memorandum'. subsequently leaked, 29 April 2000.

Blair, Tony, 'The Government's Agenda for the Future', speech at a school in Enfield, London, 8 February 2001.

*Blair, Tony, speech to the Labour Party conference, 3 October 2001.

Blair, Tony, 'Britain's Role in Europe', speech at the European Research Institute, Birmingham, 23 November 2001.

Blair, Tony, 'The Future of Europe: Strong, Effective, Democratic', speech in Cardiff, 29 November 2002.

*Blair, Tony, speech in the House of Commons in debate authorising military action against Iraq, 18 March 2003.

Blair, Tony, 'The Next Progressive Steps for Britain', speech to a Fabian Society conference, The Old Vic, London, 17 June 2003.

*Blair, Tony, speech to Joint Session of the US Congress, Washington DC, 17 July 2003.

*Blair, Tony, speech at The *Guardian* Public Services Summit, Rickmansworth, 29 January 2004.

Blair, Tony, evidence to Liaison Committee of the House of Commons, 3 February 2004.

Blair, Tony, 'Excellence for All', speech at St Thomas's Hospital, London, 23 June 2004.

Blair, Tony, speech at the launch of the Labour general election manifesto, Mermaid Theatre, London, 13 April 2005.

Blair, Tony, interview with *The Times*, 29 April 2005.

Blair, Tony, speech to the European Parliament, Brussels, 23 June 2005.

Bogdanor, Vernon, 'Devolution and the Territorial Constitution', lecture at Gresham College, 5 April 2005.

Borrie, Gordon (Lord), chairman, Report of the Commission on Social Justice, *Social Justice: Strategies for National Renewal*, London, Vintage, 1994.

Bosanquet, Nick, *The NHS in 2010,* Reform, December 2004.

Brown, Gordon, Budget speech, House of Commons, 2 July 1997.

Brown, Gordon, 'A Modern Agenda for Prosperity and Social Reform', speech to the Social Market Foundation, 3 February 2003.

Brown, Gordon, Budget speech, House of Commons, 17 March 2004.

Brown, Gordon, 'Britishness', British Council Annual Lecture, London, 7 July 2004

Brown, Gordon, speech to the Labour Party conference, Brighton, 27 September 2004.

Brown, Gordon, Budget speech, House of Commons, 16 March 2005.

Browne, Lord, speech at World Economic Forum, Davos, 27 January 2005.

Budd, Sir Alan, *Black Wednesday: A Re-examination of Britain's Experience in the Exchange Rate Mechanism*, London, Institute of Economic Affairs, 2005.

Butler, Lord, of Brockwell, chairman, *Review of Intelligence on Weapons of Mass Destruction: Report of a Committee of Privy Counsellors*, House of Commons paper 898, July 2004.

Chadwick, Andrew, and Heffernan, Richard, (eds.), *The New Labour Reader*, Cambridge, Polity Press, 2003.

Civil Service Reform, Delivery and Values: One Year On, Cabinet Office, 2005.

Coates, David, and Lawler, Peter, *New Labour in Power*, Manchester, Manchester University Press, 2000.

Cook, Robin, *The Point of Departure*, London, Simon & Schuster, 2003.

Daalder, Ivo, and Lindsay, James, *America Unbound: The Bush Revolution in Foreign Policy*, Washington DC, The Brookings Institution, 2003.

Diamond, Patrick (ed.), *New Labour's Old Roots: Revisionist Thinkers in Labour's History 1931–1997*, London, Imprint Academic, 2004.

Fielding, Steven, *The Labour Party: Continuity and Change in the Making of New Labour*, Basingstoke,

Palgrave Macmillan, 2003.

Foster, Christopher, *British Government in Crisis, or The Third English Revolution*, Oxford, Hart Publishing, 2005.

Gamble, Andrew, *Between Europe and America: The Future of British Politics*, Basingstoke, Palgrave Macmillan, 2003.

Giddens, Anthony (Lord), *The Third Way*, Cambridge, Polity Press, 1998.

Giddens, Anthony (Lord), *Where Now for New Labour?*, Fabian Society/Policy Network, Cambridge, Polity Press, 2002.

Glennerster, Howard, 'Blair's Surprise Successes', review of Toynbee and Walker, *Better or Worse? Has Labour Delivered?* (2005), *Guardian*, 12 March 2005.

Gordon, Philip H., and Shapiro, Jeremy, *Allies at War: America, Europe and the Crisis over Iraq*, New York, McGraw-Hill, 2004.

Gould, Philip, *The Unfinished Revolution: How the Modernisers Saved the Labour Party*, London, Little, Brown and Company, 1998 (revised edition, Abacus, 1999).

Hansard Society, *New Politics, New Parliament? A Review of Parliamentary Modernisation since 1997*, by Alex Brazier, Matthew Flinders and Declan McHugh, London, Hansard Society, 2005.

Hare, Sir David, interview by Rachel Sylvester, *Daily Telegraph*, 15 November 2003.

Hazell, Robert, 'Reforming the Constitution', in Auditing New Labour issue of *Political Quarterly*, volume 72, number 1, January–March 2001.

Heffernan, Richard, *New Labour and Thatcherism: Political Change in Britain*, Basingstoke, Palgrave Macmillan, 2001.

Hennessy, Peter, *The Prime Minister: The Office and Its Holders since 1945*, London, Penguin Press, 2000.

Hyman, Peter, *1 out of 10: From Downing Street Vision to Classroom Reality*, London, Vintage, 2005.

Independent Commission on Proportional Representation, chaired by David Butler and Peter Riddell, London, Constitution Unit, 2004.

Institute for Fiscal Studies, *A Survey of Public Spending in the UK*, by Carl Emmerson, Christine Frayne and Sarah Love, IFS Briefing Note number 43, September 2004.

Institute for Fiscal Studies, *Poverty and Inequality in Britain: 2005*, by Mike Brewer, Alissa Goodman, Jonathan Shaw and Andrew Shephard, IFS Commentary 99, 2005.

Institute for Fiscal Studies, *Green Budget 2005*, February 2005.

International Monetary Fund, *Article IV Consultations with the United Kingdom*, Washington, DC, IMF, 2005.

Irvine, Derry, (Lord, of Lairg), *Human Rights, Constitutional Law and the Development of the English Legal System*, Oxford, Hart Publishing, 2003.

Jenkins, Roy (Lord, of Hillhead), *A Life at the Centre*, London, Macmillan, 1991.

Jenkins, Roy (Lord, of Hillhead), chairman, *Report of the Independent Commission on the Voting System*, London, Stationery Office, Command 4090, 1998.

Kampfner, John, *Blair's Wars*, London, Free Press, 2003.

Kay, John, 'The Visible Hand of the Treasury', *Financial Times*, 7 February 2003.

Keating, Michael, Stevenson, Linda, and Loughlin, John, *Devolution and Public Policy: Divergence or Convergence?*, Economic and Social Research Council Devolution and Constitutional Change programme. Discussion paper 2, revised version, March 2005.

Keegan, William, *The Prudence of Mr Gordon Brown*, London, John Wiley and Sons, 2003.

Keynes, Lord, 'Mr Lloyd George', in *Essays in Biography*, London, Macmillan, 1933.

Labour Party, *Britain Forward, Not Back*, election manifesto, April 2005.

Lawson, Neal, and Leighton, Daniel, 'Burn the Village to Save the Village', *New Statesman*, 29 March 2004.

Lawson, Nigel, 'Cabinet Government in the Thatcher Years', *Contemporary Record*, volume 8, number 3, winter 1994.

Le Grand, Julian, *Motivation, Agency and Public Policy: Of Knights and Knaves, Pawns and Queens*,

Oxford, Oxford University Press, 2003.

Liddle, Roger, *The New Case for Europe: The Crisis in British pro-Europeanism – and How to Overcome It*, London, Fabian Society, 2005.

Mandelson, Peter, and Liddle, Roger, *The Blair Revolution: Can New Labour Deliver?*, London, Faber and Faber, 1996. (Reissued, with a new introduction by Peter Mandelson, as *The Blair Revolution Revisited*, London, Politico's, 2003.)

Maney, Patrick J., *The Roosevelt Presence: A Biography of Franklin Delano Roosevelt*, New York, Twayne Publishers, 1992.

Marquand, David, *Decline of the Public: The Hollowing Out of Citizenship*, Cambridge, Polity, 2004.

McElwee, Martin, and Tyrie, Andrew, *Statism by Stealth: New Labour, New Collectivism*, London, Centre for Policy Studies, 2002.

McKibbin, Ross, 'What Blair Threw Away', *London Review of Books*, 19 May 2005.

Miliband, David, 'New Labour in Power Again: What Next?', speech at Friedrich Ebert Stiftung, Berlin, 21 February 2002.

Milward, Alan S., 'The Rise and Fall of a National Strategy 1945–63', *The United Kingdom and the European Community*, Volume 1, London, Whitehall History Publishing in association with Frank Cass, 2002.

Miliband, David, 'Putting the Public Back into Public Services', speech at The *Guardian* Public Services Summit, 2 February 2005.

MORI, Review, December 2004.

Mount, Ferdinand, 'Thatcher's Decade', *National Interest*, number 14, 1988–89.

Mulgan, Geoff, 'Inside Blair's Machine: My Seven Years at the Centre of Power', *Prospect*, May 2005.

Murray, Alasdair, and Wanlin, Aurore, *The Lisbon Scorecard V: Can Europe Compete?*, London, Centre for Economic Reform, 2005.

National Institute of Economic and Social Research, 'Labour's Economic Performance: A Commentary', by Ray Barrell, Simon Kirby, Robert Metz and Martin Weale, *National Institute Economic Review*, April 2005, p. 192.

Naughtie, James, *The Rivals*, London, Fourth Estate, 2001.

Neustadt, Richard E., *Presidential Power and the Modern Presidents*, New York, Free Press, 1990.

New Politics Network, *Looking Back, Looking Forward, Eight Years On*, ed. Peter Facey, London, New Politics Network, 2005.

Oborne, Peter, and Walters, Simon, *Alastair Campbell*, London, Aurum, 2004.

Oborne, Peter, *The Rise of Political Lying*, London, Free Press, 2005.

O'Neill, Onora, *A Question of Trust*, The BBC Reith Lectures 2002, Cambridge, Cambridge University Press, 2002.

Organisation for Economic Cooperation and Development, *Economic Survey of the United Kingdom, 2004*, Paris, OECD, 2004.

Patten, Chris, 'Europe and America – Has the Transatlantic Relationship Run out of Road?', speech at Lady Margaret Hall, Oxford, 13 February 2004.

Peston, Robert, *Brown's Britain*, London, Short Books, 2005.

Pollock, Allyson, 'Privatisation of the NHS Is Accelerating', *Guardian*, 24 May 2005.

Public Accounts Committee of the House of Commons, *Individual Learning Accounts*, Tenth Report of Session 2002-03, House of Commons paper 544.

Public Administration Committee of the House of Commons, *On Target?: Government by Measurement*, Fifth Report of Session 2002–03, House of Commons paper 62.

Public Administration Committee of the House of Commons, *Choice, Voice and Public Services*, written evidence (including memorandum from the National Audit Office), Session 2004–05, House of Commons paper 49-11.

Pugliese, Stanislao (ed.), *The Political Legacy of Margaret Thatcher*, London, Politico's, 2003.

Rawnsley, Andrew, *Servants of the People: The Inside Story of New Labour*, London, Penguin Books, 2001.

Reich, Robert, 'The Dangers of Moving to the Mushy Middle', *Observer*, 27 April 1997.

Rentoul, John, *Tony Blair: Prime Minister*, London, Little, Brown and Company, 2001.

Riddell, Peter, 'The End of Clause IV, 1994–95', *Contemporary British History*, volume II, number 2, summer 1997, pp. 24–49.

Riddell, Peter, 'Little Brother Is Watching You', *The Times*, 22 September 1997.

Riddell, Peter, 'How No. 10 Has Become the British White House', *The Times*, 25 June 2001.

Riddell, Peter, 'Margaret Thatcher: The Lady Who Made the Weather', in *The Political Legacy of Margaret Thatcher* (ed. Stanislao Pugliese), London, Politico's, 2003.

Riddell, Peter, *Hug Them Close: Blair, Clinton, Bush and the 'Special Relationship'*, London, Politico's, 2003.

Riddell, Peter, 'Prime Ministers and Parliament', in Reflections on British Parliamentary Democracy, *Parliamentary Affairs*, Sixtieth Anniversary Special Issue, volume 57, number 4, October 2004.

Riddell, Peter, 'Bold Tony Pushes Timid Tony Aside', *The Times*, 20 January 2005.

Robinson, Geoffrey, *The Unconventional Minister: My Life Inside New Labour*, London, Michael Joseph, 2000.

Rogers, Simon, The Hutton Inquiry and its Impact, London, Politico's 2004.

Runciman, W. G. (ed.), *Hutton and Butler: Lifting the Lid on the Workings of Power*, Oxford, published for the British Academy by Oxford University Press, 2004.

Russell, Meg, *Building New Labour: The Politics of Party Organisation*, Basingstoke, Palgrave Macmillan, 2005.

Rycroft, Matthew, memorandum on meeting of senior ministers and advisers in 10 Downing Street, 23 July 2002, as disclosed in *Sunday Times*, 1 May 2005.

Sampson, Anthony, *Who Runs This Place?: The Anatomy of Britain in the Twenty-First Century*, London, John Murray, 2004.

Scott, Derek, *Off Whitehall: A View from Downing Street by Tony Blair's Adviser*, London, I. B. Tauris, 2004.

Searle, G. R., A New *England?: Peace and War 1886–1918*, Oxford, Oxford University Press, 2004.

Seldon, Anthony, (ed.), *The Blair Effect: The Blair Government 1997–2001*, London, Little, Brown and Company, 2001.

Seldon, Anthony, *Blair*, London, The Free Press, 2004 (revised paperback edition 2005).

Seldon, Anthony, and Kavanagh, Denis (eds.), *The Blair Effect II: The Blair Government 2001–05*, Cambridge, Cambridge University Press, 2005.

Stephens, Philip, *Tony Blair: The Price of Leadership*, London, Politico's, 2004.

Stephens, Philip, 'Unfinished Business', *FT Magazine*, 30 April 2005.

Steyn, Lord, 'Britain Accused of Creating Terror Fears', *Guardian*, 11 June 2005.

Strachan, James, 'Public Services Reform: Are We Getting It Right?', speech to CIPFA annual conference, Brighton, 16 June 2004.

Strategy Unit, *Briefing*, Cabinet Office, October 2003.

Strategy Unit, *Strategic Audit: Progress and Challenges for the UK*, Cabinet Office, February 2005.

Sunday Times, 'Secret Memo Says Blair Is out of Touch', and 'The Day the Magic Died', reports on Philip Gould memos, 11 June 2000.

Taylor, Matthew, 'Could This Be the End of the Labour Party?', *The Times*, 15 June 2000.

Thomson, Wendy, speech to Learning and Skills Development Agency conference, London, 16 June 2004.

Timmins, Nicholas, and Turner, David, 'Attack on "Pseudo Markets" Sparks Debate', *Financial Times*, 29/30 January 2005.

Toynbee, Polly, and Walker, David, *Did Things Get Better?: An Audit of Labour's Successes and Failures*, London, Penguin Books, 2001.

Toynbee, Polly, and Walker, David, *Better or Worse?: Has Labour Delivered?*, London, Bloomsbury Publishing, 2005.

Treasury, *Financial Statement and Budget Report*, HM Treasury, July 1997. House of Commons paper 85.

Treasury, *UK Membership of the Single Currency: An Assessment of the Five Economic Tests*, London, HM Treasury, June 2003, Command 5776.

Treasury, *Budget 2005: Investing for Our Future: Fairness and Opportunity for Britain's Hard-working Families*, HM Treasury, March 2005, House of Commons paper 372.

Turnbull, Sir Andrew, 'Professionalising Public Management in an Era of Choice', The *Guardian* Public Services Summit, 2 February 2005.

Wall, Sir Stephen, 'The UK, the EU and the United States: Bridge or Just Troubled Water?,' speech at Chatham House, 8 November 2004.

Wanless, Derek, interim report, *Securing Our Future Health: Taking a Long-term View*, HM Treasury, November 2001.

Wanless, Derek, final report, *Securing Our Future Health: Taking a Long-Term View*, HM Treasury, April 2002.

Ward, Lucy, 'Asbo Chief Rounds on Liberal Critics', *Guardian*, 10 June 2005.

Wilson, Sir Richard (now Lord, of Dinton), speech to annual conference of Chartered Institute of Public Finance and Accountancy, Brighton, 14 June 2000.

Wilson, Sir Richard (Lord, of Dinton), 'Constitutional Change: A Note by the Bedside', *Political Quarterly*, volume 76, number 2, April-June 2005, pp. 281–7.

Winston, Robert (Lord), interview with *New Statesman*, 14 January 2000.

Index

Gamble, Andrew 154

Gambling Act (2005) 180

Gaza 147

gender, race and age inequalities 92-3

general elections

(1992) 23

(1997) 9, 20-1, 30, 34, 38, 41, 71, 74, 132-3, 157, 20

(2001) 56, 62, 89, 103-4, 158, 171, 173, 179, 188, 191

(2005) 16-18, 20, 40, 59, 65, 72, 81-2, 86, 117, 171,

174, 176, 192, 195, 200-2, 207

George, Eddie (now Lord) 73

Germany 94, 130, 133, 136, 142, 166, 175

Bundestag 169-70

EU 151, 153, 155-6

Iran's nuclear programme 149

Iraq 142-3, 146

unification 128

Gershon Report 80, 83, 111

Ghent EU summit (2001) 140

Giddens, Anthony (Lord) 33, 205

Gingrich, Newt 12, 31

Gleneagles summit (July 2005) 191, 199

Glennerster, Professor Howard 113, 200-1

global warming 82, 199

globalisation 35

Goldsmith, Lord 198, 1856

Good Friday agreement 163-4

Gorbachev, Mikhail 128

Gordon, Philip H. and Jeremy Shapiro (2004)
140

Gould, Philip 21-2, 24-5, 30-1, 39, 49

'Recovery and Reconnection' 49

The Unfinished Revolution 24-5

Government Information Service 53

GPs 111-12, 121-2

fundholders 101, 109

Granita dinner (1994) 16, 70

grant-maintained schools 100-1

Greater London Council 161

green agenda 197

greenhouse emissions 199-200

Greenspan, Alan 8

Guantanamo Bay 184

Guardian 24

Hague, William 172

Haines, Joe 187

Haldane, Richard (Viscount) 41

Hamas terrorist group 147

Hampton Report 80

Hansard Society Commission 177, 179

Hare, Sir David 191

Harman, Harriet 100

Harris, Lord of Peckham 115

Hazell, Robert 162

health 126, 191, 193-4, 196, 199, 202

care 110, 202-3

and education services 114

private sector 105, 118, 203

services 50, 59, 76, 105

spending 78, 87-8, 99, 102, 106, 204

Health Department 102

health and education 88, 118

healthcare and schooling 202-3

Heath, Sir Edward 22, 127, 129, 143-4, 152

Heffernan, Richard 203

Helsinki communiqué 149

Henderson, Arthur 41

Hennessy, Peter 44

hereditary peers 162-3, 173-5, 188, 202

Heseltine, Michael 47

Hewitt, Patricia 35, 120

Heywood, Jeremy 70

Higgs Report 80

higher education 15, 108, 116-17

higher-rate taxpayers 90

Holme of Cheltenham, Lord Richard 159

Home Secretaries 182-3

Hospital for Tropical Diseases 102

hospitals 102, 108, 111-12, 120-1, 126

patient pre-booking systems 112

waiting lists 48, 100, 106

see also by name; foundation hospitals

House of Commons

modernisation 162, 169, 177

voting system 162, 171, 188

House of Lords 159-61, 169, 172-6, 188, 197

Budget of 1909; 4-5

houses 71, 81, 199

Howe, Sir Geoffrey (later Lord) 6, 9, 12

Hug Them Close 134

Hughes, Beverley 65

Human Rights Act (1998) 36, 160, 163, 166, 183, 188

Human Rights, Constitutional Law and the
Development of the English Legal System 157,
161

Hungary 142

hunting with dogs 63, 65-6, 188

Hutton and Butler: Lifting the Lid on the